On Human Needs

Open and Closed Theories in a Marxist Perspective

On Human Needs

Open and Closed Theories in a Marxist Perspective

KATE SOPER

THE HARVESTER PRESS · SUSSEX

HUMANITIES PRESS · NEW JERSEY

First published in Great Britain in 1981 by
THE HARVESTER PRESS LIMITED
Publisher: John Spiers
16 Ship Street, Brighton, Sussex
and in the USA by
HUMANITIES PRESS INC.,
Atlantic Highlands, New Jersey 07716

British Library Cataloguing in Publication Data

Soper, Kate
   On human needs. — (Marxist Theory and
   contemporary capitalism; 33)
   1. Marx, Karl
   I. Title   II. Series
   335.4'12   HB97.5

   ISBN 0-7108-0092-4

Humanities Press Inc
ISBN 0-391-02366-7

Printed in Great Britain by
Mansell Bookbinders Ltd, Witham, Essex
and typeset by
Alacrity Phototypesetters, Banwell Castle, Weston-super-Mare
in Bembo ll/12 point

For Leonie

Contents

Acknowledgements

I would like to thank John Mepham for the role he played initially in inspiring me to write this book, and for the continual assistance and support he has given me throughout its production. For discussions and comments that have contributed to its making, I am grateful to Chris Arthur, Roy Bhaskar, Andrew Collier, Ian Gough, David Murray, Geoffrey Nowell Smith, Jonathan Rée, Denise Riley and Keith Smith. I would also like to acknowledge the help and stimulus given by members of the philosophy division at Sussex University. Thanks are also due to Cora Kaplan, James Grant, Paul Soper and Erik Svarny for their encouragement and help.

I am especially grateful to Martin Ryle for all the ideas he has contributed to the content of this book and for everything he has done to enable me to write it.

Kate Soper
August 1980

1 *On Reasoning the Need*

1. The politics of human needs: some general considerations

There can be few concepts so frequently invoked and yet so little analysed as that of 'human needs'. Is one to suppose that this is accountable to some irreducibly 'primitive' and unanalysable status that the concept enjoys? Or is it not rather the case that the very regularity with which the term occurs in discourse about the individual and about society has created a certain deafness to its presence and rendered the concept itself immune to questions about its meaning and its function? At all events, we hear and read repeatedly of 'basic' needs, 'true' needs, 'false' needs, 'spiritual' needs, 'material' needs, unconscious needs, of 'needs' as opposed to 'wants' or 'desires', of 'needs' as opposed to 'luxuries', of 'actual' as opposed to 'potential' needs, but seldom pause to consider how it is that a single category can show itself so protean; on the contrary, with our needs, it is assumed, we know where we are. This book challenges that assumption; but it does not do so in order to recommend greater rigour in the use of the term or to specify some particular definition that it should be given. Its purpose is quite different: it is designed to show that all definitions of the term and all appeals to the concept of 'human needs' are, and must necessarily remain, problematic. But it also argues that it is only if the question of human needs is posed in a form that recognises this problematicity that it is posed in its full dimensions, and that means, importantly, in the acknowledgement of its *political* dimension.

Now while I shall have a good deal to say, either directly or by implication, about the failure of social theory at large to examine the various appeals that it makes to the concept of needs, my initial motivation for writing this work was frustration in this respect with a body of thought to which the concept of needs is arguably

1

more central than to any other. I am speaking here of Marxism, where appeals to the 'fulfilment of needs', to 'planning to meet needs', to 'distribution according to needs', and the like, are made in so unquestioning a fashion that one begins to suspect one must be guilty of some basic lack of insight in continuing to be plagued by the question: *what* needs? If it is heretical to pose that question, then this is a book for heretics. It is a book for everyone who has been similarly frustrated with the failure of social theory in general, and Marxism in particular, to pose the question of needs in the *form of a problem*, and with the refusal that is concealed therein to confront the fact that questions of politics are not to be solved by appeal to 'human needs', but are, on the contrary, only posed as political questions properly speaking when they are posed in the form of a question about human needs.

In stating the frustration in those terms, I am of course interpreting the question of human needs in a very broad sense: I am treating it as a question of value in human affairs — as a question concerned with the worth of human productions and their consequences and with the grounds upon which value is accorded to them. And I am suggesting that this question of value is the fundamental question of politics. In justification of this interpretation, and in full awareness of the extremely abstract level at which I am casting the discussion at this point, I offer the following considerations:

(i)   Every actual or possible form of social organisation is value based. It is underwritten, that is to say, by some 'theory of human needs', however 'unconscious' or implicit this may be, and even when the particular form it takes is that of a defence of the correctness (the value) of a certain form of social organisation precisely on the grounds that this organisation is 'value-free' in respect of needs. In other words, the defence of a given form of society on the grounds that so far from imposing any set of values or policy of needs it is dictated in its form by the 'needs' of its members, itself constitutes a particular 'theory of needs'— a 'theory' that would have us regard economic production and patterns of consumption as conditioned by human needs, in whose service they operate, and would ultimately persuade us that any deliberate social policy on needs must infringe the autonomy of individual needs and thus represent a form of political tyranny. I want to suggest that this is, paradigmatically, the underlying 'theory of needs' that sustains a liberal politics and is subscribed to by defenders of a social organisation based on a market economy and capitalist production, and it will be one of my aims to make explicit the political dimension to this apparent neutralisation of the question of needs. But here I would merely indicate its two main arguments. These are (a) that the question of 'value', or the question of what is 'truly' needed is an improper question, or rather not at issue at all, since human beings simply have their needs and these are sovereign; and (b) that, granted (a), the only 'proper' question is the question of means — the question of *how best to satisfy* the existing pattern of needs that is found to hold in society.

But if this is paradigmatically the theory of need that justifies a capitalist society based on a market economy, it is also, as I have already suggested, all too frequently the implicit justification of a 'planned' economy based on socialist principles. For arguments in favour of planning that appeal simply to the more adequate satisfaction of needs that this permits are equally guilty of a neutralisation of the question of needs in their assumption that the existing pattern of needs is a sovereign dictate from which the economic and social organisation of society must take its cue. In other words, a socialist politics that appeals only to the *satisfaction* of needs promoted by a socialist economy, and fails to confront the fact that any planning to meet needs is always, whether it be admitted or not, a planning of what will be needed (a decision about values) is evading the politics of need: it is refusing to admit the question of ends, the question of 'true' needs.

This of course raises the issue of the scientificity of 'scientific' socialism, and of the extent to which Marx and Engels themselves, and subsequent exponents of their thought, regarded their socialism as scientific precisely because it refuses to offer a theory of 'true' need. I shall have more to say on this later. But whatever the answer we give to this question, we must recognise that the refusal to confront this question of 'true' need — the attempt to avoid involvement in the politics of a laying-down of value, whether it forms part of a justification of the realities of capitalist society or of the realism of a socialist theory, is itself deeply enmeshed in the politics of needs, and argues from the standpoint of value-laden assumptions regarding human needs.

(ii) A second point I would want to make is that if the very attempt to deny the politics of need is itself a form of politics, then perhaps we can distinguish between a politics of need that exists in the form of a suppression of that politics, and a politics that explicitly recognises itself to be involved in that politics. One might characterise the latter as an 'authentic' politics in the sense that in the actions it takes to control the forces that control society, it recognises that these forces are themselves a product of human decision and action, and that society is in the last analysis in a position to determine upon the forces that will determine it. It is in this sense, then, that I refer to the 'decision' about these forces, the confrontation with the question of value or 'true' need, as itself the fundamental political act. But if it is, in this sense, the first political act, it is also, no doubt for that same reason, the act we are most reluctant to undertake, and the question that it poses is the question we are most anxious to repress. The fear here is of the *imposition* of values that is entailed by any answer to it; it is the fear of the *subjection* to decisions that is the other side of assuming responsibility for them. Regarding all options and decisions about our needs as potential impositions or 'manipulations', we choose instead to think that 'no one' can or should prescribe for them. This fear that we are controlled in the very act of taking control, and that we lose autonomy in the very process of self-determination, expresses the tension of political action itself and the capacity to experience it would have to enter into any explanation of what it is to be a political being. But it is a fear that can be experienced either in and through acknowledgement of the tension that creates it, and thus in open confrontation with the grounds of its production, or else in such a way that it becomes an excuse for evading that tension. Bringing to light the full political dimensions of the question of needs means, among other things, that the grounds of production of this fear can be directly and openly experienced as necessary but essentially enabling conditions of political action, rather than merely felt in the form of the anxiety they effect. It permits us to realise the potentially liberating effects of overt political dialogue on those questions and tensions that are thought to be the very expressions of our actual political impotence; it permits us to question, for example, whether self-imposed values *are* impositions, and whether 'no one' does not hold us in just as tyrannical a political dictatorship as that it is designed to avoid. After all, on a global scale it might be said that 'no one' has brought everyone to the brink of nuclear annihilation.

This question of the imposition of values that is deemed to be the undesirable consequence of any conscious political decision upon them can be fruitfully (and less metaphorically) discussed in the light of the distinction between 'needs' and 'wants' (or 'desires') that is registered somewhat ambiguously in ordinary language, and whose underlying logic has tended to engross such philosophical attention as has been paid to the question of needs. For the temptation to suppose that any political programme that openly commits itself on the question of needs is of its nature illegitimately presumptuous (in claiming to know what is 'really' needed) is clearly linked to an erosion of the distinction that the language of 'needs' and 'wants' is thought to express. For example, if the grounds for insisting upon a difference between needs and wants are, broadly speaking, thought to consist in the greater objectivity of the former whereas the latter are merely subjective in status, and in the fact that agents' statements and beliefs about their needs are corrigible in a way that statements about their wants are not (i.e., you can be mistaken about your needs in a way that you cannot be about your wants), then we can say that the inclination to object to the 'presumption' of a politics of need is based on an assimilation of needs and wants; or, in other words, maintaining the subjectivity of needs and the incorrigibility of agents' professions of them.

The problem here is whether, politically speaking, we can be said to have wants which we do not need and needs which we do not want. On the whole, liberal theory in vaunting the sovereignty of individual wants or felt needs has tended to deny that we can. Whereas a Rousseauesque politics based on the notion of 'forcing people to be free' moves from the antithetical position. And of course just as totalitarian implications have been imputed to Rousseau, so they have to Marxism, and perhaps in particular to its theory of alienation, for presuming to suggest that the 'perfectly contented' worker under capitalism 'needs' to be emancipated from the conditions of his existence and is the more alienated from his 'true needs' for failing to recognise this need.

Now if, as I earlier suggested, a genuine politics is involved in a conscious decision on value and itself recognises that the 'facts' upon which it bases its claims to know what is needed are themselves value-impregnated (and thus in a sense pre-interpreted in the light of a 'theory of need') on what grounds can it be maintained that the conditions it judges to be 'needed' are not merely what it 'wants' to implement? How can it claim that the needs for which it speaks have that objective status that was deemed to distinguish needs from wants? If any statement of needs is a statement of value, and if any 'genuine' statement of needs is made in acknowledgement of its normative character, then what distinguishes statements of need from statements of want?

Well, one short way with this, is to point out that nothing necessarily does or necessarily has to dintinguish between them, and one is only led into thinking that it must if one treats the ordinary language of needs and wants as if it had to express polar concepts that are logically exclusive. Nonetheless, it might be objected that if ordinary language does not register an exclusive relationship between wants and needs it does record the restrictive nature of needs relative to wants, the point about wants being that we can (and frequently do) want more than we need. I shall discuss the assumption on which this objection is based, namely, that our needs can be defined in terms of 'what is essential' more fully in the next section. Suffice it to say here that if we do comnmonly talk about our needs in this sense, we also, quite typically, make use of a concept of human needs that belies it: the concept of human needs is commonly invoked not as a concept of what we cannot do without but as a concept of the possibilities of gratification over and above what in any restrictive sense we 'need'. When Marx talks about the 'fulfilment of needs unmeasured by any predetermined yardstick' he is talking not about the minimum 'needed' but about the maximisation of pleasure. It is true, of course, that any philosophical analysis that aimed to produce a rigorous definition of the concept of needs might find itself in the position of having to disallow this 'Marxist' concept on the grounds that it was logically confused, and no doubt this book will be criticised for the extent to which it takes it for granted that it makes sense to talk about human needs in the 'Marxist'sense. But my refusal to be drawn on the question of definition has its polemical side, for I want to argue that the attempt to define what is meant by 'needs' and to demarcate definitively between needs and wants must tend to the neutralisation of the political dimension of the question of needs to which

I am throughout objecting. This point can be exemplified by reference to a recent piece of philosophical analysis of the logic of needs and wants,[1] on the basis of which it is contended that statements of need are distinguished by their non-normative character. The conclusion arrived at is that:

(statements of need)...are certainly elliptical; that is, if something is needed, it is needed for...or in order to...or because of...or...etc; that is, with reference to some end-state. Furthermore, needs can be logical, legal, moral, economic, psychological, etc. But it is the existence of the end-state, not its *value* or *desirability* that makes something needed...nor does the statement that A needs X become normative just because what A needs X for is itself something normative. 'A needs care and affection' has exactly the same (elliptical) role whether A needs it in order to become a good citizen or in order to become a wealthy citizen. The confusion between the *existence* and the *desirability* of an end-state has only arisen from a confusion between *specifying* the end-state in virtue of which the need arises and *justifying* it. One cannot decide whether A needs X unless one knows what he is alleged to need it for; but one does not have to pronounce on the merits of the latter.

This position would apparently countenance such oddities as, for example, a doctor claiming: 'This patient needs a blood transfusion — but in saying that don't take me to be in favour of her survival'. But let us leave this aside and merely note that the same author in the course of his argument also claims that: '...it is arguable that, in some sense, we always know what we want, but not at all plausible to suppose that we always know what we need. We have no hesitation in allowing that experts know better than ourselves what we need...'; and that 'Whitehall may know better than we do what is in our interests' (NB interests are said to be a sub-class of needs); and that 'educationalists have to distinguish, e.g. between a pupil's needs and his wants...'; and that 'It is because modern industry needs a large body of consumers that joining the Common Market may be in our interests even if we do not want to join...' It is clear from these claims that the supposed opposition between needs and wants, and between what is in our interests and what we are interested in, can only be maintained because the ends which allow 'Whitehall' or the 'educationalist' to ascribe needs which the citizen or pupil does not in fact have are themselves evaluated more highly than any supposed ends in relation to which the individual feels his or her needs. It is, in short, impossible for the author to comply with his own argument, since a covert normative judgement of end-states is a precondition of the required distinction between needs and wants. The appeal to need here is made in order to justify the incorrectness of the end-states we merely want or merely think we need. The mistake lies not in arguing that we cannot judge whether X is a need unless we know what the end-state is in virtue of which it is said to be a need, but in thinking that end-states can be justified without reference to needs, or that in *specifying* the end-state *as a need* one is not at the same time justifying it *as an end*. If Whitehall informs the country that it has a 'need' to join the EEC in virtue of the end-state of the 'expansion of wealth' it relies upon a positive judgement on that end-state. And let us note in this connection that it is an essential condition of the success of Whitehall rhetoric that it specifies end-states in such a way that it becomes possible for anything to be justified as a need by reference to them. Thus, it will inform us that it is in virtue of the 'common good' that the country needs the Cruise missile (and whoever was so perverse as not to approve the 'common good'?) 'Knowing' end-states in virtue of which we are supposed to judge our needs means knowing the 'theory of needs' in terms of which the end-state is cashed. And similarly one cannot challenge any claimed need independently of one's judgements upon the end-states in virtue of which the need is claimed to be a need. Thus, for example, my acceptance or rejection of the need to chop down a particular avenue of trees will depend upon my theory of environmental needs. I may accept it on the grounds that one of the trees is suffering from elm disease, but reject the grounds that it will interfere with overhead electric cables (which I may argue ought, albeit at greater cost, to be put underground). The question, in short, of what is needed can never be settled by appeal to some common and incontrovertible range of needs as simple factual conditions for the attainment of X independently of questions about the 'need' to attain X, or about the effects as by-product end-states of attaining X in a given way.

Now this, I think, has some important implications for the supposed distinction between needs and wants. I would want to maintain, in fact, that it is a condition of an agent having a need properly speaking that the agent acknowledges it and is openly committed on the choice of value that it states. This would mean, for example, that an oppressed class or group does not need to revolt until it feels that need, until it 'chooses' the end-state of emancipation from its existing conditions. In this sense, it is the 'choices' that *are* made, rather than those which any political theory approves or recommends or claims to be needed, that constitute human needs and realise their 'truth' at any point in history. But this does not mean than any political or social theory that openly commits itself to the rightness or wrongness of certain forms of social organisation, a certain utilisation of natural and human resources, certain methods of material production, and so on, is open to the charge of *imposing* a pattern of need and thus of being politically coercive in a pejorative sense. If it is a condition of having a need that it is experienced as such then there can be no question of theory enforcing practice, and the suggestion that any theorisation of needs is, by virtue of its very theoretical activity, politically suspect is based on a confusion between theory and practice and a conflation of the argument of any theory with its efficacy. Political theory can certainly be implemented concretely, but there can be no question of it automatically, by virtue of its being implemented, actually eliciting the needs that it speaks on behalf of. The suggestion furthermore that an explicit choice or laying-down of value is 'coercive' of people's actual needs neglects the fact that actual needs are not spontaneously self-generating in the breasts of individuals, but always exist in the context of a particular social-economic organisation and series of institutions and are thus necessarily subject to and moulded by the 'coercion' and 'constraints' of the theory of needs which underlies that organisation, however implicit and unstated that theory may be. Thus any theory of human needs that challenges that organisation and those actual needs which it conditions must tend to the removal of those constraints if it enlarges the understanding of those who have the needs of the grounds upon which they have come to have them. Any enlargement in understanding of the formation of the needs that one in fact has is potentially transformative of the needs one has, in that it removes the straitjacket of a theory of needs that would persuade one of their inviolable (i.e., unalterable) status. And if explanation of this kind engenders conflict between the needs that are actually experienced and the needs that might have been had or could be had, it is a conflict that itself represents an expansion of needs, a breakdown of the coercion of an unthinking and spontaneous acceptance of who one is and of the social context in which one is who one is, and thus moves in the direction of a genuine politics of need.

The stress that liberal theory places on the 'truth' of felt needs or wants is not mistaken as such; what has to be attacked is the coercive force of the theory of the autonomously chosen and unconditioned nature of those needs or wants that is expressed through this emphasis. And since the other side of this notion of the unconditioned and autonomous nature of felt needs is the impossibility of changing such needs, it is hardly surprising to find that liberal theory in fact lends itself to political systems based on 'experts' serving the 'real' needs of individuals who are 'incapable' of seeing beyond the nose of their wants. The supposed incorrigibility of 'wants' is here doing (liberal) service as a theory of the incorrigible stupidity of the mass of human beings, and thus justifying the pointlessness of any expansion of their possibilities of self-understanding. But any individual who has been enabled to appreciate the role of social forces in the formation of his or her needs, and thus in a profound sense to appreciate the otherness of self, is immediately placed in a position to demystify the supposed transgression of individual political rights in the move from 'I need' to 'we need' and thus to 'you (as the other in society) need', and thereby to remove the block to any political action of a supposed political impotence.

2.   On the essentiality of needs

Now someone might object at this point that not only are these reflections overabstract and metaphoric, but also that they have little or no bearing upon needs as normally understood. After all, it might be said, the question of needs has nothing to do with decisions on values, whether explicit or implicit; it has to do with what is *essential*, and that in turn has to do with certain quite straightforward facts about the biology and psychology of human beings. The concept of needs is the concept of what we *must* have or consume. But, of course, since this immediately invites the question: 'must have as a condition of what?' it is clear that this solution only raises once again the question of what we need, and that the 'facts' of biology and psychology to which it appeals are themselves interpreted in the light of the answer given to that question. Aristotle, it seems to me, saw this point about needs very clearly. Amplifying his definition of the 'necessary', he writes: 'when life or existence are impossible (or when the good cannot be attained) without certain conditions, these conditions are "necessary", and this cause is itself a kind of necessity';[2] rather than condemn the circularity of his definition, we should accept it as a salutary reminder that in all attempts to argue for or against certain conditions as needs (i.e., as conditions of survival and the acquisition of the 'good') we are already involved in judgements of what constitutes 'life' or the 'good' for human beings. In other words, it is a reminder that all apparently value-free claims presuppose judgements/decisions/assumptions about conditions for survival and the acquisition of the good (in short about our needs). It is, of course, our physiological nature and the causal processes upon which we are dependent for biological survival that supply the grounds for any claim of the form 'human beings need to eat'. My only point is that in passing from these facts of biology to statements of that form, one is implicitly asserting some statement of the form 'the survival (happiness) of human beings is a good thing', and we interpret the facts or select them as pertinent facts in the light of that implicit assumption.

But still, it might be objected, granted that the data of human biology are interpreted from the standpoint of the needs they express only in the light of certain assumptions about survival or the good, this does not mean that the data are not quite adequately spoken for in terms of our possession of what can be termed 'biological' needs; no one can seriously dispute that we have these 'basic' needs for food, shelter, sleep, and so on. Accepting this for the time being, let us turn instead to consideration of the much greater degree of uncertainty we experience in the face of claims about our 'psychological' needs. Here I have in mind claims to the effect that we need love, security, autonomy, solitude, privacy and so on. What are the grounds for uncertainty here? Why do we regard it as more controversial to claim a need for, e.g., 'autonomy' than a need for food? Precisely because, I suggest, we regard the truth or falsity of such claims as depending upon the interpretation that is placed on the invoked psychological concepts. When the child-psychologist tells us that experiment or observation shows it to be a 'fact' that the young child needs the 'security' of close and continual contact with the mother, we accept this to be a fact only to the extent that we concur with the definition and evaluation of the invoked 'security'. If the deprivations of the child placed in the care of the child-minder are to become evidence for the child's need for security, they must first be interpreted as deprivations and not as mere events or neutral effects. In other words, the child's misery, so far from 'speaking for itself' is spoken for by us who interpret it and thereby imply the need it bespeaks, and in this case it is clear that in postulating this need we are engaged in an act of interpretation of our 'nature' involving judgement and decision about its import. And these judgements are historical and relative. What counts as security in the eyes of the psychologist is itself only definable in terms of the structure of social (and in this case specifically familial relations holding in a given society.

In a much more blatantly prejudicial interpretation of the facts, the present Prime Minister claims that the people of Britain have a need for security in their property and possessions. Here the appeal to the general psychological need embodies an entire politics of what is good for society, whose main article of faith is the continuation of relations of production based on private ownership and excessive inequalities of wealth.

But this should hardly surprise us. If, as I have argued, all talk about human needs is political in the sense that it involves a laying-down of value (a decision about what conduces to survival and the good), then we should expect different political ideologies to reflect this in the different sets of 'facts' about our needs that they put before us. (And in this respect, we might note that these sets of facts are possessed of a certain internal coherence and systematicity — thus, for example, in the light of the need for security of possessions other needs will be discovered and defined: the need for young people to be subject to greater parental authority, the need for more discipline in the schools, and so on.)

To insist upon the historically relative and socially conditioned-contextual nature of the values appealed to in general claims about what I have termed 'psychological' needs is not to suggest that it is mistaken to make any such appeals. I want to insist, on the contrary, that such appeals are inevitable in human society and are the profound mark of its political status. To deny, on the grounds that it commits us to 'non-scientific' claims, that we can pass normative judgements of this kind is ultimately to deny our status as political agents. What it does suggest, however, is (a) that we must continually examine the credentials of any such claims and challenge (on the basis of an alternative 'theory of needs', which has to be argued for — see (b)) the necessity of the use that is made of them in justifying a given form of social existence; and (b) psychological investigation of the springs of human motivation and action, of the ways these affect our 'reception' of a given world and are in turn conditioned by it, and of the possibilities and limits of their manipulation and transformation. From such an investigation, it may well emerge that there are grounds for speaking of abstract psychological needs rather as there are grounds for speaking of abstract biological needs. I shall have more to say on this elsewhere. Here I am only concerned to stress how circumspect we must be in proceeding to any claims about universal needs for 'autonomy', 'security', 'self-development' and so on. For appeal to such needs is made to justify the most heterogeneous and antithetical political programmes, and it is all too likely that the concepts of 'autonomy', 'individuality' and the like that are invoked in such claims will themselves derive their particular content *from* the social-political theory which wants to appeal to them as if they were external to it and represented 'neutral' facts about our needs. We must consider, for example, that thinkers as diverse as Marx and Mill both insist upon the need for the development of individuality and yet argue for utterly different political programmes on its basis. If this is so, it obviously points to the need for an investigation that will show us the grounds for the production of the competing concepts and thus afford us some basis from which to assess their respective claims to represent authentic needs. I suggest that in all such investigations, we shall be correct to privilege the more adequate explanation, that is to say, the body of theory which can provide, on the same grounds that it explains the production of its own concepts, explanation of the concepts of any theory incompatible with it. Thus Marxism, in explaining the grounds for the production of the Millian concept of individuality, is to be privileged over liberal theory, even though the Marxist concept may well stand in need of further investigation itself. Likewise, I would suggest that any adequate theoretical justification for positing abstract needs for 'privacy', 'autonomy', 'security' and so on, will be one that reveals the grounds for the psychologistic-empiricistic content so frequently given these needs by social and political theory. Any claim that we need 'privacy' will have to take its distance from prima facie similar claims that justify the atomisation character- istic of capitalist society; any claim that we need to develop our individuality will have to take its distance from prima facie similar claims that in fact justify measures designed to secure the reproduction of individuals possessed of the intiative and entre- preneurial spirit so essential to the maintenance of capitalist production.

So, to sum up, any discourse about the individual or about society that invokes the concept of needs will be involved in a process of selection of pertinent data, interpretation of that data, explanation-critique of data, that in a profound sense constitutes its particular theory of needs — its laying down of value, its politics. It is thus necessarily involved in a certain circularity. But this does not commit us to a straightforward subjectivism or relativism of needs (and thus to political voluntarism) since social theory can itself provide the grounds for assessing the validity of social theory, thus for assessment of opposing theories and thus for choice of a given theory or theoretical framework in terms of which to understand ourselves (including the formation and nature of our needs).[3]

In the following chapter I shall speak in more specific terms about the contribution of Marxism in this respect, and I shall attempt to place it and non-Marxist economic and social theory within the context of these rather abstract considerations. But at this point it is important, I think, to look a little more critically at two assumptions that have supported my discussion so far. In the first place, I have assumed that it is legitimate to speak of 'abstract universal needs'. The epistemological grounds for doing so will be discussed in some detail in the course of this book. In order, however, to avoid misunderstanding and to provide some signals for the reader, I should like to make it clear at this point that in speaking of abstract needs I am speaking of conceptual abstrac- tions, and not referring to needs that are concretely instantiated. The only needs that are experienced, and the only products that enter into their gratification, are specific, particular, historic needs and products. This of course, is Marx's crucial insight upon them; it is usually expressed in terms of his recognition of the 'historically developed' nature of needs, or in terms of his rejection of any essentialism of needs (his rejection of the view that treats needs as attributes of a general, transhistoric, unchanging 'human nature'). In his own words: 'Hunger is hunger, but the hunger gratified by cooked meat eaten with a knife and fork is a different hunger from that which bolts down raw meat with the aid of hand, nail and tooth.'[4]

Actual hunger is always specific. But 'hunger' nevertheless 'is hunger', or, in other words, conceptualisation of the common and abstract need for food is essential to specifying the distinct concrete needs for food that exist historically *as* instances, precisely, of hunger. It is essential rather in the way that the general abstract concept of 'production in general' is essential to the specification of actual, historically existing modes of production, and of it, we may say as Marx himself says of production in general that it is '. . . an abstraction, but a rational abstraction in so far as it really brings out and fixes the common element and thus saves us repetition.'[5] But, as he goes on to say, one fixes the common element only in order to isolate in any particular instance the elements which are not common and general, and which 'must be separated out from the determinations valid for production as such, so that in their unity — which arises already from the identity of the subject, humanity, and the object, nature — their *essential difference* is not forgotten'. Now exactly the same epistemological points can be made about the concept of an abstract universal need: the category of 'hunger'/'need for food' fixes the element common to all experiences of it (and which owes its identity throughout these particular instantiations to the biology of human beings); but if we then proceed to account for all instances simply in terms of this identity we shall lose sight of precisely those determinations of them which are not common and general and which provide them with their specificity.

My second assumption — and this bears directly upon the analysis of needs in terms of 'what is essential' — is that talk of abstract 'biological' needs is uncontroversial relative to talk about abstract 'psychological' needs. I now want to query this assumption on two grounds. Firstly, is it in fact possible to draw this kind of distinction between two sets of needs? Are not all so-called biological needs possessed of a psychological dimension, and vice-versa? Is it not obviously the case that certain needs which we would want to account no less 'basic' than the need for food (sexual needs, for example) escape any analysis in purely biological or purely psychological terms? In this connection one might consider evidence to suggest that gratification of the supposedly primary biological needs is dependent on certain other conditions being fulfilled, these conditions themselves arguably bespeaking psychological needs. In situations of intense fear or despair 'biological' needs will go ungratified,[6] and certain disorders (insomnia, anorexia nervosa) appear to testify to the capacity for the psychological need to prove more 'urgent' than the biological.

Secondly, is it in fact the case that there are clear cut criteria for determining what is to count as the 'biological' as opposed to the 'psychological' element in our needs? As a way into discussing this second ground on which I would want to query my original assumption, we might recall Aristotle's two criteria of x being necessary: x is necessary when it is (i) essential to life and (ii) essential to the acquisition of the good. Now it might seem that it is in such terms that one could attempt to distinguish the 'biological' from the 'psychological' need. Biological needs would then be those essential to physical survival, psychological needs those essential to the good (whatever the good might be deemed to be). But such a distinction is clearly question-begging — and not simply because it provides no criterion of the good, but because the same is true of the invoked concept of 'survival'. After all, what does constitute the 'existence' of life or 'survival' for the human being? Even at the abstract conceptual level at which the discussion is currently being conducted there is clearly room for debate about the use of the criterion of 'survival' for demarcating between supposedly primary or basic biological needs and other 'secondary' needs. Why otherwise is there the inclination to speak of the 'vegetable' as opposed to human survival of those deprived of everything except physical reproduction? When it is said that man 'cannot live by bread alone' should we not treat this as precisely a claim about survival? Can one be said to have survived experiences that have driven one insane? I leave these queries as queries; they are intended here only to indicate the problematic nature of the appeal to the notion of 'essential to survival' as the criterion for designating some set of basic, abstract needs.

In any case, even if we do adopt some criterion such as 'reproduction of the physical organism' as a good enough working definition of so-called biological needs, we must recognise that *actual* biological needs will be extremely complex and sophisticated in most societies today, and also very divergent between individuals. For the mass of those living in Britain today, for example, biological survival is dependent upon the vast and highly complex structure of production and distribution that delivers the loaf of bread to the supermarket; persons suffering from kidney disease or diabetes must surely be allowed to have 'biological' needs for kidney machines and insulin;[7] an old person's biological needs will differ from those of a young person, a baby's from those of its parents, a woman's from those of a man, and so on.

The suggestion, then, that we can isolate either at the abstract or at the concrete level some set of 'primary' needs on the criterion of their being 'essential to survival', though not entirely incoherent, is far more problematic than might be supposed. For depending on the way in which it is interpreted it tends to be either misleadingly restrictive or vacuously uninformative. When applied in restrictive fashion, it will lead to the absurdity of claiming that bread and water are needs, while bread factories and antibiotics are 'luxuries'; when employed vacuously it will lead to the position of claiming that everything we currently consume in the reproduction of our bodies, and the entire system of social activities which deliver the products to us, are all equally needed. Both of these positions do less than justice to the concept of needs, which I suggest both overspills biology and yet remains restrictive relative to any and every consumption. Our needs are arguably both more than a matter of biology and both more and less than what we actually consume. This is a point which, it seems to me, King Lear appreciated well enough when he protested:

> O, reason not the need! Our basest beggars
> Are in the poorest things superfluous.
> Allow not nature more than nature needs,
> Man's life is cheap as beast's. Thou art a lady;
> If only to go warm were gorgeous,
> Why, nature needs not what thou gorgeous wear'st,
> Which scarcely keeps thee warm. But, for true need —
> You heavens give me that patience, patience I need.

But to accept this is, of course, to be returned precisely to the question of 'true' need, and to be brought face to face with the impossibility of providing any answer to the question: 'what do human beings need?' or 'what are human needs?' in terms of some set of 'facts' whether about our 'nature' or about what we in fact consume. We are forced, in other words, to recognise that if these questions are answerable, they are so only in the form of a series of political decisions-acts, in the form of a series of choosings-positings of values beyond which there can be no further appeal, and which themselves must reveal the 'truth' of our needs.

It is, then, already a decision of this kind that rejects any account of needs that attempts to suppress the political dimension of the question it poses, and which argues both against the restriction of human needs to certain biological attributes, and against their identification with actual consumption. And if we accept King Lear's suggestion that human beings have needs for more than what 'nature' needs but not necessarily for all that artifice has happened to provide, then this itself involves a choosing-positing of value, and is expressive of certain convictions about human potentialities and about human needs. But it is, at the very least, a standpoint from which we can raise the question as to why contemporary scientists of man and of his politics are bent on the suppression of the politics of human need, and begin to see the politics of this suppression.

Notes

1   Alan White, *Modal Thinking*, Oxford, Blackwell, 1975, Chap. 8.
2   Aristotle, *Metaphysics*, ed. D. Ross, London, Dent, 1956, p. 10.
3   In this connection, the reader is referred to R. Bhaskar, *A Realist Theory of Science*, Sussex, The Harvester Press, 1978, and in particular to his arguments for a naturalist conception of the social sciences in which these are seen to be critical, self-reflexive and totalising, in *The Possibility of Naturalism*, Sussex, The Harvester Press, 1979 and in his article 'Scientific Explanation and Human Emancipation', *Radical Philosophy*, no. 26, 1980.
4   K. Marx, *Grundrisse*, Harmondsworth, Penguin Books, 1973, p. 92.
5   *Ibid*. p. 85.
6   As a recent instance of this, one might cite the widespread failure of women to menstruate in Kampuchea in the aftermath of the terrorism of the Pol Pot regime. According to doctors, this could not be accounted for wholly in terms of malnutrition.
7   Though these are, of course, needs that do not feature among the 'biological' needs of earlier generations, and this suggests the intentional character of a need, i.e., that one cannot be said to have a need except on the condition that there exists an object towards which it is directed. Hence, prior to the discovery and production of antibiotics there can have been no

need for them, even though, had they been available, they would have ensured the survival of many who died for lack of them. But perhaps it will then be said that since antibiotics were lacking in this sense, they were 'needed'? Here we need to distinguish between 'needed' in the sense of 'essential to the reproduction of the physical organism' and 'needed' in the sense of a feeling intentionally directed towards a specific object. But strictly speaking, I think it must be admitted that the patient whether conscious or unconscious, can only 'need' a serum injection if serum is available. The intentionality of need relates to the existence of the object towards which it is directed, rather than to any conscious 'intention'.

2 Marxism and the Question of Human Needs

I want now to speak in somewhat more concrete terms about the orientation of this work. I opened, in my introductory chapter, on a note of frustration, and then went on to suggest that this was nowhere more acutely felt than in relation to Marxism. And I further suggested that the acuteness of the frustration was due to the fact that when the question of needs is neutralised or depoliticised in the name of Marxist thought, it is neutralised or depoliticised in the name of a body of theory that shows more clearly than any other the full dimensions of the question of needs and the impossibility of suppressing its politics. Counter, then, to any suggestion that Marxism offers a solution to the question of human needs, or else must be seen to have disentangled itself from that question, I shall argue that its value lies precisely in the fact that it poses that question in the form of a problem.

It does so, in the first place, because it recognises the historically developed and therefore specific nature of human needs and theorises this development and specificity. But this recognition of the historically developed and expanded nature of needs is only as fruitful and as problematic as it is because of the other aspect of Marxist thought: its critique of the specific, historically developed needs (or pattern of consumption) to which capitalism, as the latest form of development of the productive forces, has given rise, and its advocacy of a socialist, and ultimately communist alternative form of development wherein needs will progressively expand 'without limit' and distribution will be 'in accordance' with them. In other words, the question of needs is posed as a problem by Marxism as a result of the way it combines an epistemological reorientation of thought about needs with a prescriptive and political programme whose fundamental article is the development and satisfaction of human needs.

But secondly, and directly as a result of the way in which the question is posed by Marxism, it is also a question that is posed *for* it. There is no doubt that Marx in a sense foresaw this secondary posing of the question. He argues, for example, in the *Grundrisse*[1] that the historical process is a process of transformation of what was previously superfluous into what is necessary, and is thus constantly 'suspending' our 'natural needs' as well as our 'former luxuries'. But he also argues that the development of industry in bourgeois society only operates this 'suspension' in 'antithetical form', in that it itself 'only posits another specific social standard as necessary, opposite luxury'. He thus recognises here that there is a further question — a question of the critique or assessment of this standard, a question of absolute or 'true' need, which it is implicitly suggested cannot be automatically 'read off' from, or identified with, the 'needs' developed by the productive forces of capitalism. But he never expressly poses this problem of 'true' need as a problem or aporia created at the heart of his own thought, nor does he ever attempt to confront it. Indeed with a certain irony that his frustrated reader is bound to feel even more forcefully today, he concludes the passage from which I have quoted with the remark: 'These questions about the *system of needs* and the *system of labours* — at what point is this to be dealt with?'

Moreover, though he may recognise that a problem is posed in principle by the merely 'antithetical' development of needs in bourgeois society, it is doubtful that he ever envisaged what this might involve in practical terms, and almost certain that he never perceived how the actual development of capitalism might be such as to call in question certain fundamental tenets of his account of the transition to socialism. We today, however, living as we do in the context of a global system of capitalism that has proved more tenacious and more resilient to its own contradictions than Marx ever predicted, have no choice but to confront the question that this poses in practical political terms for us and for future generations, and poses theoretically for the standard Marxist interpretation of the passage to socialism and for its standard account of the nature of socialist-communist society. For though there is little general recognition of the fact, there is some growing awareness on the left that the emphasis on production that has characterised both bourgeois and revolutionary thought for so long must cede to an emphasis upon consumption. It is clear now, at least to some, that the questions we should be asking are not about how to expand production with a view to meeting a body of needs that are left to take care of themselves and allowed to develop as the *post eventum* complement of the goods produced for consumption, but questions about what in fact we do need to consume; questions about the form this consumption should take and about the limits to be imposed upon it. They are questions about our 'true' needs, and about what in terms of these we can afford to consume in the way of material goods and services. And these are questions, of course, that are intimately bound up with, and in a sense only arise in the form that they do because of, the failure of capitalist economies to satisfy even the 'basic' needs of large numbers of people, and the failure of the socialist nations to innovate, except to a minimal degree, upon the patterns of consumption, the life-style, the expectations and values of capitalist society. Indeed, contrary to what we might have hoped, and what Marx perhaps expected, the socialist countries have come increasingly to reflect, rather than to diverge from capitalist society in these respects. And what is more depressing is that one finds them justified by Marxists precisely on the grounds that they do so. Thus, in a recent text, an orthodox economist is castigated for the 'facetiousness' of his suggestion that the USSR has an 'ideological need to avoid any obvious imitation of capitalist methods', and the non-orthodox, Marxist author claims approvingly that the Soviet Union in fact 'abounds in examples of learning from capitalism'.[2]

But when learning from capitalism means implementation of technologies that live only for the day and have no thought for the ecological disasters of the morrow; when it involves materialising increasing amounts of social labour time in armaments whose only use-value is to destroy all value and the agents of its production a thousand times over; when working for the socialist Age of Plenty means toiling eight hours a day on an imported Togliatti assembly line, then the time has perhaps come to consider the wisdom of the 'master' and to reclaim an imagination about consumption that has for so long now been crushed by the all too palpable exemplar of capitalist life-styles and 'standards' of living.Even without the absurdity of the destruction of value involved in the arms race (whose damage and horrors are not exhaustively retained in a present cold-storage, but are lived daily in the form of what could otherwise have been consumed, and in an actual dread whose psychological toll is being extracted now), it has become ecologically impossible to pursue a path of continual expansion of material production, and the traditional Marxist argument that it is only capitalist relations and no problem of material resources that stands in the way of such expansion[3] must be dealt with no less severely, though with greater seriousness, than Ronald Reagan's recent suggestion that the energy crisis is a conspiracy of President Carter.[4]

In the light of the shift of emphasis to questions of consumption that is forced upon us by this impossibility, we must seriously question the longstanding Marxist faith in the development of the productive forces to usher in the communist era of abundance. And we must appreciate the extent to which Marx's own conceptions of this development — his reliance upon the 'civilising' influence of capitalism, his commitment to technology to overcome social evils, his appeal to the 'unlimited expansion of needs' — are impregnated with the 'productivist' values that inspired the political economists of whom he himself was so critical. For Marx's attack on Smith and Ricardo could be said to be directed not so much against their faith in production, which indeed he regarded as a definitely enlightened aspect of their thought (as opposed to the nostaligic-regressive character of romantic critiques of capitalism), as at their failure to appreciate that the capitalist mode of production was itself but an historical and limited form of that productivity, whose barriers would progressively be overcome with the emergence of socialism and passage to communism.[5] The fact is, however, that while the productive forces of capitalism have long ago accomplished their civilising mission (in the sense of a development of scientific and technological knowledge to a point where in principle the earth's resources could be harnessed in a fashion that allowed its population an unprecedented standard of living and an unprecedented allocation of free time), capitalist relations have yet to quit the stage of history; indeed, they still occupy its centre, and so far from having been burst asunder by the expansion of the productivity they have promoted, they have come to assert an ever tighter stranglehold upon global production to the point where certain nations — and especially a certain class within those nations — are increasingly privileged to the detriment of all the other peoples and nations of the world. Capitalist accumulation, in fact, has superseded the limitations imposed by individual consumption to the point where surplus-value can only continue to be realised in products which are increasingly removed from concern with day to day consumption and can scarcely be credited with satisfying anything that would qualify as a *human* need. As mere mortals, we need the stock-piling of armaments like we need a hole in the head — for which, indeed, a gun is quite adequate. The suspension of our 'former needs and former luxuries' has incontestably proceeded 'antithetically'.

The reason for this inhuman proliferation of production is, of course, capitalism's capacity to maintain its relations of production and to harness labour-power and natural resources in ways that accomodate and confirm these relations. Crucial to an understanding of this capacity is an understanding of the ingenious and prejudicial application of technologies which serve the purpose of exploitation in the self-same moment that they serve the purposes of a more efficient production. Also crucial to it is an understanding of imperialism and of the role of the State as protection-cum-mitigation of capitalist development. As for its effects, we know them well: impoverishment and underdevelopment of two thirds of the world, ecological attrition of such severity that its effects are fast becoming irreversible even in principle, the continuance of a capitalist economy in most of the developed nations. And as I have suggested, even when we turn to those countries which have experienced a socialist revolution, we see that the hand of capitalist civilisation lies heavy upon them both economically and ideologically: economically in respect of the limits that global capitalism places on any autonomous planning to meet needs, ideologically in respect of the permeation of the techniques and institutions of capitalism, its goals and values, to every aspect of their societies. Such is the force of the actual economic constraints imposed by this global context, and such is the influence of the value attached in such a context to *economic* considerations, that economics remains the dictator even in socialist countries, which have in principle opted for the subordination of 'blind market forces' to conscious political decisions. The failure on a global scale to achieve any subordination of economics to politics has tended to subvert whatever attempts have been made on a national scale to set that process of subordination in motion, and the politics of the socialist nations have themselves become underpinned by a notion of politics as a secondary and *a posteriori* form of adjustment to economic forces rather than as the prime moment of choice of the forces that will 'control' society.

In other words, it is not only capitalism but the relative absence, either in the practice of the socialist nations or in the 'Marxist' theory that interprets and endorses that practice, of any thorough-going reversal-critique of the practices and values of capitalism, that reproduces the dislocation between an area of production (of 'economics', of determinants of the system, of 'the level of development of the productive forces') on the one hand, and an area of consumption (of 'politics', of intervention in the deter-minants, of conscious decision making) on the other. But a genuine critique of both capitalist and socialist societies must appreciate the actual unity of the production-consumption relationship that underlies this apparent dislocation, and the way that this disloca-tion is reflected and reproduced in the divorce between 'economics' and 'politics'. A genuine socialist practice must be based on this understanding and in a sense incarnate it, for in a 'planned' economy, conscious political decision and intervention is part of the very structure of production, of the 'economic base', of the 'infrastructure' that in the last analysis is determinant. And this, of course, means that it is a practice that is constantly posing questions from the standpoint of its consumption, its 'needs', about the nature and purposes of its production.

The question of needs, then, is posed *by* Marxism through its critique of political economy and liberal theories of man which would silence it or present it as in some sense already resolved; and also because of the central role that is played by the concept of needs in the Marxist characterisation of future communist society. And it is posed *for* Marxism in and through the failure of the 'forces of progress' in which Marx placed his trust to have issued in anything very much today that a Marxist can regard as 'progres-sive'. Viewed in that light, it is not a question than can be resolved by Marxist doctrine, but a question about the coherence of that doctrine from the standpoint of a re-thinking about human needs and their fulfilment that has gradually been forced upon those of the left by the events of the post-war period. If to be Marxist is to be committed to social progress, then it is also to be committed today to a serious questioning and reconsideration of the tradi-tional Marxist notion of progess. In this respect, it matters little whether we see it as a question posed for Marxism or as a question posed for human society as such, and if it is the former that first put it on the agenda, it is the latter that has now to confront it, and to do so more or less unaided by the 'solutions' to it that Marxism is frequently credited with providing.

I have spoken above of the 'silencing' or presumed resolution of the question of needs by political economy and liberal theory which provided the context in which Marxist theory was created, and I have associated that silencing with a re-posing and re-opening of the question that is the outcome of Marx's critique of those bodies of thought. I shall explain more fully what I mean by that in the next chapter. But here I want to say something about the way in which the Marxist 'opening up' of the question has in turn been silenced in our own day, in the first instance by 'bourgeois' theory, and in the second by a Marxology whose theorists have themselves succumbed to this bourgeois theory. The main tenet of this 'theory' is the distinction between 'facts' and 'values', and the argument in support of this distinction is familiar enough: science, if it is to be science (as opposed to speculation or 'metaphysics'), must confine itself to a 'neutral' description of facts, a description that is freed of any normative force, and never involved in any evaluation of the facts in which it deals. Hume and the logical positivists are the main architects of this theory, and a great deal of subsequent thought — despite the extent of its internal disputes — has been its coping. Had Marx himself been less an inhabitant of its edifice he might have realised the dynamite that his thought (*dunamei*) contained to explode it. Unfortunately, being as concerned as he was with establishing the scientificity of scientific socialism, and too ready to accept that this must have positivistic credentials, he never managed to pose the problem that is raised by the co-presence in his thought of a 'factual' and an 'evaluative' discourse, let alone theorise that co-presence explicitly as the mark of what was most progressive and revolutionary about it. Marxism has suffered greatly as a result. It has suffered firstly because in leaving its evaluative dimension unanchored and without support, it has made it too easy for positivism to relate to the fact that it is there at all as a piece of theoretical confusion or naivety, a metaphysical hangover that contaminates its 'science' and in the end, therefore, must be seen to undermine its claim to provide knowledge. And it has suffered because it has produced a lesion within its own ranks separating those who have been convinced, like Marx himself, that he was in the busines of 'science', but have, again like him, accepted the positivist interpretation of science and therefore done their uttermost to rid Marxism of its contamination with values, from those who, convinced that Marx was in the business of 'humanism', have produced ad nauseam its normative-humanist themes in blissful ignorance or perverse denial of the fact that in order for them to have real import they must be kept in their problematic liaison with the scientific strand of Marxist thought rather than severed from it and continually retailed in their unanchored and unsupported form.

Let us deal firstly, however, with the silencing of the question of needs in the form that Marx raised it by current bourgeois thought. Marx raises that question through insisting that 'needs' are historically developed and thus in a sense to be 'read off' from or seen reflected in actual consumption, and then allowing that claim to confront another to the effect that what we consume may not be what we 'need' and what we need may not be gratified in what we consume. Bourgeois thought silences it by saying: the confrontation is illegitimate — the second claim is evaluative and never resoluble by any investigation of facts; it must therefore not be allowed to confuse the purely descriptive account of needs that we are offered in the first claim. Hence to the extent that the contemporary human sciences offer any 'theories' of needs themselves these tend to move either in the closed circle of the identification of needs with an actual, specific historical consumption, or else attempt to provide purely factual answers to the evaluative question as to what it is that human beings 'truly' need.

Economics is a prime representative of the first line of approach when in order to preserve its scientificity it refuses to countenance any concept of needs except one defined in terms of 'effective demand': needs, it will tell us, are revealed through sale. The prior methodological evaluation that underlies this economic definition of needs is obvious enough — for if it is clear that the attraction of this definition lies in the fact that it disallows two value-laden questions (do human beings fulfill their needs in what they in fact consume ('buy')?; and do they have needs which they cannot satisfy through their consumption, i.e., by means of their purchasing power?), it is also clear that this is itself only so because of the value attached to a 'value-free' account of needs. Even more obvious is the political import of this definition, and the extent to which it could only satisfy one who was already up to the ears in a whole series of evaluations of the society whose 'needs' can be slotted so easily into an economic calculus. It is a definition based on the presupposition that the only matter of concern is the satisfaction of an unquestioned, already existing body of needs. The economist who refuses to entertain any but the effective demand definition of needs clearly has no interest in how the needs· so defined come into existence. It is of no concern to him or her why it is that individuals are possessed of different purchasing powers; and though there may be considerable concern with what it is that motivates the consumers to exert their varying purchasing powers in the way that they do, it is clear that this concern cannot entertain concern for whether 'x is motivated to purchase y' is equivalent to 'x needs y'. All that matters from the point of view of the economic calculus of needs is that the consumers, for various reasons, have their motivations and that a body of commodities is sold. Seen in this light, the instrumental nature of the identification of needs with commodities sold is apparent enough, and could only be accepted by one who had already accepted the correctness or 'value' of a given pattern of consumption and a given distribution of income (or at least the correctness of the idea that it was not the business of an economist to question that 'correctness' or value). I would argue, therefore, that the definition of needs in terms of effective demand forms part and parcel of a scientistic ideology that would persuade us that one can divorce the question of the satisfaction of needs from the question of their determination and assessment, and the question of means (*how* best to satisfy an existing body of needs) from the question of the ends served by that 'satisfaction', but which is in fact an ideology that is itself a means serving a quite definite end: the reproduction of a particular socio-economic system together with its particular mode of distribution of wealth.

But if the economic definition of needs seems the most blatantly pernicious attempt to 'decontaminate' the question of needs of any evaluative-political dimension, the attempt to settle that question by referring our needs to 'facts' about our biological and psychological 'nature' is, as I have already indicated, equally confused methodologically. For it is in fact impossible to supply this supposedly 'neutral' or purely factual account of needs. The concept of needs, that is to say, must enter right at the start as a criterion of the pertinence of the physiological and psychological data selected for investigation, and it is only because in a certain sense we have already decided what constitutes the needs (as opposed to the whims, or 'less necessary' or indeed undesirable gratifications) of human beings that we can in turn decide which aspects or manifestations of our nature are those which reflect our needs. In short, it must be recognised that any data about the biological or psychological constitution of human beings has itself to be interpreted, and can only be interpreted, from the standpoint of a certain 'theory of needs'.

Similar points hold in relation to the 'facts' about our needs that sociological studies present us with, at least to the extent that these studies are confined to cataloguing the 'needs' of 'lesser necessities' or 'luxuries' of a given society or social grouping. For while it is true that the data offered are intended to be purely descriptive of patterns of consumption, it remains the case that they could only be collated because the researcher had already adopted a particular criterion or definition of need. For the most part, such sociological studies base themselves on the criterion of need that the society or grouping under investigation is itself felt to adopt. It is of course a moot point whether this sensed 'norm' does in fact reflect extensive agreement between the individuals of such a society or grouping or is based on any shared criteria or value system. (It may well be that some sociological definitions of need are no less ad hoc than that of the judge in a recent maintenance case who allowed the divorced wife adequate money for a black and white television but disallowed her enough to use a colour television on the grounds that the former was a need but the latter a luxury). But what is clear is that any sensed norm which is used as a criterion of needs already incorporates the value-judgements of the society in which it is sensed.

It should be said, however, that though sociology shares with economics a positivist tendency to think of needs in terms of actual consumption, it has also tended to recuperate the concept of need from economic theory precisely in order to designate a demand that is not effective and thus to mark areas of consumption for which there is a 'need' but for which there is no provision — therefore no 'need' in the strict economic sense. There have been sociological studies, for example, that have wanted to chart the dislocation that — counter to the supposed ideal of market relations — always emerges in a market economy between actual ('non-effective') demand and 'effective demand'. This concept of needs thus becomes the concept of a demand (eg. for housing, health, education and other welfare services) that even the most successful market economies are incapable of satisfying, and whose gratification therefore falls to the public sector.[6]

It is clear that this concept of need bears directly on the Marxist distinction between the (essentially economic) dictate of the law of value that holds in a capitalist economy and the (essentially political) 'planning to meet needs' that characterises a socialist economy, since the term functions as an index of the recognition that the market economy is an inadequate mechanism for satisfying needs. It is therefore a recognition of the role that can be played in consumption by a conscious and deliberate intervention in contrast to the 'blind' determinations of the market. But it is precisely for that reason that it invites the same kind of questions that the Marxist account of ' planning to meet needs' invites — questions, of course, which would be meaningless from the standpoint of the economic identification of needs with effective demand, and which are silenced by that definition: questions of the philosophical kind about what it is that human beings really need, about the extent to which needs must be felt and expressed in order to qualify as needs, about the relationship between social and individual needs, about the extent of the dependency of the latter on the former — but also about the extent of the divergence between the two — and about the 'creation' of new needs.[7]

But this similarity in the questions raised by the Marxist recipe for socialism-communism and by the existence of an island of state planning in the sea of capitalist 'anarchy' should not blind us to the very relative nature of welfare state planning under capitalist economies, since in all its initiatives it remains ultimately determined by and answerable to the law of value. State intervention is confined to an area of adjustment between social needs and economic production that will assure the exercise of the law of value, and the very divorce between 'social' and 'economic' factors is a symptom of this restriction.

*   *   *

So much, then, for the silencing by contemporary bourgeois thought of the question of needs in the form that it is raised by Marxism. Let us now turn to the effects of obedience to the fact-value distinction within Marxist thought itself. I have already suggested that it is in terms of this obedience that we must understand the polarisation between humanist and anti-humanist interpretations to which Marxist thought has been subjected. I now want to add a word about the way in which this polarisation has resulted in antithetical closures of the question of needs.

Broadly speaking, the humanist tendency has wanted to argue that Marx provides a 'theory of needs' or 'solves' the question of needs in his theory of alienation, dealienation and realisation of species-being (a state identified with the fulfilment of 'true' needs), and it has in the past been more or less assumed that any discussion of Marx and the 'theory of needs' wll be premised upon the theory of alienation. In fact, almost all such discussion has indeed based itself upon the concepts and themes of the philosohy of man which Marx outlines in the *Economic and Philosophical Manuscripts* of 1844.[8] But though some of this book will be concerned with the theory of alienation, it is written in the conviction that it is mistaken to regard that theory as in any sense a solution to the question of neds. I shall try to show, in fact, that this Marxist humanism closes the question of needs at precisely the point where historical materialism discovers and opens up its full dimensions, and in its own way, therefore, is involved in a suppression of its politics.

But while I believe that anti-humanist interpreters of Marx have served a useful purpose in forcing us to recognise the epistemological objections to any 'solution' to the question of needs that starts out from a presupposed 'theory of man' or human nature, in regarding their criticism of humanist Marxism as itself an alternative 'solution' to that question they have adopted an equally dogmatic attitude towards it. For the most part, anti-humanist Marxism has simply evaded discussion of any of the questions about needs that are implicitly raised by the Marxist critique of capitalism and its advocacy of the socialist-communist alternative. In its feverish anxiety to purge the science of historical materialism of any normative content, it has refused to countenance any but a positivistic definition of needs in terms of actual consumption — the only definition having the required neutrality — and has suggested that any evaluation of consumption belongs to a separate domain of 'ideology'. In this sense, the very posing of the question: 'what is it, that human beings need?', let alone the attempt to answer it, is regarded as fundamentally mistaken and can only form part of an ideological project — at its worst consisting in the reproduction of a Feuerbachian speculative anthropology that cannot be reconciled with the 'scientific' problematic of historical materialism, at its best a doomed attempt to transcend the 'non-scientific' status of speculative anthropological categories while still having recourse to them and while still trying to accommodate the ethical or ideological aspect of Marxist social criticism within its scientific aspect. Anti-humanism, then, either abstracts altogether from the evaluative aspect of Marxism and from its 'anthropological' discourse, since it is not clear how and where they fit into its analysis, or else it regards them as part of a humanist discourse to be found running in tandem with Marx's 'scientific' discourse but operating on a different level. That is to say, the scientific content of the latter is said to direct us to the ideological status of the former. Thus we have historical materialism on the one hand, and Marxist humanist ideology on the other, and the discovery of the former is the exposure of the non-scientific status of the latter.

What is depressing about anti-humanism (and this, in its particular way, is equally true of Marxist humanism) is its constant suggestion that it is some 'betrayal' of Marxism to do anything less than reveal it as wholly consistent, its failure to consider that there might be virtue in the very fact that it presents itself as aporic, that it is both factual and evaluative, that it is using the concept of needs in differing ways. This is not to deny that this failure is encouraged by Marx himself. And this is so, firstly, because he himself never explicitly confronts the aporic nature of his doctrine or expressly recognises the epistemological tension which his different but co-existing discourses create at its centre; and secondly, because the only instance of a complete and coherent discourse that we are offered is the economic analysis of the capitalist mode of production. The temptation, then, is to regard this analysis as an epistemological 'model' into whose straitjacket we must, lest we sacrifice scientificity, attempt to confine all other supplementary discourses however remote their subject matter from that of economics. Hence the obsession with the application of the 'bearer' or *Träger* conception of the subject to the understanding of class, politics, ideology, psychology, art, literature, and so on.

Marx himself, of course, never suggests that such a conception of individuals would be adequate to an analysis of other domains of human activity. On the contrary, the stringent anti-humanist ought rather to find fault in the extent to which Marx simply assumes that in such matters men and women are not bearers of their relations in the way that they may be said to be of economic functions. Marx, after all, just intuitively accepts that human beings as *agents*, rather than simply as personifications of social roles, would have to enter into any understanding of politics and ideology. This is because, in a profound sense, their very substance is human action and affectivity. An ideological system only functions as ideology because of the nature of human beings, or, in other words, it is because human beings are as they are that ideology functions as what it is. Likewise the political relations of power, dominance and subordination are not the relations of an inanimate system, but the product of human action, and what they express is conflicts of will and motivation. To suggest, therefore, that a study in terms of 'bearers' and 'personifications' could in any sense exhaust this substance of politics is to fall into idealism: it is to suggest that will and consciousness are produced externally to the human subject.

Nevertheless, if nothing that Marx says licences an anti-humanist approach to human affairs generally, it remains the case that he is relatively silent on the issues of politics and psychology that must be brought into relation with what he says about economic activity and its effects by any genuine and comprehensive study of the problem of human needs. At least one anti-humanist has sensed this uncharted terrain of 'anthropology' that the theory of alienation cannot speak for but which lies as a background to the economic analysis, always perceptible but seldom remarked upon. But even he, as if fearful to venture outside the haven of historical materialism and its scientificity, has relegated its study to the ever receding future of the last study that never comes. Of Marx's analysis in *Capital*, he writes:

The only needs that play an economic part are those that can be satisfied economically: those needs are not defined by human nature in general but by their effectivity, i.e. by the level of income at the disposal of the individuals concerned — and by the *nature* of the products available, which are, at a given moment, the result of the technical capacities of production. (...) The direct relationship between these 'needs' thus defined and an anthropological basis becomes therefore purely mythical: or rather, we must invert the order of things and say that the idea of an anthropology, if it is possible at all, must first take into consideration the economic (non-anthropological) definition of those 'needs'.[9]

But if a link between actual consumption and an anthropological basis is merely 'mythical' or at best no more than a 'possibility', what grounds remain for thinking (as Althusser himself clearly does think) that Marx is offering an account of *human* consumption? Why are the products that the bearers of this economic system purchase with their income bread and cheese and not gnats and grass?[10] And what of the evanescent status of anthropology under socialism and communism, where we understand that economic production, so far from itself exclusively determining the needs it satisfies, is itself determined by the need of *human beings* and not by the 'needs' that capitalism would elicit in them?

There are others, as we shall see, who have had even fewer qualms about expurgating Marxism of any discourse about human nature or human happiness. I shall try to show that this stringent anti-humanism can only rid Marxism of its humanist dimension at the expense of ridding its science of social relations of any necessary connection with human society, and that it purchases consistency only at the cost of closing off from questions that it is precisely the value of Marxism to have brought to light.

In future chapters I shall argue this case on the basis of an examination of two distinct and apparently autonomous discourses in which discussion of human needs can be and has been conducted. These can be specified as follows:

A.   The Cognitive Discourse
This argues that human needs are historically developed and discoverable in or identifiable with existing historical patterns of consumption. They are the effect of producton and their explanation refers us primarily to the relations of production.

B.   The Normative Discourse
This argues that history hitherto has failed to satisfy the authentic needs of individuals. Capitalism as the historic condition for the full satisfaction of needs is yet a barrier to that satisfaction. The aim of social production is the 'richly developed individual'.

I shall argue that Marxism employs both of these discourses, and indeed brings them into confrontation in such a way that questions that each discourse raises for the other, but which each, taken in isolation, respectively denies, are necessarily forced into a relationship with each other. This double discourse, as I have shown, is reproduced in the alignments and particular biases of contemporary Marxology, where anti-humanist and humanist readings of Marx's work are able to confront each other while each claiming the credentials of Marx himself because they privilege one of these discourses at the expense of the other. In this sense, the 'theory of needs', or rather the absence of such a theory, is itself the absent centre of Marxism. For while both humanist and anti-humanist Marxisms can be said to offer their respective accounts of needs, both of these are only coherent to the extent that they express one side, while suppressing the other, of an issue which, with the advent of Marxism, precisely becomes an issue because both sides of it are presented conjointly. Neither the humanist nor the anti-humanist account is an account which itself arises out of the tensions between these two aspects and whose content is the consideration and expression of those tensions. It may well be that there can be no such thing as a *theory* which is the expression of such tensions; for a theory is always, in its way, a form of resolution; it may well be that the 'absent centre' which I have suggested is the rightful object of a 'theory of needs' is not the kind of object that can be thought in the coherency of a single theory. But at the very least, there is a discourse about needs to which Marxism invites us, a discourse which can explore the different and at times antithetical discourses about human needs which appear to co-exist in the texts of Marxism and which, I would argue, reflect the tensions and oppositions to be found in social and political thought at large. It is, as I have suggested, because it functions as a mirror in this respect, because it is unique in exposing to view the full dimensions of the question of human needs, and unique in the understanding that it brings to that question, that I devote so much attention to Marxism. But another way of putting this point might be to say that, precisely because of its uniqueness in these respects, it plunges us into previously unthought of difficulties about needs, introducing problems to which it itself provides no real solution and upon which it is not a little confused and confusing.

Notes

1   K. Marx, *Grundrisse, op. cit.*, p. 528.

2   P. Sloan, *Marx and the Orthodox Economists*, Oxford, Blackwell, pp.19-20. Elsewhere in this book, the socialist economies are commended on the grounds of their 'parallel' developments with the capitalist economies in a number of areas, such as their formation of an International Investment Bank comparable to the IMF (p. 9), or their systems of graduated wages (p. 72f); and the backwardness of these economies in comparison with the advanced capitalist nations (and thus their need to 'catch up and surpass' the latter) is accepted without qualification. Given all this, the author leaves himself little option but to stress the 'theoretical differences' between an 'orthodox' economics and Marxist political theory (p.9), and while he argues for these convincingly enough, his work as a whole exemplifies that neutralisation of the question of needs in the name of Marxist doctrine which I have criticised above. Thus he writes, for example, that 'errors will continue to occur for a long time even under a planned economy with regard to estimates of wants and resources, production and coordination' as if it were just a question of accurate calculation of means towards ends that are assumed to take care of themselves.

3   An argument whose mistakes are well exposed by Hans Magnus-Enzensberger in his article 'Critique of Political Ecology', *New Left Review*, no. 52. Enzensberger writes that the ecologists, for all their blindness and naivety, 'have one advantage over the utopian thinking of the Left in the west, namely the realisation that any possible future belongs to the realm of necessity not of freedom and that every political theory and practice — including that of socialists — is confronted not with the problem of abundance, but with that of survival'. And one might note here that even if it were simply a matter of replacing capitalist by socialist relations of production the argument would be academic so long as the socialist economies themselves failed to reverse the path of capitalist production or to think in terms of any radical alternatives in technology.

4   At a recent election meeting, Ronald Reagan was reported (in *The Guardian*) as saying: 'President Carter wants you to adjust your thermostats so as to make you uncomfortable in your homes ... that's nonsense! We've got all the energy we want ...'

5   In this connection, see L. Colletti, *Rousseau and Marx*, London, New Left Books, 1972, Part Three.

6   Ken Coates and Stephen Bodington, in their interesting introduction to Agnes Heller's book on *The Theory of Needs in Marx* (for my views on which see *Radical Philosophy*, no. 15, 1977) point out that the Seebohm report speaks of the social services as 'large-scale experiments in ways of helping those in ned'; they also discuss researches carried out by CREDOC in France with a view to determining the extent to which the public sector provides for needs, and with a view to differentiating between the types of need so accommodated. See A. Heller, *The Theory of Needs in Marx*, London, Alison and Busby, 1974, p. 14.

7   On the question of the Welfare State's creation of needs, Ken Coates and

Stephen Bodington again have some interesting remarks (*ibid.*, pp. 14-15). Referring to the public controversy over the need for false teeth and spectacles triggered by their free provision by the National Health Service, they comment: 'It was argued at the time that this rush for aid reflected the privation previously imposed by the system of market provision on those too poor (or too mean) to exercise "effective demand". But in a similar way the elaboration of medical technology constantly creates new and newer needs, some of them involving far more investment than teeth and glasses. No one could "need" a kidney machine until there was one'. Cf. note 7 Chap. one.

8   K. Marx, F. Engels, *Collected Works* (CW), London, Lawrence and Wishart, 1975 - , Vol. 3.

9   L. Althusser, *Reading Capital*, London, New Left Books, 1970, pp. 166-7.

10 This is not to deny that there is an 'anti-humanist' conception of the subject that is quite consistent with the recognition of human agency in human history, and is, indeed, committed to the assumption that there must be human sciences other than the science of social formations. Althusser's anti-humanism is arguably open to more or less extreme interpretations in this respect. For a very useful clarification of these issues, see J. Mepham, 'Who Makes History?', *Radical Philosophy* no. 6, 1973.

3   The Cognitive Discourse I: Production and Consumption

It is frequently said that what is 'revolutionary' about the Marxist conception of human needs is that these are shown to be 'historically developed', specific in content, and the attributes, not of any 'dumbly general' human nature, but of particular, concrete, historical individuals. Now there can be no doubt of the importance of Marx's break with the essentialist view of human nature which underlay both the political economy and the philosophies of man current in his day and whose themes are still very much a presence in our own. In this and the following chapter I shall be concentrating on the positive import of this break from the standpoint of any theorisation of human needs, and I shall try to show that its revolutionary force lies in the fact that it poses for the first time, or allows us for the first time to pose in correct form, the question of the production and determination of needs. It thus poses questions that are foreclosed when political economy and liberal theories of man appeal to the concept of human needs as itself the explanatory concept of the production of wealth and social development. I shall refer to this Marxist displacement of the concepts of human needs and of human nature from the position they occupy as original, unexamined and unexaminable presuppositions in the evolutionary accounts of political economy and liberal theory in terms of the 'opening' that is operated by historical materialism upon the question of needs. I shall examine it in two stages, first from the standpoint of Marx's critique of bourgeois economic theory, and secondly from the standpoint of his critique of essentialist 'anthropology'. At the same time, however, I shall be arguing that the discourse of political economy is underwritten by the discourse of essentialist anthropology, and that the two are parasitical upon each other, operating complicitly in the 'closure' they effect upon the question of human needs ; and also, inversely, that the two aspects of Marx's 'opening' complement each other.

But before proceeding to this analysis, I should, perhaps, give some indication of how this 'opening' relates to the openness with which I credited Marxism at the end of the last chapter, and which I suggested was accountable to the co-presence within it of two types of discourse about needs. Now it is only *one* of these discourses, or themes, that is constituted or represented by Marx's critique of political economy and liberal theory. It is 'open' where bourgeois economy and essentialist theories of man are closed in its insistence (a) that needs be related to a given structure of production, and (b) that it be a precondition of any study of human needs that we recognise these to be historically developed in their content.

But the general openness of Marxism relates to the fact, as I argued in the previous chapter, that when Marx presents us with this discourse, and thus opens our eyes to the historical and relative character of human needs, he does not, as a good positivist might do, close down on the question of their evaluation. Or perhaps this is better put by saying that from the standpoint of any fact-value distinction, when Marx exposes the historical and relative character of needs, he thereby appears to remove the grounds for the critique of any given pattern of actual consumption. In other words, in default of any theory of absolute needs, the very theory which is denied by the arguments which reveal their relative character, it appears impossible to deliver judgements of a kind that might condemn a given pattern of consumption in favour of its replacement by one that was more 'human' or self-fulfilling. In actual fact, as we know, Marx is constantly involved in a critique of a given pattern of social consumption — namely that of capitalist society — and certain of his condemnations quite directly imply the absolute standpoint of needs that other of his arguments equally directly imply we must reject. Thus, despite the fact that, when contrasted with the political economy and theories of man against which it mounts its stand, the cognitive discourse presents itself as a solution to the question of human needs, when placed in the context of Marxism itself it must be viewed not so much in terms of the resolution it offers but in terms of the role it plays in constructing a problem. I shall delay consideration of that problem to later chapters, and shall here be concerned only with the terms of the critique itself.

1. 'Production is dominant'

It is not my intention here to offer any comprehensive account of the nature and terms of Marx's 'break' with classical political economy; nor shall I have much to say about its general epistemological implications. Given the extensive literature on those issues, such an account is not necessary here. But what has been less discussed, or only discussed in marginal fashion, is the import of Marx's critique from the standpoint of the conceptualisation of human needs, and it is upon this aspect that I shall focus here. I shall argue that in the course of this critique, Marx empties the bourgeois concept of needs of any of the apparent cognitive content it appears to have in the discourse of political economy — disarms it, so to speak, of its apparently explanatory power — and in so doing provides a quite different framework for thinking about needs. Broadly speaking we can say that within the terms of this framework we are directed to a concept of needs (whether the term be applied to the affective attitudes of the consumers, or, in a form of short-hand, to the objects towards which those attitudes are directed[1]) in which these are thought of as effects which can be analysed and theorised in terms of various determinations upon them, rather than unanalysable, pre-given causes.

I have said that the implications of Marx's critique of political economy from the standpoint of the 'theory of needs' that follows from it have received little or only marginal attention. More forcefully, I might say that it is not uncommon to find Marxists who, if questioned on the matter, would no doubt agree that Marx 'breaks' with the entire problematic of classical economy, but who nonetheless in expounding what was enlightened about Marx's approach to needs will couch this in over-general formulae (eg., 'the dominance of production over consumption', the 'historically developed' nature of needs) which themselves stand in need of criticism or further specification in the light of the fully-developed problematic of Marxist economic theory. And those who are quite rigorous and systematic in their exposition of the distance that separates the concept of 'labour' from that of 'labour-power', or Ricardo's 'production' from Marx's 'discovery' of the concept of surplus-value, tend to be rather less so when it comes to specifying the effects of this change in problematic from the standpoint of any theorisation of human needs.[2]

I believe, moreover, if only on the basis of my own experience, that it is easy to be misled into oversimplifying the issues here by over-concentration on one of the rare passages in which Marx explicitly theorises the formation of needs. I am thinking here of the passage on Production and Consumption to be found in the 1857 Introduction to the *Grundrisse*.[3] In other words, it is very tempting, if one is looking for express messages about needs, to fix upon this section from the Introduction as if it were *the* enlightenment, and to relate to it as a final and definitive statement. To do so, however, is to overlook the fact[4] that neither in the Introduction nor in the *Grundrisse* as a whole does Marx manage to establish that distance from the 'problematic' and categories of political economy that informs the writing of *Capital* right from the beginning of its first chapter. In this sense, the *Grundrisse* cannot be seen as a stage in the evolution of *Capital* except in the sense that it records the theoretical struggle with political economy and with Hegelianism that was a necessary prerequisite to Marx's seeing that he could no longer conduct that struggle on *Grundrisse* terrain or with *Grundrisse* concepts. Likewise, and more specifically, there is a break rather than a continuity between the framework for thinking about needs that is provided by *Capital* and that we are offered in the *Grundrisse*. If this is so, it might seem more economical to overlook the latter and proceed directly to an exposition of the former. And this I might be inclined to do, were it not for the fact that it may well be via a critique of Marx's account in the 1857 Introduction that one can best appreciate the more adequate framework established in *Capital*. On the assumption, then, that it may prove more informative, I propose to proceed in two stages: firstly to expound and examine the terms and implications of Marx's account in the 1857 Introduction, and secondly to relate the 'findings' of this examination to the analysis of the capitalist economy we are given in *Capital*.

As is well known to readers of the 1857 Introduction, the main point that Marx is anxious to establish in the section entitled 'The general Relation of Production to Distribution, Exchange, Consumption' is the *dominance* of production over the 'totality' of production, distribution, exchange and consumption, and, specifically in regard to the formation of needs, the *dominance* of production over consumption. Thus he writes:

with a single subject (i.e. society taken as a whole) production and consumption appear as moments of a single act. The important thing to emphasise here is only that, whether production and consumption are viewed as the activity of one or of many individuals, they appear in any case as moments of one process, in which production is the real point of departure and hence the prodominant moment. Consumption as urgency, as need, is itself an intrinsic moment of productive activity. But the latter is the point of departure for realisation and hence also its predominant moment ...[5]

and he contrasts this subordination of the moment of need to that of production with the 'trite notion' that in production 'the members of society appropriate (create, shape) the products of nature in accord with human needs'. Now what is odd about this assertion of the predominance of production over consumption is that nowhere in the section in question is it effectively argued for. Marx produces a number of arguments to support his claim that production, consumption, distribution and exchange are all members of a 'totality' and must be understood as 'distinctions within a unity' — i.e., arguments to the effect that it is mistaken *either* to regard these economic acts as disconnected, discrete elements *or* to conflate them together in an Hegelian identity (as do the economists who argue that since there is no production without consumption, and no consumption without production, consumption and production are the *same* thing); but very little, it seems, to convince us of the fact that within this totality of distinctions between which 'mutual interaction takes place' as in 'every organic whole', it is the moment of production that predominates. It is true that in support of this claim he states that 'the process always returns to production to begin anew', but really that amounts to no more than a restatement of the claim it is allegedly arguing for; for why should we accept that it is production, rather than, say, the needs of consumption, that is the 'starting point' of the process? In short, why pick on production as ultimately predominant when, as Marx has shown, the structure of distribution, exchange, production and consumption is one of mutual interdependence and determination wherein it is only possible to view any of the elements as dominant over the others if one, precisely, views it 'one-sidedly'?

And after all, in thinking himself through the relations between production and consumption, Marx appears to produce exactly the arguments that might convince us of the mistakeness of any attempt to posit one as dominant over the others. For, *on the one hand*, as he points out, though it is production that alone creates the material for consumption, it is consumption tht alone creates for the products the subject for whom they exist as products, consumption that, in a two-fold fashion, produces production, (i) in that a product only becomes a real product in being consumed (a that a product only becomes a real product in being consumed (a house is only a house if it is lived in, a railway where no trains run is not a genuine railway), and (ii) in that it creates the need for new production. Thus, *on the one hand*, it appears that consumption creates both the motive (need) for production and its object: 'if it is clear that production offers consumption its external object, it is equally clear that consumption *ideally posits* the object of production as an internal image, as a need, as drive and as purpose'[6] — a remark echoed, it would seem, in the footnote in *Capital* I where it is suggested that what differentiates man from the bee is that the former erects his constructions in the imagination prior to their concretisation.

But, then, and *on the other hand*, and 'correspondingly', production, says Marx, must be seen to produce consumption, firstly by furnishing the object for it, secondly by determining the manner of consumption, and thirdly by creating the products initially posited by it as objects, in the form of a need felt by the consumer. In regard to the first determination it is argued that it must be recognised that there can be no consumption without an object which is consumed; in regard to the second, it is argued that it is 'clear' that the object of consumption is always a specific object and that it is production which is responsible for its specificity; and in regard to the third determination it is argued that production creates the need for an object, since this need requires its prior existence. Marx cites the object of art which 'like every other product creates a public which is sensitive to art and enjoys beauty'.

Now at this point, the reader might, I suggest, feel somewhat bemused. For the logic of Marx's argument appears to have been somewhat as follows: (i) consumption (need) looked at one way produces (determines/predominates over) production;

consumption (need) looked at another way is produced (determined/predominated over) by production; (ii) forget that dialectic: after all, the correct way of looking at the matter is in terms of production predominating over consumption. And yet nothing, it would seem, has been said to convince us of the superiority of (ii) over (i).

Why, then, is Marx so convinced of it? I suggest that the answer to this question must lie in a truth that is repeatedly stated in this text, a truth that Marx himself has already clearly perceived, of which, in a sense, he might be said to be too aware in that it makes him blind to the fact that he has not actually produced the conceptual apparatus to explain it and cannot do anything with it so long as he continues to speak the language of the political economists, albeit it in 'inverted' form. The truth, namely, that production and consumption are always determinate and historically specific. One is always dealing, as Marx says, with a definite form of production, a definite form of consumption, and therefore with a definite form of relations between them; to stay, then, with the political economists is to stay at a level at which it is impossible to begin to theorise this determinacy. Marx's insistence on the predominance of production should be seen as the register of an epistemological reversal that is an essential precondition of thinking the historical specificity of production and consumption. It is inadequate as it stands in the sense that what it is designed to explain, namely, the historically developed and specific nature both of the objects of consumption and of the consumers, cannot be explained unless and until concepts are introduced allowing us to think the historical specificity of production itself; and we shall see some of the effects of this inadequacy when we put the principle of the dominance of production over consumption to work in explaining the particular pattern of consumption of a particular society. But what it does do, as I say, is to register Marx's recognition of a basic failing of the discourse of the political economists, namely their assumption that the concept with which you grasp the genesis of a process must be that whereby you grasp the process of its development. In arguing for the dominance of consumption over production, for the primacy of need over the product which satisfies it, the economists assumed that what is true of an abstract point of genesis is equally true and applicable to the understanding of the actual history of production and consumption. Marx himself recognises this initial priority of need over product in the famous passage from the *German Ideology*:

the first premise of all human existence ... men must be in a position to live in order to be able to 'make history'. But life involves before everything else eating and drinking, housing, clothing and various other things. *The first historical act* is thus the production of means to satisfy those needs, the production of material life itself;[7]

and this recognition of 'the first historical act' is reflected in the reference in the 1857 Introduction to consumption's 'initial stage of natural crudity': 'As soon as consumption emerges from its initial stage of natural crudity and immediacy — and, if it remained at that stage, this would be because production itself has been arrested there — it becomes itself mediated by the object.'[8]

There is, in other words, a 'natural' or 'crude' stage or initial point at which it is correct to think in terms of the primacy of need over product; but these terms would only be appropriate if there were indeed no historical development of production. Marx's point is therefore epistemological; or, if preferred, it is both epistemological and historical: *if* consumption had remained in its crude immediacy (which in fact it did not) — and this would involve an arrested state of production (a state at which it did not in fact remain) — *then* the account in terms of initial need begetting 'production' (and note that the production involved would scarcely deserve the name, since it would be no more than a matter of gathering fruit, and so on) would be adequate, and it would be appropriate to what was in fact a non-expanding, simple reproduction. But this is a purely hypothetical state of affairs: real history has been the history of a development of needs and of an ever-expanding reproduction. In order to understand and explain this, the real process of social history, one must understand the predominant role of social production in the needs-product relationship. In this sense, then, the *expansion* of needs might be said to be the 'first historical act' — which is interestingly enough precisely what we are told in the 'second point' made in the *German Ideology*: 'The second point is that the satisfaction of the first need (the action of satisfying and the instrument of satisfaction which has been acquired) leads to new needs; and this creation of new needs is the *first historical act*.'[9]

That consumption does not stay in its 'crude immediacy', and that production, therefore, is not arrested, points to important differences in the development of human as opposed to animal life. Suffice it to say here that they are differences that can only be correctly specified and understood on the basis of an understanding of the essential characteristic of human productive activity: all animals reproduce themselves, only human beings hitherto have reproduced themselves in the form of an ever-expanding social and objectively existing patrimony. And this suggests, of course, that there is no form of production that we can characterise as distinctively human — no production in general, but only determinate forms of production corresponding to different stages of our existence as consumers, as 'needing' subjects. Or again, as Marx says in the *German Ideology*: '... the production, as well as the satisfaction ... of needs is a historical process, which is not found in the case of a sheep or a dog ... although sheeps and dogs in their present form certainly, but *malgré eux*, are products of an historical process'.[10]

I suggest, then, that in this confusing reference in the *German Ideology* to two historical acts, both of which are said to come 'first', Marx is struggling to capture conceptually the reversal in our manner of thinking the needs-products relationship that is an essential precondition of our bringing our thought into correspondence with the reality of our needs — i.e., with their always historical and specific nature. And it is, I am suggesting, the necessity of this reversal that is being registered in Marx's claim about the dominance of production. Failing to appreciate the truth about our needs that is recognised in this reversal, the political economists must necessarily remain deaf to the epistemological demand it imposes; and when they assume that what is true at the most abstract and general level of all production (that there would be no production at all were it not for the existence of needing subjects) is also the truth that explains the actual development of production, they entirely abstract from the real object of knowledge. To suggest, as do the political economists, that the history of development of production can be accounted for as the effect of changes in the form of basic pre-given 'needs' — an account which conceives production as ultimately determined by consumption, as effected by the needs it must fulfil — is to assume an essence of needs that is auto-developing in its form. For if production is the mere effect of these needs it cannot provide the dynamic of the changes that they undergo: these changes must be self-generating — a 'natural' but unexplained result.

Nevertheless, the insistence upon the predominance of production over consumption with its associated notion of products producing or creating needs is inadequate to the task whose necessity its registers — the task of thinking consumption in its historically developed existence, in its existence in bourgeois society.

Let us look a little more closely at the account of the formation of a need that Marx provides in the 1857 Introduction. Throughout his account Marx employs the term 'need' as a concept designating the subjective feeling evoked in the consumer by the 'perception' of the object of its gratification, and the main point he appears to want to make is that once past the stage of crude immediacy, this subjective urge that he is characterising as 'need' is aroused only through a definite production. He speaks of this need in the following terms:

... consumption creates the need for *new* production, that is, it creates the ideal internally impelling cause for production, which is its presupposition; it also creates the object which is active in production as its determinant aim. If it is clear that production offers consumption its external object, it is therefore equally clear that consumption *ideally posits* the object of production as an internal image, as a need, as drive and purpose. It creates the objects of production in a still subjective form. No production without a need. But consumption reproduces the need.[11]

The need which consumption feels for the object is created by the perception of it.[12]

Consumption ... produces the producer's *inclination* by beckoning to him as an aim-determining need.[13]

Consumption accomplishes the act of production only in completing the product as product by dissolving it, by consuming its independently material form, by raising the inclination developed in the first act of production through the need for repetition, to its finished form ...[14]

Despite the plethora of terms ('ideal internally impelling cause', 'ideal positing', 'internal image', 'drive', 'purpose', 'inclination'), the sense that Marx wishes to convey is clear enough. In these passages Marx is referring to a psychic effect produced by a previously consumed product within the consumer. This effect, he suggests, takes the form of an image or perception of that product — an ideal reproduction of it in the mind's eye; but it is not merely a static picturing but possessed of a certain energy — it takes the form of a drive or purpose, it is 'aim-determining', it 'beckons' — and the impulse behind it is for 'repetition' of the earlier gratification. Thus it 'aim-determines' new production because it urges it on to a repeat performance. Now obviously this repetition cannot be literally a repetition in the sense of a sameness; the new product to which the need for repetition gives rise cannot be identical with the product which inspired the 'ideal internal image'. In this respect the 'need' which Marx is here attempting to distinguish is ungratifiable, or rather, the only possible sense we can give to the notion of its 'gratification' is that which takes place via the detour of the new, and specific production which it inspires; in this sense, it has no real object, for it is its own object, that is, the lack of a real object, the merely internalised image of gratification trapped in the perception which is its only existence.

Here, to digress temporarily, one might call attention to the parallel between this account of need and that which Freud offers in *The Interpretation of Dreams*.[15] For Freud, too, speaks in terms of internal perceptions, and claims that the precondition of the satisfaction of a need, and an essential component of it, is a particular perception 'the mnemic image of which remains associated thenceforward with the memory trace of the excitation produced by the first need'. And he claims that as a result of the link established between the excitation and the perception stemming from the original gratification, next time the need arises it is produced along with a psychical impulse (which, of course, Freud, unlike Marx, precisely distinguishes as a wish or desire rather than a need) to re-evoke the perception of the object that originally gratified the need. The reappearance of the perception is the satisfaction of the desire. As Freud points out, the nature of desire in this account is such that there is nothing to prevent wishing originally ending in hallucination: 'Thus the aim of this first psychical activity was to produce a "perceptual identity"' (i.e., something perceptually identical with the 'experience of satisfaction' — a *repetition* of this perception, which was linked with the satisfaction of the need). However, the 'bitter experience of life' changes this merely thought (ideal image of) gratification into a more expedient secondary one because satisfaction — upon which survival depends — does not follow from perceptual identity: the need persists. From this Freud concludes that 'reality-testing' takes place allowing for the pursuit of paths which lead to the desired perceptual identity being established from the direction of the external world. Where desire evokes a merely internal response and the merely 'thought' adjustment of hallucinatory gratification, need demands its satisfaction through reorganisation of the real world. Or, to put this in Marx's terms, the need cannot be gratified in the mere image or perception of the product, but only through the new production which attempts to repeat the original product of the original gratification. And this suggests a non-static, non-repetitious, innovatory quality of need in contrast to the regressive and static quality of desire (in contrast, that is to say, to what would be an eternal repetition, or falling back upon the sameness of itself, if desire were ever — which it cannot be — the sole mode of gratification).

But let us return to the main issue in hand: let us ask how this psychological account of needs stands in relation to the general principle of the dominance of production over consumption. It suggests the following model:

Product (1)➤evoked need (A)➤product (2)➤evoked need (B)

This in turn suggests that it will follow automatically that product (2) will be the object of consumption which corresponded to (i.e., was the appropriate gratification of) the evoked need (A) and that therefore even though the evoked need only arose because of the existence of Product (1), it was nevertheless that which directly caused the attempt to repeat Product (1) through the production of product (2). But the inadequacies of this model are clear enough, and can be summarised in four points.

(i) Since it offers no principle of explanation as to why Product (2) should ever differ in kind (as opposed to being a new product of the same kind), it fails to explain what it is designed to explain, namely the qualitative expansion of needs. It might be objected to this that a given production is capable of 'intimating' other, quite different forms of production, evoking a need which, so to speak, 'over-leaps' the absence of any concrete production (cf. 'the erection of the object in the imagination' of which Marx speaks in *Capital*[16]) to meet it, and stands as a pre-formed need to a merely potential production. But this hypothesis rests in fact on what the Product-Need-Product model as it stands is denying, namely on the supposition that potential consumers have complex motivations determining their needs whose source is external to the product offered to their 'perception'. Marx's account of a need with which we are here concerned, suggesting as it does a 'tabula rasa' theory of human affectivity, cannot be defended by suppositions which presume a non-tabula rasa theory.

(ii) This model fails to explain the diversity of either needs or consumption between individuals. For on the tabula rasa view, it would seem that all members of a given society in 'perceiving' the same products will automatically conceive the need for them, 'urge' on the repeat production and proceed to the consumption of the products of this new production. Nothing, as we know, could be further from the truth in any actual society, and least of all in bourgeois society.

(iii) The model fails as it stands to account for unfulfilled needs — unless the explanation be in terms of a total breakdown of production. But as again we know, human production has proceeded perfectly consistently with (and might even be said to have depended upon!) experienced but unfulfilled needs. (That some individuals might want to deny this, thus making a virtue out of necessity, and congratulating themselves upon the fact that they are 'persons of few needs' and 'what they can't have, they don't want', by no means gainsays the general truth of this.[17])

(iv) The model fails to allow for the possibility of products for which there is no need, since according to the model, the only products produced will by definition have come in answer to a previously elicited need.

I conclude, then, that since all the features it fails to explain are strikingly obvious characteristics of consumption of any society that has progressed to any degree beyond the stage of 'crude immediacy', and are clearly features of bourgeois society, the mere inversion of the production/consumption relationship is cognitively inadequate as an explanation either of the formation of needs or of the patterns of their gratification, and advances us but little *as it stands* upon the position of the political economists; and furthermore, that to shift the burden of explanation away from needs to an earlier production is not in itself to argue for the dominance of production over consumption, but merely to state it.

And in conclusion, too, we should recognise that it does not in fact constitute a genuine break with political economy, for Ricardo himself recognises the dominance of production over consumption, and as Althusser has said:

Marx's whole discovery is often reduced to this basic theory (i.e. of the dominance of production over consumption and distribution) and its consequences.

But this 'reduction' runs into one small difficulty; this discovery is as old as the Physiocrats, and Ricardo, the economist 'of production *par excellence*' (Marx), gave it systematic form! In fact, Ricardo proclaimed the primacy of production over distribution and consumption.[18]

If, then, the account that Marx offers in the *Grundrisse* not only fails to theorise what it wants to theorise, but is too little distinguishable from the most advanced position reached by that political economy which he is submitting to critique, then it is clear that we must look elsewhere for his own, definitive theory. Elsewhere, both in the sense of to a different text (namely *Capital*) and in the sense of 'to different concepts'.

2. 'Value is dominant'

In *Capital*, Marx starts, not with 'production', but with the commodity. Thus, it may look at first sight as if he is starting with exchange, as if he is taking the relations of exchange as predominant. But in fact, behind this initial interest in the commodity, there lies his interest in a different question. His concern is no longer with which of the economic 'moments' predominates, but with the form of production of social wealth, and in particular with why it is that, in the form of production under examination, this takes the form of commodity production, of a production of products which must be transferred to others, in order for those others to make use of them, by means of exchange. His concern, then, is the value-form of the commodity: why this form? Now it is clear that to pose this question is immediately to undermine the assumption of the political economists that commodity production is the only possible form of production. It is to undermine any suggestion that it is a necessary and natural law of the production of social wealth that it must be produced in the form of exchange-value.

What has happened between the *Grundrisse* and *Capital* is that

Marx has finally managed to conceptualise the distinction between a material-technical process of production and its social forms, i.e., to ask, and respond to the question: why does the production of social wealth (and thus the pattern of consumption it permits) take the form that it does in any society? To answer that question it is insufficient merely to invert the relations posited by political economy between production and consumption, since that is to retain the concept of production as a concept of production in general (or rather it is to accept political economy's generalisation-eternalisation of a specific form of production: commodity production). Indeed, merely to ask the question of the social forms of production is to move out of the circle of terms in which political economy poses its questions, since it is to ask what *is* specific, and why, to the form of production (capitalist commodity production) that political economy takes to be the only form of production. It is not that Marx denies the common factors that enter into all production, but his specific concern is with the form of existence of these factors in capitalist society (with the fact that means of production exist in the form of capital, land in the form of an object of purchase and sale, labour in the form of wage labour) and with what this form of existence represents in terms of the development of the value-form, namely, a stage in society's development at which the labour spent on the production of useful articles has come to be expressed as one of the objective qualities of those articles, as their *value*. The dominant concept now is not that of production, but that of the *social relations of production* as the relations in which the factors of production are brought into combination with each other, as the relations of distribution of the forms of value of capital and labour, and of the exchange of products in the form of commodities.

From this standpoint, the errors of political economy are specified not so much in terms of the relations they posit between production, consumption, distribution and exchange, as in terms of their conflation of the technical and social aspects of production. They assign the 'economic definiteness of form' to 'an objective property of things'[19] — thus the ability of capital to yield profit, which presupposes the existence of particular social classes and production relations among them, is explained in terms of the technical function of capital in the role of the means of production; or else, inversely, they assign material or technical properties inherent in the instruments of labour to the social form of the instruments of labour — thus, for example, capital is credited with the power to increase the productivity of labour when this is in fact a technical property of the means of production. And even an economist like Ricardo, who sees that it is not capital but labour which is the source of value, cannot explain how or why it is that this value is expressed in the form of exchange-values. Marx says,

Political economy has never once asked the question why labour is represented by the value of its product and labour time by the magnitude of that value. These formulae, which bear it stamped upon them in unmistakable letters that they belong to a state of society in which the process of production has the mastery over man, instead of being controlled by him, such formulae appear to the bourgeois intellect to be as much a self-evident necessity imposed by Nature as productive labour itself.[20]

If labour-power is the source of value, why is it not directly realised as such, and what are the effects of its realisation only in the form of exchange-value upon the nature and structure of consumption? In other words, why is it that Marx says of these 'formulae' cited in the quotation above that they bear it stamped upon them unmistakably that they belong to a state of society in which production has the mastery over men, rather than vice-versa, and what are the effects of these relations of mastery for any theorisation of needs and consumption in capitalist commodity society?

The question can be considered in quite basic terms. Let us take it as incontrovertible that any society, at a given level of development of its productive forces (that is, of its material-technical resources, including the skills and capacities of its main productive resource: the working population) has at its disposal a given body of social labour time. The fundamental question, then, from the standpoint of its 'form of life', its pattern of consumption, the 'needs' it does or does not satisfy, the 'needs' that do or do not emerge, is the mode of allocation of this body of social labour time. And here, it would seem, there are basically only two alternatives. Either a society can calculate aforehand the amount of social labour time it has at its disposal and the body of needs requiring satisfaction and can then proceed to allocate its labour time to the various branches of production in accordance with those needs (and can furthermore decide where it will allocate any labour time left over once those needs are satisfied and indeed can decide whether to allocate it to further production or allow it to exist in uncrystallised form — in the form of free time) or else a society can have its allocation of labour time decided for it 'behind its back'. The second, 'irrational' alternative is that of commodity societies, where it is left to independent producers to decide what goods and services to produce and it is only at the point of their exchange, on the market, that the 'wisdom' of that allocation of society's labour time is decided on the basis of the extent to which the value of products is realised. In commodity societies, it is the law of value which operates 'behind the backs' of the agents of production, rather than any conscious decision, which regulates the allocation of social labour time and in doing so ensures some sort of correspondence between existing levels of need and social production. But since it asserts itself only *after* the expenditure of social labour time to a given branch of production, it asserts itself in and through the facts of over and under production of goods relative to existing needs, in and through the disproportions in the allocations of social labour time, in and through the deviation of prices from values, or in other words, in and through the wastage and destruction of value, of social labour time. Since the only index of need in such a society (and 'need' here means need that can pay) is the actual sale of goods, the correspondence between the existing body of need and the production of use-values to satisfy them is achieved in *a posteriori* fashion through the act of sale. Or, in other words, one only discovers what proportion of social labour time at a given level of productivity should have been assigned to a given branch of production in order for its particular use-values to meet existing needs for them after production has in fact taken place, after a proportion of social labour time has actually been absorbed in 'meeting' them; and the reason for this is that the only index of the social labour time that should have been apportioned to the production of a given commodity is the extent to which that commodity in fact sells at the value of the social labour actually incorporated in it. This means, of course, that such correspondence as is achieved between the allocation of social labour time and the satisfaction of an existing body of need will be a matter of contingency, and that in the absence of any principle to guarantee this correspondence the actual result will be a continual disproportionality between existing social need and the allocation of labour time to meet it — a disproportionality only adjusted to *post festum*, through the sale of goods above or below the value of the labour time incorporated in them, through a constant deviation of prices from values, through a wastage and in some cases (if the goods fail to sell altogether) a destruction of the value represented in the product as a result of the labour time spent in its production.

Every individual article, or every definite quantity of a commodity, may indeed, contain no more than the social labour time required for its production and from this point of view the market value of the commodity represents only necessary labour, but if the commodity has been produced in excess of the existing social needs then so much of the social labour time is squandered and the mass of the commodity comes to represent a much smaller quantity of social labour in the market than is actually incorporated in it. (It is only where a society is under the actual predetermining control of society that the latter establishes a relation between the volume of social labour time applied in producing definite articles, and the volume of the social want to be satisfied by those articles).[21]

It is only, then, in a society that plans its allocation of social labour time in accordance with 'social want' that excesses or deficiencies in production can in principle be overcome and the social labour time that is lost as a result can be recuperated for society at large:

... to say that there is no general over-production, but rather a disproportion between the various branches of production, is no more than to say that under capitalist production the proportionality of the individual branches of production springs as a continual process from disproportionality because the cohesion of the aggregate production imposes itself as a blind law upon the agents of production, and not as a law, which being understood and hence controlled by the common mind brings the production under the joint control.[22]

It is important to stress the 'blindness' of this law against any suggestion I may have given that it makes itself consciously felt in the exchange of goods. I spoke of the extent to which a commodity sells at its value as being the 'index' of the social labour time that should have been expended in its production, but this should not be taken as meaning that the various producers themselves become aware at the point of sale of the underlying relationship between the expenditure of social labour time and the price that their product happens to fetch on the market (for them the value of the product is itself the price it will fetch); or, in other words, the law of value is not a law that the various producers act consciously in accordance with; it is the law that explains their acts.

Two points can be made here, and they both relate to what I shall argue is the more complex, but for that reason more adequate, framework for theorising the formation of needs that follows from the analysis in *Capital*. In the first place, it is clear that there are certain effects upon production and consumption that are intrinsic to any society in which the necessity for social wealth to be brought into some sort of correspondence with existing levels of need is never directly recognised by the producers but only imposed upon them 'behind their backs'. For as we have seen, the mechanism of this imposition is the continual over and underproduction of goods that is reflected in the constant deviation of prices from values. And this means some destruction of value — some squandering of social labour time — will be a necessary condition of the satisfaction of the body of social needs. This in turn means that commodity society is depriving itself, in the very process of meeting its needs, of the potential permitted it by its technical capacities to develop and satisfy further needs. By wasting social labour time, it is, quite obviously, restricting the consumption of labour time it potentially permits, whether this consumption takes the form of a 'consumption' of free time or of various products and services in which it could be crystallised. For society taken as a whole, then, commodity relations of production impose their 'mastery over man' in the form of a restriction on the consumption of free time or products that it is actually in a position technically to accommodate.

However, it can, and I think should be objected at this point, that if the irrationality of capitalist commodity production is thought to consist merely in the inefficiency with which it accommodates an existing structure of social needs then this cannot be considered a very damning objection, and in any case not a very realistic one, in that it is based on the questionable assumption that it is efficient in principle and possible in practice to assess *a priori* the entire body of social needs (including all the vagaries of individual consumption) that a socialist production consciously sets itself to meet. When Marx, for example, writes of production being brought under the control of the 'common mind' one might be forgiven for questioning whether this appeal to a vague and metaphoric concept should not be regarded as an index of the extreme abstraction, or even purely speculative nature, of the premise that underlies this line of Marx's critique. For Marx here, it might be said, is damning capitalist production from the standpoint of an ideal that it is impossible to achieve in practice under *any* relations of production, which is to say even in a society whose prime concern *is* to plan to meet needs.[23] Certainly such a society is in a position to assess quite accurately a large range of relatively stable and homogeneous needs and to allocate its labour time accordingly; the socialist economies have proved quite successful in fact in doing so. But whether *a priori* assessment can be extended so as to accommodate any and every consumer need, subject as these needs are to quite rapid transformation, and whether it is desirable to do so from the standpoint of allowing individuals the measure of choice and control over their particular pattern of consumption that would seem both democratic and a condition of the development of 'rich individuality', is another question. Again, in practice, as we know, the socialist economies have had to resort to a limited market economy as the most efficient method of satisfying many such needs on the grounds that it is the sale of goods that provides the most adequate index of these.[24]

But the real question here, it would seem, concerns the criterion of efficiency itself. Marx tends to present the issue as if efficiency were a question of maximum out-put for minimum expenditure of labour-time — as if the 'efficient' economy were one that never allocated more than the social labour time necessary at a given level of productivity to a given branch of production in order to meet the needs for its products. But it may well be 'efficient' from the standpoint of other needs that can be gratified under a truly socialist economy (needs, for example, for variety in the labour-process, needs relating to the abolition of the division of labour, needs for the 'inefficient' elements of society — the old or handicapped — to be centrally involved in the productive life of their society, and needs arising from concern for the long-term ecological effects of certain short-term, albeit highly productive, uses of resources) for a wide range of technologies to be employed in the production of a given product, having very different degrees of efficiency in terms of the labour input-product output ratio. Here the important difference between a capitalist and a socialist economy is seen to relate to the fact that the latter is no longer subordinated to the law of value: it can accord worth to its productive activities independently of their value, independently of considerations about the social labour time actually incorporated in its products. Any society that is conscious of the fact that value comes to be accorded to products on the basis of the labour-time incorporated in their production is immediately placed in a position to directly value its labour-time, and thus to allocate it as it chooses, to allocate it in accordance with what it 'values' or deems worth producing, in accordance with its needs. The real mastery of capitalist commodity production lies, then, not so much in its irratonal allocation of labour time to a body of products that it has decided upon as worth producing, as 'needed', but in the fact that the 'needs' in acccordance with which it irrationally allocates this time are themselves decided by the exchangeability of products, and that in turn by its specific relations of distribution of social wealth.

This brings us to the second point. Hitherto, account has only been taken of the intrinsic effects of the irrational allocation of labour time upon society taken as an aggregate; and the suggestion has been that this irrationality relates to the wastage of social labour time incurred in meeting a body of presupposed social needs. From this standpoint, it is as if the entire 'mastery' of capitalist production consists in its inefficiencies in meeting the pre-given, homogeneous needs of 'society' for bread or shoes or cotton or steel, the idea being that when it is left to independent producers to decide themselves what they 'fancy' producing, they may well end up producing all shoes and no bread or all cotton and no steel, and it is only in the form of a refusal to buy shoes at their value, or a preparedness to buy bread at well above its value, that the expenditure of social labour time is forced back into the quasi-correspondence with needs that is necessary to the reproduction of society.

But the mastery of capitalist society over man extends, of course, far beyond this, for it is a mastery both over the *structure* of consumption and over what might be termed its *ontology*, that is to say, the actual nature and type of use-values consumed. This mastery, it should be said, is not total, for it is, of course, a condition of the reproduction of any society, including capitalist society, that it satisfy certain needs accountable to the nature of its members — who must, for example, be in a position to feed, clothe, house themselves and so on. These needs impose certain limits both qualitatively and quantitatively upon the use-values that any society can produce. By virtue of the biology of human beings, a certain amount of food has to be consumed, only a certain amount of it can be consumed and only certain substances can function as food. Such needs, then, can be seen as a series of limit conditions upon the possibilities of human production and it is a condition of production being a human production that it remain subject to their constraints. The same limit conditions apply in the case of the productive forces: any production, no matter what its technical capacities, is subject to the constraints imposed by inorganic nature in the form of the physical properties and availability of the raw materials harnessed in productive activity, and in the form of the physical and psychological capacities of the human agents of production. But these limits are extremely elastic, and it is within the area of 'free play' provided by their elasticity that societies can be masters or mastered. All the emphasis in understanding the mastery of capitalist production must therefore fall on its *form*, on its particular relations of production, which include, of course, its relations of distribution and exchange.

While nature, therefore, plays its part in determining the body of social needs that is presupposed by capitalist production, it is capitalist relations of production that have the dominant say over their specific structure and content. Insofar as its structure is concerned, it is important to recognise that this is already fixed by the relations of distribution: the only needs that are presupposed, the only needs to which, *post festum*, capitalist production adjusts, are those which are effective, i.e., equipped with purchasing power. In this sense, its productive activity proceeds in abstraction from any needs it may elicit, either for the use-values it produces, or in reaction to them and the methods of their production, that cannot be converted through the exercise of purchasing power to actual consumption. There is no need for it to recognise needs that do not assert themselves economically via the

detour of the acquisition of money to back them. Hence it is that
the struggle for the fulfilment of needs is essentially a struggle for
increased wages: it is only when you have the power to buy
whatever you need, whether it be more goods, or more time, that
society recognises its accountability to it — that you have a 'need'.
A given structure of income means a given structure of 'fulfillabi-
lity' of needs and this in turn means a given allocation of labour
time that has definite material effects, qualitatively and quantitatively, upon the products produced. To recognise this is to
recognise and incorporate within the terms and framework of
economic theory a simple but essential distinction between
unfulfilled and fulfilled needs; to recognise the distinction
between needs which are felt and persist irrespective of whether
the objects upon which they are intentionally fixed (and which
may be tangible or intangible) enter into the consumption of the
individuals experiencing them, and needs which are converted to
actual consumption because they are effective. The definition of
needs in this latter sense is such that nothing counts as a need which
is not equipped with the capacity (the purchasing power) to attain
its object. Given that the object is available then, *ceteris paribus*,
effective demand will always be converted to actual consumption,
which is, in fact, its only index. This distinction can be expressed
in a more shorthand way as a distinction between felt needs (to be
referred to in future as needs (A) and actual consumption (to be
referred to in future as needs (B)). As we have seen, orthodox
economic theory wants to concern itself only with needs (B) on
the grounds that this is the only operational concept of needs. But
though this exclusion of other concepts of need is justified in the
eyes of the economists by the demands of their science, it does, as I
have also suggested, serve the quite definite political end of
allowing a society's needs (A) to be 'read off' from its actual
consumption. In other words, it simply denies the gap between the
two. As we shall see, classical political economy, though with
somewhat more concern for its moral justification, does so too. It
is the great value of Marx's 'opening' upon political economy that
it recognises this gap and explains the reasons for it. And in doing
so, it at least allows us to formulate certain fundamental questions
about the relations between needs (A) and needs (B), about the
differences and similarities in their content and in the factors
responsible for that content, and about the role that each plays in

determining the content of the other. Above all, in recognising the gap between (A) and (B) one is automatically adopting a critical standpoint about (B) for one is directing attention to the fact that unfulfilled needs are consistent with the satisfaction of needs provided in (B). It is important to distinguish this critical standpoint, which as it stands is merely condemnatory of the fact that there are needs (A) which are not converted to needs (B), from the question whether either needs (A) or (B) are indeed 'needed', i.e., from the standpoint that questions the 'truth' of the needs expressed for and in actual consumption. I shall postpone consideration of the question as to whether judgements upon unfulfilled needs commit one to judgements about 'true' needs till a later chapter, where I discuss the extent to which arguments which Marx adduces in explanation of the gap between (A) and (B), or, if preferred, the arguments that force us to recognise its existence, commit him directly or indirectly to a judgement about the very nature of consumption in a society which reproduces that gap. Here, however, I shall be concerned only with the reasons for the reproduction of this gap and the effects that it has on the structure and ontology of actual consumption.

Now since the only access in capitalist society to the social wealth produced is via possession of the representative of exchange-value, namely money, it is clear that the structure of actual consumption will be the effect of the distribution of income between the members of its population; and this in turn follows directly as an effect of capitalist relations of production. These relations constitute the social form in which the factors of production are brought into combination and set to work in the production process, and their character is familiar enough: private ownership of the means of production in the hands of a select few, to whom the mass of the population is forced to sell its labour power in order to realise a wage, in order, that is, to reproduce itself. In selling this labour power, the non-owners of the means of production also 'sell' any value it creates over and above the value of commodities represented by the wage. And since the owners of the means of production, who through this 'fair and equal' contract with the labourer have gained the power of disposing of the portion of labour time that is not needed to produce the value of the wage, can do nothing with this portion if it exists merely in the form of surplus labour time, it must be transmuted into the only form in which it is possible for the value of labour power to be represented in capitalist society, i.e., it must be embodied in products which can exchange on the market, this exchange enabling the owner of the means of production to realise the surplus labour in the form of surplus-value (profit).

Insofar, then, as concerns the structure of actual consumption, it is clear that, regardless of the similarities in the needs (A) experienced by the different members of society, there will be considerable divergence in their needs (B), which is precisely accountable not to the 'nature' of the consumers — not to any natural difference in their needs — but to capitalist relations of production. These relations, in determining the level of income at the disposal of individuals, determine their effective demand, and thus their respective contributions to consumption — the poorer you are, the less you consume, the fewer your needs (B).

Let us now turn to the rather more complex question of the determinants upon the nature of the products that satisfy needs (B). And here again, there can be no immediate appeal to the nature of the consumers. For though it is true that no economy can literally produce anything it wants, and that a precondition of its reproduction is the satisfaction of certain requirements (for food, shelter, clothing, education, recreation, and so on) accountable to the biology and psychology of human beings, it would clearly be mistaken to reduce the explanation of the manner in which these abstract needs are concretely satisfied in any given society, or the differences between individuals in the manner of that satisfaction, to a question of biology or psychology. If we want to know why it is that at the self-same moment that his boss is toying with chocolate profiteroles at the Savoy, his worker is reconstituting a dehydrated Chinese dinner, we shall not be greatly informed by being told that they both need to eat. This point seems obvious enough, but it is not always appreciated. Thus E. Mandel, failing to see the full range of determinants upon consumption that stem from the mode of production, commits himself to a wholly psychological account of changes in consumption. Arguing that, after all, the infinite variety of means to satisfy our 'few basic needs' is only apparent, he writes:[25]

Between the stout country squire of the early nineteenth century stuffing himself with roast beef, and swilling port wine, or the big bourgeois of the 'Belle Epoque' with his twenty course dinners, on the one hand, and, on the other, the rich capitalist of today, slim, devoted to sport, and constantly watching his weight, the change is undeniable. With the increase in income, *the increasing consumption of food has given way to a more rational kind of consumption*; the criterion of health has superseded that of blind or showy self-indulgence. This change does not so much reflect an ethical progress as it reflects the demands of self-preservation, the self-interest of the individual himself.

What Mandel neglects to mention is that whether the capitalist stuffs himself on a feast of Lucullan proportions or dines 'in the interest of self-preservation' on asparagus and out of season strawberries, he does so at the expense of his worker, and it is quite possible to consume twenty times as much social wealth on a meal of 300 calories as on a meal of 6,000 (a consumption about as self-restrained as the fat woman gambler in Jacopetti's film *Mondo Cane* who eats only the smoked salmon in her sandwiches). Nor does Mandel mention the fact that the criterion of health (which no doubt is *a* factor in eating habits) is itself being satisfied by the (rational?) consumption of a vast range of 'slimming' products on the profits of which some capitalist can slake his thirst tonight on low calorie champagne.

Considerations of the kind mentioned by Mandel do, of course, enter into the explanation of changes in the nature of the use-values that satisfy 'basic' needs, but always within the context of the determinations exercised (a) by the material-technical capacities of a given society (the level of development of the productive forces) and (b) the distribution of income (though it is the material effects of this upon what is produced with which we are here concerned rather than the unequal *structure* of effective demand in which it results.)

In respect of (a) we shall immediately have to recognise that the development of the productive forces, so far from being autonomous, is itself determined by capitalist relations of production whose logic they serve. In other words, the type of goods is directly the effect of certain specific, material-technical production processes, but these processes are themselves developed under the dictate of the law of value: only those technologies will be evolved which further the maintenance of capitalist control over the labour-process and the accumulation of capital. Capitalist relations of production, then, are continually exerting their influence, through their influence upon the development of the productive forces, upon the very nature of the commodities offered for consumption, and thus imposing a series of limitations on the possisble manner in which even our effective needs can be gratified. A technology geared to the production of x product rather than y product will always be favoured if it promises greater overall profitability from the combined standpoint of the efficient operation of the labour-process it incorporates and the cheaper costs of production, installation, maintenance, and so on — and this will be the case even though had y been produced it would have found a buyer (we are all familiar with this restrictive effect of the law of value even where our need is effective and we would pay if we could. It is banally reflected in that classic response so favoured by retailers : 'We don't have any call for that anymore'). And that one's need for a vacuum cleaner or a bicycle pump, or whatever, is better satisfied by the 'old line' of production than by the 'new line' that the manufacturer is so concerned to assure one is 'superior' is something that capitalist production is constantly forcing one to 'deny' or override : if one is to satisfy the need at all it will have to be satisfied in the form dictated by capitalist production. Similarly, it is just too bad if all that one needs to repair one's oil stove is a flame spreader that is no longer available as a spare part now that the manufacturer has ceased production of that 'obsolete' model. And what is more, of course, it is all too likely that the new model one will be forced to buy if one is to satisfy one's need for an oil stove will have been 'improved' by the addition of a measure of 'built-in' obsolescence, the phenomenon of built-in obsolescence being one of the more striking instances of the stranglehold of capitalist relations of production upon the nature of actual consumption. A society which refuses itself the benefits of its technical capacity to pro-duce 'durable' goods, and ensures instead that such goods will do rather less than endure, is surely one in which 'production has the mastery over man'.

Insofar as conerns (b), i.e., the determination exercised upon the content of actual consumption by the distribution of income, we shall clearly have to link this once again to the effects of the law of value, and in particular to the necessity for the owners of capital to appropriate the labour-time of their workers in an exchange-able form — in the form of exchangeable products. Now we know very well that whether or not a product realises exchange-value depends (i) on its having use-value and (ii) on the need for it being backed by purchasing power. Any distribution of income, then, such as characterises a capitalist society (and it is a distribution which must of necessity be unequal since the accumulation of capital depends on the extraction of surplus-value and that in turn on a limitation upon what is to count as 'necessary' labour) will have a quite definite effect on the actual products produced and consumed. For it is clearly pointless for any capitalist producer to devote his enterprise to the production of goods (whatever their use-value — i.e., even when there is a need (A) for them) for which the relevant effective demand is absent. Hence the intrinsic tendency of capitalist production to devote itself increasingly to the production of luxury goods: a capitalist society is one that must of its logic tend to produce use-values for the wealthy since it is only they who have the purchasing power necessary for such articles to prove themselves as use-values, to realise exchange-value. In the *Grundrisse*,[26] Marx speaks of this material effectivity upon consumption of the distribution relations of capitalist society in terms of 'surplus-value as a limit on surplus labour', and in *Capital* he writes:

Since the aim of capital is not to minister to certain wants, but to produce profit, and since it accomplishes this purpose by methods which adapt the mass of production to the scale of production, not vice-versa, a rift must continually ensue between the limited consumption under capitalism and a production which forever tends to exceed this immanent barrier . . .[27]

Now such remarks as these are not merely concerned with the structural inequalities of income resulting from capitalist relations of distribution, but with its material effects upon the use-values consumed: Marx is here saying something quite specific about the restriction imposed on the expansion of the productive forces, and thus on consumption, that results from the need, under capitalism, to transform value (labour-time) into exchange-value, or, in other words, to incorporate it in the form of products distinct from value itself, distinct from the labour-time incorporated in them. And since, as we have seen, in order to sell, these products must meet not just a demand, but an effective demand, and the effective demand is, beyond a certain point, the privilege of the minority, social labour time will tend to be incorporated into products satisfying increasingly refined, non-'basic' needs, i.e., in luxuries. Of course, there are certain limitations upon this tendency, because the production of luxury items cannot be allowed to proceed at the expense entirely of the gratification of the body of presupposed needs essential to the reproduction of society, and this is a limitation which is reflected in taxation policies which serve to limit the possible luxury consumption even of the wealthiest members of society. In other words, the production of luxuries can proceed quite consistently up to a certain point with the non-fulfilment of quite ordinary needs of the mass of the population; but it can do so only up to a certain point, and beyond that point State intervention to control the 'anarchy' of capitalist production will be essential if certain needs necessary to the reproduction of society as a whole and to the maintenance of its mode of production are to be met. Hence the growth of the state sector, assuming responsibility for those areas of production (e.g., transport, communications, some heavy industries) which provide goods essential to the reproduction of society, but are 'casualties' from the standpoint of the relations of competition in which, *strictu senso*, capitalism takes place. Hence, too, the provision by the State of 'essential' services (housing, health, education and so on) which would not otherwise be satisfied — 'essential' here meaning just so much as is essential to the reproduction of society and the health of capitalism. (We should note that it is important from the standpoint of that health that money is not 'wasted' on satisfying needs that capitalism can afford to neglect, so that a failure to satisfy needs (A) — a low standard of living of many members — is integral to the reproduction of a capitalist society).

So much, then, for the determinants exercised by capitalist relations upon actual consumption in capitalist society, which we have seen to consist in a double determination by the level of development of the productive forces and the distribution of income, both of these being themselves ultimately accountable to the relations of production. But what of needs (A) and their relationship with actual consumption? We have seen that capitalist production is not only consistent with, but in fact dependent upon, the existence of a 'gap' or non-equilibrium between the satisfaction of (A) for the mass of the population and the satisfaction of needs (B). Obviously for the mass of the population we can think of the proportion of their felt needs that are converted to actual consumption in terms of the goods and services covered by the wage — in terms, that is to say, of a historically specific necessary subsistence level, this specific level precisely coinciding with that quantity of social value that is deemed 'necessary' as opposed to 'surplus'. This shows us that the relationship between needs (A) and needs (B) is not one of opposition or mutual exclusion, but rather one of containment and overlap. Needs (B) are included in the range of needs (A) but not vice-versa, and the 'gap' between the two is created by the excess of (A) over (B). The question then becomes a question of what determines the character of those needs which are felt over and above those needs which are gratified. To what extent, for example, are people conditioned in respect of their needs by the actual consumption of their society — by the products made available in their society even though these may not be made available to them as individuals? I think in answer to this it would have to be granted that felt needs are very largely conditioned by actual consumption and thus ultimately by all the economic factors responsible for the form taken by actual consumption. And it is here that Marx's point about the elicitation of needs upon the 'perception' of products comes into its own, for some such theory would seem to be implied by the very possibility of needs being conditioned by the structure of production (and likewise by the possibility of capitalism being able to elicit 'new' needs by its production of new products for consumption). In other words, if we recognise, as it seems we must, that it is mistaken to think of needs (A) as escaping all economic determinations and as standing opposed to actual consumption as some kind of purely 'anthropological' set of needs accountable directly to human nature, then we must give some credit to the idea that needs are open to manipulation by the products offered for consumption.

Does this mean, then, after all, that both needs (A) and needs (B) must be understood as the effect of economic determinations, and the affectivity of the consumers as some tabula rasa in itself without content and only given content through the imprint stamped upon it by the actual consumption of products and by the 'perceptions' of such other products as exist but are not in fact consumed? Now it is certainly true that this view of the matter appears to some extent confirmed in capitalist society where felt needs (A) typically appear to be directed towards products

actually available but for which the effective demand is lacking —
that is, towards goods that already feature in the actual consumption of the wealthier classes — and where any failure to
convert needs (A) to needs (B) is explained in terms of a lack of
effective demand.

On the other hand, though there would appear to be some truth
in this conception, it must, I think, strike us as over-simple for all
the reasons adduced earlier in criticism of the notion of the simple
dominance of production over consumption. In the first place, it
appears to assume a homogeneity of needs (A) when it explains the
actual heterogeneity of needs (B) wholly in terms of economic
determinants. In other words, it seems to assume that *if* there were
equal distribution of social wealth, then at any particular stage of
social production the actual consumption of individuals would be
identical. And yet clearly, even between individuals possessed of
the same purchasing power there is enormous difference both in
their needs (A) and in their actual consumption. How, it might be
asked, can we explain this if it is assumed that the contemplation
of products automatically evokes the needs for them, when the
same collection of products is offered for contemplation to these
different individuals? In the second place, it seems to preclude the
case of products which are not needed, of products which instead
of invoking a need (A) are met with rejection or indifference. And
yet, for all its market research, only a small percentage of the
products that capitalism invents for our consumption actually
manage to establish themselves on the market.[28] In the third place,
this tabula rasa view suggests that there can be no needs (A) except
in the perception of products, which it is therefore assumed must
already exist. But it is clear that we experience needs for many
kinds of 'product' that the production of other products serves to
render less and less available (such products as more space, more
free time, more diversity in work, and so on).

So while there is no doubt that the theory of the elicitation of
needs by the 'perception' of products must enter into the explanation of needs (A) (and also, of course, into the explanation of
needs (B) as contained in, and overlapping, with these), the
psychology of needs/absence of needs in relation to the products
that are the objects of acceptance and rejection is far too complex
to be satisfactorily accounted for in terms of that theory. It is
inadequate as an explanation of the formation of needs in a capital-

ist society, for even though it is certainly true that capitalism does manage to elicit needs that exist only in virtue of the appearance to the consumer of the products it throws on the market, and in this sense it is constantly creative of needs, it is also true that capitalism presents products to the consumer that fail to elicit needs, and that the consumer experiences needs for which there are no products available. And its inadequacy is even clearer if we attempt to invoke it as the sole explanation of the expansion of needs in a planned economy. For where production is not under the determination of the law of value, but takes place in response to existing needs, what is the motivation for the production which according to this theory is the essential presupposition of the elicitation of any new needs? What replaces the 'creativity' of the law of value in such an economy? We want to reply: the needs of the members of society. But if that answer is correct, it is clear that the analysis of needs simply in terms of products and their perceptions is incorrect.

Any attempt, then, to explain consumption in terms of the natural, pre-given needs of the consumers in neglect of the role played by economic determinants stemming from the relations of a given society is fundamentally mistaken. The 'opening' that Marx operates upon the question of needs as a result of his critique of political economy, and his analysis of capitalism as a particular form of social production, lies precisely in the fact that he exposes its errors and the reasons for them. But I have also tried to show the deficiencies of any corrective to this account which attempts to explain all features of consumption simply in terms of the needs that are invoked by the 'perception' of products on the one hand, and the economic determinants that might intervene between those needs and their conversion to needs (B) on the other. Over-emphasis on the role played by economic determinants results in a naive psychology of the formation of needs that denies the genuine interaction between production and consumption, the genuinely psychological element in that interaction, and thus its necessary presence and autonomy as that over which economic determinations can assert their dominance in the first place. If human needs or the anthropological element in their formation are attributed wholly to the influence of earlier productions which have moulded them, then there is no material at all to be subordinated to production in the dynamic process of its expansion.

The value and superiority of the analysis provided in *Capital* lies in the fact that it enables us to recognise the full range of determinations that must enter into the explanation of any concrete pattern of needs and any pattern of actual consumption, to recognise that there are both 'anthropological' and economic forces at work in the formation of both, and that there can be no adequate explanation of the divergence between felt needs and actual consumption that does not refer to the work of both forces. Capitalist production not only fails to fulfil needs that are elicited by the 'perception' of the products that enter into actual consumption; it also 'distorts' (and in a sense, therefore, leaves ungratified) effective felt needs in the very process of their conversion to actual consumption, since it imposes certain definite and limiting forms on the objects that gratify them; and it also gives rise to products which fill the 'perceiver' with repulsion, which elicit the need to be rid of them, and beget the need to consume in alternative ways on the basis of an alternative system of production. Needs do not merely follow as mirror images to a given pattern of production; they also emerge in reaction to it. This reaction takes complex and even contradictory forms reflecting the complexity and contradictory determinations upon the formation both of what we feel we need and upon the actual patterns of our consumption (both of which in turn, to add complexity to complexity, are mutually conditioning).

This is a reaction whose unfulfilled needs or 'dis-needs' find various expression. They can be openly articulated and spoken for; or they can exist merely in the form of a vague malaise whose sources are either misrecognised or else are so entirely lost to sight that it never even occurs to those who sense it that there may be any reasons for it. But whether they find expression in the full emergence of a political discourse and political action, or whether they exist only in submerged fashion, veiled from those who have them by their own experiences of depression and anxiety, by their 'inexplicable' resentments and 'inexplicable' feelings of lethargy, by their 'pointless' acts of violence or their sense of the 'pointlessness' of any action, these needs are the other face of capitalism, the grim visage from which we are screened by the radiant televised smile of the delighted consumer. If it were not so, there would be little point in raising the question of human needs at all, and the entire discourse of the left would be as utopian as it has often, in reaction to the contradictions of its own production, accused itself of being.

Granted, however, the importance of recognising the 'anthropological' forces at work in the formation of needs and their necessary presence as that with which economic forces interact, what does this imply from the standpoint of Marx's attack on any essentialism of needs, and thus from the standpoint of the absence that that attack implies of any theory of 'true' needs upon which assessments of actual patterns of consumption can be based? As a preliminary to discussing that question, I shall devote the chapter which follows to an exposition of that aspect of the cognitive discourse which is represented by the critique of liberal theory, and of its essentialist account of human nature.

Notes

1 Thus it is said, for example, when x needs y that y is x's need. The shorthand form it accountable to the intentional nature of the concept of need (to the fact that it is part of the logic of needing that a need is directed towards an object). Likewise, a person's desires or interests are what they desire, or are interested in.

2 Cf. in this respect, L. Althusser's somewhat dismissive and cursory remark quoted at the end of the last chapter. A similar charge, it seems to me, can be made against E. Mandel (*Marxist Economic Theory*, London, The Merlin Press, 1962; see esp. pp. 170-1 and Chap. 17), though he errs in the opposite direction from Althusser. Whereas Althusser tends to place all the emphasis on the determining role of the relations of production and distribution upon the formation of needs, to the neglect of an anthropological category of needs, Mandel tends to neglect the real formative influence of a given system of production upon what people come to experience as their needs. Neither of them, it follows, can *pose the question of* the 'truth' or 'falsity' of actual consumption under capitalism: Althusser wants to suppress the anthropology that would make it meaningful to do so, while Mandel assumes that the question has already been answered.

3 K. Marx, *Grundrisse, op. cit.*, pp. 99-108.

4 Which has to be argued for, of course. But some beginnings have been made in this direction. The reader is referred to the essays in *Issues in Marxist Philosophy*, ed. J. Mepham and D.-H. Ruben, Sussex, Harvester Press, 1979, Vol. I (*Dialectics and Method*) and in particular to that by J. Mepham, 'From the *Grundrisse* to *Capital*: The Making of Marx's Method'.

5 K. Marx, *Grundrisse, op. cit.*, p. 94.

6 *Ibid.*, pp. 91-92.

7 K. Marx, F. Engels, *The German Ideology*, CW, *op. cit.*, pp. 41-42.

8 K. Marx, *Grundrisse, op. cit.*, p. 92.

9   K. Marx, F. Engels, *The German Ideology, op. cit.,* p. 42.

10 *Ibid.,* p. 80.

11 K. Marx, *Grundrisse, op. cit.,* p. 91.

12 *Ibid.,* p. 92.

13 *Ibid.*

14 *Ibid.,* p. 93.

15 S. Freud, *The Interpretation of Dreams,* Standard Edition of the *Complete Works,* ed. J. Strachey, London, Hogarth Press, 1953, Vol. 5; see Chap. 7, sect. (c) on 'Wish-fulfilment'.

16 K. Marx, *Capital, op. cit.,* Vol. I, p. 174.

17 It does, however, raise complex questions about the criteria for ascribing needs, about the incorrigibility of agents' accounts of their needs, about the propriety of talking of 'unconscious' needs, and about the 'ideologies' in which people think about their 'needs'. These are issues touched upon in Chapter One. Consistently with the position I adopt there, I would have to maintain that if such talk is true, and the needs are unexperienced, then they are not had. But this in turn raises the question of whether the needs are unexperienced, or whether the denial of them is not an instance of a kind of Freudian negation. It might be argued that those who profess 'not to need' in this sense are necessarily involved in a recognition that what they 'do not need' is something they 'could do with'. Refusals of charity might be considered in this light, since it would seem that a tacit acknowledgement of the need for it is a condition itself of having 'enough' pride to reject it.

18 L. Althusser, *Reading Capital, op. cit.,* p. 168.

19 K. Marx, *Capital, op. cit.,* Vol. II, p. 164.

20 *Ibid.,* Vol. I, pp. 84-85.

21 *Ibid.,* Vol. III, p. 187.

22 *Ibid.,* pp. 256-57.

23 For a discussion of the actual difficulties encountered in this respect in the Soviet Union and of the extent and limits upon *a priori* assessment of needs, see C. Bettelheim, *Transition to a Socialist Economy,* Sussex, Harvester Press, 1978.

24 Again, see C. Bettelheim, *op. cit.,*

25 E. Mandel, *op. cit.,* p. 661.

26 K. Marx, *Grundrisse, op. cit.,* p. 415 and cf. p. 402f.

27 K. Marx, *Capital, op. cit.,* Vol. III, p. 256 and cf. p. 244.

28 A reading of the Business supplements of the Sunday papers provides many examples of such failures. They range from the (trivial?) flop of asparagus flavoured crisps to the (serious?) crisis of demand encountered by Concorde.

4 The Cognitive Discourse II: the Critique of Essentialist Theories of Human Nature

1. The moral justification of political economy

I suggested at the beginning of the last chapter that political economy and liberal theories of man operate complicitly to effect a closure upon the question of needs, and in spelling out the viewpoint of the former, its reliance upon the assumptions of the latter has no doubt emerged fairly clearly. Or, at the very least, what has emerged quite clearly is the assumption that underlies the argument that production takes place in response to needs, namely, that these needs are pre-given to the consumer as an essentially natural rather than socially acquired possession. And it is, of course, but a short step from that assumption to the explicit talk about the essential nature of man that is to be found in seventeenth and eighteenth century liberal theory.

But in order fully to understand the complicity of political economy and liberal theory, we must see the way in which the latter provides a moral basis for what would otherwise remain a positivistic or merely descriptive account of needs that is offered by the former. For in one way of looking at the matter, all that political economy is telling us when it tells us that production takes place in order to satisfy needs, is that we can discover our needs in the products we consume, or in other words, that our needs are identifiable in our consumption: if products are always evoked by needs, and come in response to them, the consumption of those products must be viewed as the satisfaction of needs. Taken by itself, however, that way of looking at the matter provides no guarantee that the 'needs' revealed in consumption are indeed what is needed in order to ensure satisfaction, in order that consumption be a fitting and appropriately human consumption. What, then, provides this guarantee and renders the production that takes place a genuinely 'human' production in response to intrinsically 'human' needs? Well, the answer, of course, is the nature of the needs themselves that evoke production: it is Nature itself which ensures the 'rightness' — the humanity — of the system of production as a whole and of the pattern of consumption that it is designed to accommodate.

One index of the shallowness of this conception has already been mentioned: its failure to account for the expansion of needs; it human needs are a pre-given, natural endowment which finds an automatic confirmation in the products whose production they inspire, then it would seem that this production must be limited to a simple rather than expanding reproduction. But that is far from being true of most societies and least of all of bourgeois society. How, in other words, using this model of the relation between needs and production are we to think of the emergence of new needs except in terms of the alteration to the *form* of gratification of already existing needs? The fact that the history of social production has been a history of diversification and elaboration of products can only be understood, on this model, as a diversification and elaboration of *modes of satisfying* a set of essential human needs given for all time. But that, of course, fails to explain why there should be diversification and elaboration in the first place. If needs are just needs, and production is production to satisfy them, why should that production ever 'evolve' the form of their gratification?

But another, equally important, objection to this moral endorsement of capitalist production via appeal to the naturalness of needs lies in the fact that *as it stands* it fails to account for the actual diversity of consumption between different consumers. For while the appeal to an essential set of human needs suggests that each member of the human species is such a member by virtue of equal participation in that essence, and equal participation thereby in the intrinsically 'human' set of needs, this seems quite at odds with the actual differences in levels and types of consumption that characterise bourgeois society. If Nature ordained that all men are equal, how can Nature also provide the justification of the inequalities in the consumption of individuals?

It is in accommodating this striking disparity between the facts of bourgeois society and the presumed equality of men, that the essentialist anthropology of liberal theory acquires its particular complexity. And this complexity corresponds to the particularly difficult task it sets itself, namely, to provide a moral justification of social inequalities on the basis of the natural equality of men.

Earlier epochs felt no need to set themselves so apparently intransigent a problem. Slavery, for example, or feudal relations, could automatically be given their justification on the basis of the natural differences between persons and their allotted place in the divine order of things. Why, then, is it only bourgeois society that must set itself to solve a paradox that earlier societies felt no need to entertain? The answer, we know, of course, lies in the 'enlightenment' of capitalist relations themselves, for which it has become impossible for the abuses of slavery and thralldom to be conducted in the slave or feudal mode; for which it has become necessary that private ownership, exploitation, minority appropriation of the surplus, should be carried out a little more discreetly, veiled, as it were, behind the consciousness that the individual[1] is no one's chattel, but a free and independent agent, the sole proprietor of his body and the voluntary participant in all his contracts and exchanges. Capitalism, the market economy, both express and depend for their maintenance on the belief in the freedom and equality of all individuals in their exchanges with one another, and the morality of slavery and feudaldom is anathema to it, for no individual can be owned by another, and no individual forced to alienate his body. The market economy, that is to say, is characterised by the 'free and equal' exchange of individuals both in respect of the sale of their labour-power, and in respect of the purchase of the products in the market place to satisfy their needs. The social bond, the cohesive force of this society, is no longer the personal ties of slave and master, of serf and feudal lord, but *money*, 'the individual of general wealth',[2] the symbol of the indifference to the particular form taken by this general wealth, and which, by virtue of this indifferent character, seems to represent the communality of men, all of whom are equal in their use and possession of an identical commodity. As the owner of this undifferentiated product, each individual appears alongside every other individual as equal participant in social wealth (for is not the form of money common to all?) and as equal in his needs — for is not each individual equally in a position with every other to concretise this general representative of wealth in the form of his choosing?

The relations of the market economy, premised as they are upon the belief in the freedom and equality of individuals, and in a sense incarnating that belief, thus set the stage for the production of a theory of man that both endorses that egalitarian conception and at the same time uses that very endorsement in order to explain (and thereby justify) the actual inequalities that are as much a feature of the relations between men under a market economy as of those relations in earlier modes of production where money and the exchange of commodities played little or no part.

The progress of this 'anthropology' designed to accommodate the specific character of the market economy (and which I shall exemplify with particular reference to Hobbes and Locke) is as follows. Basically, the endorsement must take the form of showing that what appear to be specific, historical, social effects are in fact the reflection of a natural state of affairs. Firstly, then, bourgeois civil society is 'read back' or reflected in a hypothetical 'state of nature'. Within this 'state of nature' all men are seen as equal, as equal participants in a common humanity or 'human essence' and therefore equal in their needs. Bourgeois society, it would follow, must be regarded an enlightened advance upon slavery or feudalism because the freedom and equality of market relations correspond with, rather than conflict with, this original equality and freedom. The other aspect of this conception is the view that the freedom and equality of market relations are themselves the proof and mark of the original equality of men. In other words, to posit an original, natural inequality of men — an untroublesome supposition for earlier epochs — would render the equality of market relations in apparent conflict with the natural order of things, and the whole point is that bourgeois society does, and must be seen to correspond with that natural order. So, in the first instance, there is a reading back of bourgeois equality into nature, and a reading forward of natural equality into its complement under bourgeois society, which sanction and endorse the moral correctness of the market society.

But how then are the actual inequalities of contemporary society, and the actual differences between individual consumption that it manifests, to be accommodated within this framework? How are these glaringly obvious empirical features to find their appropriate reflection and ultimate moral justification in a 'state of nature' whose fundamental character is the equality of all individuals living within it?

The answer, very crudely, is that the very concept of 'human essence', which we might, in our naivety, have suspected to be common to all members of the species *homo sapiens*, and to be that by virtue of which they could be said to be 'men', and 'human' in their needs, appetites and aspirations, is *itself* the read back reflection of the (human) essence of the well-to-do bourgeois individual. In other words, the solution to the particular dilemma that the market economy presents for this philosophy of man, is a solution to the effect that all men are born equal insofar as they are men, that is, insofar as the level of development of their needs and their actual consumption complies with that of *bourgeois* man; but while all such men are born equal and equal in their birthright, not all members of the species *homo sapiens* are born 'men'. Some, that is to say, are less than human, not participants in the allegedly original, but in fact reflected, concept of human essence. Let us give two examples of how this unconscious 'sleight of hand' is affected.

Hobbes

According to Hobbes, all men are equal in the state of nature firstly by virtue of their equality in insecurity (even the weakest can kill the strongest), and secondly by virtue of the equality of their hopes in attaining the satisfaction of their wants. The 'war of all against all', which is seen to be the natural outcome of these natural equalities (each man equally liable to the invasions of the other, each equal in his desire for *bonum sibi*) is, however, none other than the 'bellum omnium contra omnes' that characterises the market economy, and these supposedly natural 'facts' about man become the moral justification of that market society because they reflect and are reflected in the character of bourgeois man: the covetous, self-seeking, entrepreneurial spirit of the market society is thus justified by reference to man's natural appetitiveness in the pursuit of his private goals in the state of nature. But then, of course, this covetousness, this spirit of accumulation (and the commodious living associated with it) is the privilege only of the bourgeois class, of the landowners and owners of capital, and the supposedly natural character of men, by virtue of which they are all equal, is in reality the exclusive property of the merchant and capitalist entrepreneur. Their covetousness is the essence of humanity itself, which thus comes to be defined in terms of the self-seeking, individualistic, competitive nature of men. Anyone, then, who falls short on covetousness (who is incapable of accumulation for himself), falls short of humanity itself. That, in the crudest terms, is the deduction to be made from the Hobbesian position. The actual inequalities of men in the market economy therefore follow *naturally* from a natural deficiency in the character (the humanity) which is the hallmark of their equality.

Locke

For Locke things are not quite so simple. Their complexity is explored in some detail by C. B. MacPherson,[3] who has argued that where Hobbes found no problem in abandoning traditional moral law in favour of a fully materialist doctrine of utility, Locke was more in tune with the public opinion of his day in thinking such a doctrine to be too dangerous to the fabric of society. Too cavalier as he is with traditional conceptions of morality, too quick and uncircumspect in the treatment he accords the doctrine of natural inequality, Hobbes fails to prove himself a satisfactory ideologue, and it is Locke, both more respectful and more pains-taking, who weaves the more complex and more adequate fabric for reconciling all the facts of bourgeois society with its subscription to an apparently conflicting system of human values.

Rejecting Hobbes' celebration of covetousness, and his too apparently 'immoral' condonation of greed and self-seeking appetitiveness, Locke moves in two stages. (a) Men are seen to be rational ('humane') to the extent that they appropriate the earth in the satisfaction of their needs without any *wasting* of its resources. Accumulation beyond the limits of one's needs is immoral and unjustifiable if and only if it results in a squandering of the natural riches of the earth. (b) Wastefulness of the earth's bounty is circumvented with the introduction of money, which allows the individual to appropriate the earth beyond the limits of his needs in a permanent form of wealth not subject to decay. Unrestricted accumulation then becomes the natural *modus operandi*.

Thanks to this second move, a justification of capitalist accumulation based on greed is supplanted by a justification based on the rationality of an accumulation that makes use of money as a store of value. It is true, of course, that at the point at which it becomes morally and expediently rational to appropriate beyond one's immediate needs, this appropriation must proceed by way of the labouring of others (who, of course, do not appropriate), so that what is rational is weighted towards the appropriation of the surplus of others rather than towards the labouring which produces the surplus.[4] But it is also precisely at that point, and indeed by virtue of his unconscious biasing of rationality in the direction of appropriation, that Locke can be seen to have arrived, albeit by way of a more complex detour, at the reconciliation between natural rights and social inequalities that Hobbes achieves. The only difference is that, with greater moral respectability, Locke stresses the rationality of a monetary accumulation, which precisely in using money avoids the excesses and consequent waste of a consumption motivated by greed, whereas Hobbes, who had rested his case on the natural urge of each and everyone to pursue his own good and to desire commodious living, had in fact appeared to offer too directly a pragmatic justification — for it still left accumulation tarred with the brush of amoralism, if not of irrationality. Or, to put it slightly differently, Locke's picture was more acceptable because it was more precise, and where it was more precise was in the mirror it held up to the specific nature of accumulation under the conditions of capitalist economy. Hobbes' justification could, after all, have tolerated the gulping down of salads of pearls, which the abstemiousness required for the accumulation of *capital* must necessarily frown upon.

Yet in the end, and to return to our main point, they both achieve the desired reconciliation between natural equality and social difference by covertly identifying the essence of man with the essence of bourgeois man. Whereas for Hobbes, it is the covetousness of bourgeois man that is read back into the state of nature, where it becomes the mark of the equality of man, and can thus function as a sanction for the competitive relations that hold in a market society, for Locke it is the rationality of appropriation that is thus read back, becoming the defining characteristic of man's 'humanity', and thus in turn enabled to function as the sanction for the 'humanity' of bourgeois society. In both cases, the non-propertied classes, the labouring classes, who are an all too obvious feature of seventeenth and eighteenth century England (and the more moral Lockean liberalism remains the dominant ideology even up to our own day) are justified in their actual inequality, in the relative paucity of their needs, and in their relative deprivation of 'commodious living', by virtue of their failure to participate in the 'original' humanity — a 'humanity' that is the characterising feature of men in the state of nature and in which all men are equal, but which, of course, is none other than the derived 'humanity' which is the exclusive endowment of the propertied classes. Or, in other words, the labouring classes do not attain to the full 'rationality' which is precisely the attribute of anyone who is truly 'human': they are, in fact, a little less than human. In the words of MacPherson:

The assumption that men are by nature equally capable of shifting for themselves was not an idle one. It enabled Locke in good conscience to reconcile the great inequalities of observed society with the postulated equality of natural right. If men are by nature equally rational, in the sense of equally capable of looking after themselves, those who have fallen permanently behind in the pursuit of property can be assumed to have only themselves to blame. And only if men are assumed to be equally capable of shifting for themselves, can it be thought equitable to put them on their own, and have them confront each other in the market without the protections which the old natural law doctrine upheld. The assumption that men are equally rational in capacity of shifting for themselves thus makes it possible to reconcile the justice of the market with the traditional notions of commutative and distributive justice.[5]

Needs and Human Nature
There is a quite definite theory of needs that follow logically from this Hobbesian-Lockean rationale of class society. And it is a theory, as I have already suggested, which brings economy full circle and supplies it with the moral basis without which its positivistic identification of needs with actual consumption would otherwise remain unanchored. The actual inequalities of consumption, and importantly the relative deprivation of the labouring classes, do not in any sense point in the direction of some category of 'unfulfilled' needs — a category that would be at odds with the positivism of the economic theory — for these irregularities in consumption now follow from the *nature* of the consumers, whose consumption is by definition that appropriate to their nature. That the lesser and simpler consumption of the labouring classes does not match the elaborate consumption of the well-to-do is not an instance of an inegalitarian distribution of social wealth, nor does it suggest that, pace the economists, production does not take place entirely in accordance with human needs, for the only needs that are properly speaking *human*, are precisely those that are met in the consumption of the average

bourgeois individual. Just as the very notion of what it is to be human is read off from the alleged humanity of bourgeois man, so, too, is the concept of what constitutes human needs. Those who fall short of humanity fall short also of the consumption proper to man, and it is no accident that it is to animal and bestial metaphors that recourse is had in order to describe the needs, the life-style and the satisfactions of the exploited classes under capitalism. Marx himself, of course, makes deliberate recourse to these metaphors even in the moment of inverting the liberal con- ception: for the working-class has indeed sunk to the animal level as a result of the *social* forces that have deprived them of the humanity that was their *natural* birthright).[6]

I have tried to show how the myth of the equality of man, which is essential to the reproduction of the system of capitalist economy, is used to reindorse the traditional conception (that could formerly be espoused quite openly) of the natural inequal- ities between men and between their levels of need. In this respect it plays the role that in earlier epochs was played by the myth of the divine or transcendent order of things or natural purpose, in accordance with which individuals had their particular natural endowments, and the particular functions and allotted place in society that followed from them. And, indeed, despite the enormous difference between these mythologies (for the belief in the autonomy of man seems directly opposed to belief in his divine determination, and in contrast to the transcendent ethics of naturally predetermined inequalities we have the secular ethics of individual freedom and equality) they share an underlying logic, a logic without which they would lack the consistency essential to their successful functioning as ideology. For if a large part of the purpose of these mythologies is to reconcile individuals to the differences that characterise the consumption and life-style of different classes and individuals, their success must depend on showing such differences to be indeed natural and *not* the effect of forces of social coercion beyond the individual's control. For the myth of the divine order of things, which corresponded to a stage in history for which there was no obvious social or economic need to ascribe to the belief in the equality of men, it was enough simply to state the fact of this natural difference. But with the birth of the market economy, which reflects, expresses and depends upon an ideology of individual freedom and equality, individuals had to be shown to be placed as apparently in situations of equal opportunity in order for them to be prepared to accept that the actual inequalities characterising their social existence were the result of natural factors — and importantly of natural factors over which they themselves had some control, and for which they themselves were responsible. The secular, rational, enlightened ethics of capitalism, which cannot stomach the idea of a divine assignation of natural differences (for to do so would be to undermine the very principle of its enlightenment: the belief in the freedom of man) must replace divine order and natural purpose by the agency of man, the measure of all things. But if, at the same time, the results of the social activities of man, the results of his active agency and freedom of will, must be seen to be natural in order to be morally justifiable, one's allegedly natural station in life, since it cannot be attributed to God or divine decree, must be that which it is in one's nature to be able to choose. Belief in the autonomy of the individual from society thus becomes the corner-stone of the secular and rational ethics of liberal theory: if people are to be convinced that what are in fact social determinations are natural givens, this naturalness must be seen to be a matter concerning themselves alone, literally a question of their own nature. When divine ordinance becomes discredited, there is a risk that the effects of social determinations will be seen for what they are, as indeed the effects of *social* forces. The myth of the essential freedom of the individual serves to pre-empt that subversive move; by insisting that men are the masters of their destiny and not the playthings of social forces, liberal anthropology can make it truly a matter of one's nature who one is and where one happens to be placed in civil society.

The picture, of course, is not entirely convincing, and it scarcely bears a very close examination. Symptomatic of the cracks it is papering over is the infinite regress of its argument: man himself is responsible for his nature, and in that sense 'chooses' who he is; but it is his nature that determines this choice of himself and which is reflected in the way that he finds himself ... The theory of the freedom of the individual from social forces in fact, therefore, is a theory of his wholly determined existence, for it follows that if society has no control over the ways in which individuals 'naturally' find themselves, it is equally the case that there are no determinations over which these individuals can exert control: intervention would be as pointless as the individual is powerless.

2. Contemporary justification of the market society

No doubt, it will be said, this is all very well as an exercise in the history of ideas, but it is now a fairly familiar and well-trodden terrain, and in any case it is scarcely relevant to modern society or to its economic and anthropological theories.

Now there is no doubt that when it comes to 'justifications' of contemporary capitalist society, any overt attempt to present a coherent ethics in terms of 'human nature' and its intrinsic needs has been more or less abandoned. Rather than face the question of the extent to which class differences and the ensuing differences in consumption are ultimately accountable to the 'nature' of individuals, the emphasis falls not on the 'nature' of man but, more pragmatically, upon the efficiency of capitalism in reproducing the society to which it happens to have given rise. The stress on capitalism's capacity to deliver the 'goods' serves to divert attention from the question of the 'goodness' (or 'humanity') of the goods. And this form of justification is further reinforced by the suggestion that any attempts in socialist countries to emulate the degree of satisfaction of individual needs permitted by capitalism have either failed (and there are a thousand tales to tell of the wastefulness and inefficiency of the socialist economies, of their failure 'to meet needs'), or else have only achieved such success as they have at the expense of sacrificing those values of individual freedom, self-determination and autonomy of choice, which capitalism alone is able to reconcile with its continued productivity, and for whose maintenance it must, therefore, be the appropriate — the provenly 'scientific' — system. Capitalist production, then, no longer has to be defended by reference to the intrinsic humanity of the needs it accommodates; the needs to whose satisfaction it is devoted are justified simply by virtue of their existence. Indeed, capitalism can now be justified as the historical system that has created those needs and as the mode of production that is best fitted to meet them. For has it not allowed for material satisfaction undreamt of by earlier epochs, and has it not endowed man with an ability to choose his gratifications and his style of life in general, that was denied to earlier generations?

In place, then, of the essentialist and overly moralistic-anthropological endorsement of bourgeois society, which depended for its force on eternalising that society and so presenting it as the appropriate reflection of a state of nature, there arises a 'scientific' justification, which so far from eternalising the system of capitalist production, can recognise its specific and historical character and the developed human aspirations that it alone evokes and satisfies. Within the framework of this justification, issues of morality are 'scientifically' seen as referring to relative factors, not to givens of a transhistoric kind, and the moral element that in the ideological discourse of the seventeenth and eighteenth centuries underpinned the positivism of the too overtly pragmatic account of political economy, and mitigated the 'realism' of its approach to matters of *human* concern, is able, in an era that privileges 'scientific' explanation above all others, to be unashamedly absorbed within that positivism becoming one aspect of it.

This is not to deny, of course, the measure of critical discourse that often accompanies the defence of capitalism. It is fashionable these days, to speak of the 'consumerism' and 'fetish of materialism' that capitalism has bred; to acknowledge even that it can be 'wasteful' of resources and have undesirable ecological consequences. But if all that is meant by such talk is that a few deformities must be expected of any monster that has proved so fertile, and that certain, less fortunate by-products are the inevitable condition of the immense benefits it bestows, it is devoid of any genuine critical edge. It is clearly hypocritical to voice regrets about the 'mindless consumerism' begotten by capitalism if one is still persuaded overall that capitalism alone can deliver the goods. And all too often, in fact, this gestural acknowledgement of the evils of capitalist society is doing service in an argument that would convince us of the far more important and more damaging implications of any alternative to it: thus, it is suggested, granted the mindlessness of much consumption, what Socialist God or tyrant is to dictate what commodities we want, and what socialist economy, has managed in fact to satisfy the needs of those for whom it plans?

So while it is true enough that any convincing defence of capitalism must choose today to stress its pragmatic rather than its natural necessity, this only indicates the extent to which the original positivism of political economy's discourse about needs is not only alive and kicking, but has flourished to a point where it no longer requires the direct complement of a moral discourse or theory of man: the facts of supply and demand speak for themselves. This is not to suggest that were those economists who offer their wholly factual defences of a capitalist system of production to be pressed upon the question of the justification for the unequal distribution of wealth and the differences in consumption that typify capitalist society, they would not in the last analysis have recourse to the values of individual freedom and equality, and that in order to reconcile these values with the facts of contemporary society, they would be forced to introduce all the lumber of a Lockean liberalism, or something very akin to it. I believe, in fact, as I earlier suggested, that however inadequate that framework of thinking may have proved to the realities of the modern capitalist nations, it is still the pervasive, albeit now more convert, justification of the status quo. In other words, if we scratch deeply enough, we shall still find this kind of naturalism lurking beneath the veneer of scientism and positivism that protects the social scientists from what might prove a distressing confrontation with the value-system they sustain.

That much said by way of defence of the continued pertinence of the Marxist critique of liberalism, let us now turn back to consideration of its terms. The core of the attack on essentialism lies in the displacement of the individual subject as the object of study in favour of the 'ensemble of social relations', which is, and always has been, the context of human existence and production:

The more deeply we go back into history, the more does the individual and hence the producing individual, appear as dependent, as belonging to a greater whole. (. . .) The human being is in the most literal sense a *zoon politikon*, not merely a gregarious animal, but an animal that can individuate only in the midst of society. Production by an isolated individual outside society . . . is as much an absurdity as is the development of language without individuals living together and talking to each other.[7]

According to Marx, then, individuality is itself the outcome of an extended process of development out of the gregariousness of the animal state — a process of hominisation. This process of individualisation will always be at a particular stage at a particular time and is itself the effect of a determinate stage of production.

The implication here, clearly, is that to have knowledge of human beings and their needs is to have knowledge of them in their specificity. Marx's whole concern is to break with the political economy and philosophy of his predecessors and contemporaries by 'not confounding or extinguishing all historical differences under general human laws'[8] either with respect to the production of social wealth or with respect to its consumption. He is prepared to operate with a concept of 'production in general' only insofar as it is recognised that there is no such thing, nor ever has been, nor ever will be, in reality. Production is always a 'specific kind of production'; and so, too, are the needs to which it gives rise, and so are the human beings who are reproduced as a result of their own production.

This suggests that any proper understanding of the nature and formation of needs, must base itself on a study of the forms of unity between a humanity which is the outcome of constant unification with a nature that is likewise constantly changing and developing as the outcome of that interaction with human activity. Just as the distinction between individual and society must be seen as a historical product having its particular expression correlative with the stage reached in individualisation, so must the distinction between humanity and nature, the nature appropriated in production being as much the product of a prior appropriation as the humanity which appropriates. In this sense, as Marx says in the first Preface to *Capital* I: 'the evolution of the economic formation of society is viewed as a process of natural history'.[9] It is from this standpoint, that he can dismiss the idea that in production the members of society appropriate nature in accordance with human needs as the 'obvious, trite notion'.[10] The trite way of looking at things, that is to say, is to regard the purpose and motivation of production as lying in the gratification of predetermining needs, and as we have seen it gives rise to only a 'shallow coherence' when bourgeois economy attempts to analyse the relationship between production, consumption, distribution and exchange.

Likewise, this 'trite' notion both underlies, and is given confirmation in the 'dumbly general' concept of human nature that lies at the heart of the account given in liberal anthropology. For just as the affective characteristics of this 'human nature' (its 'appetitive' spirit, or its spirit of 'rational accumulation') are derived from the observed features of contemporary society, so, too, is its set of essential needs, which it then follows all too automatically must determine the production of the day.

But let us note here that this attack on the notion of an abstract human essence is not just directed against the pseudo-human essence of the Hobbesian-Lockean account, but against essentialism *tout court*. Indeed, the main target of the *Sixth Thesis*, in which this attack is summarised, is, of course, Feuerbach, whose secular view of the human essence was regarded by Marx and Engels themselves as a significant advance on the spiritualism of Hegel, and a first step towards a materialist understanding of society. But even Feuerbach's sensuous-materialist and genuinely universal concept of human nature remains abstract, a-historic and therefore epistemologically vacuous. So whether Man's essence is conceived in spiritual, in hedonistic-materialist or in purely biological terms, Marx's insistence on the primacy of human productive activity in determining both the objects of consumption and the 'nature' of the consumers — his insistence, that is, that needs must be understood as historic and specific contents rather than as mere forms of a pre-given essence — equally applies, for it denies the validity of any a-historic, universally defining characteristics of man, no matter how these are conceived.

Let us pause for a moment to consider the implications of this Marxist attack on essentialism, for these, it seems, have not always been fully understood even by those concerned to expound the Marxist position. E. Mandel, for example, has written in reference to the 'alleged variety of needs' that 'any moderately serious study of anthropology and history will show, on the contrary, how remarkably stable they are; food, clothing, shelter, etc. . . . there are half a dozen needs which do not seem to have changed since the beginnings of homo sapiens'.[11] But it is, of course, precisely against this abstract conception of human needs in terms of 'basic biological drives' that the insistence on the historical content even of human hunger is directed. In complete contrast to Mandel's suggestion, Lucien Sève, in expounding the message of the *Sixth Thesis* has written:

The natural point of departure, in the life of individuals as in that of social formations, is something quite other than the *real basis of* the developed totality, the formation of the totality consisting precisely in the reversal of the relations between the natural and the social, in the progressive transformations of natural givens into historic results . . .[12]

There is no doubt, I think, that this is true to the spirit of the discourse in Marxism that is here being examined. Indeed, it is more or less true to the letter of those remarks we have already discussed in the 1857 Introduction to the effect that 'as soon as consumption emerges from the initial state of natural crudity . . . it becomes itself mediated as a drive by the object', or of the claim in the *German Ideology* that 'the production of new needs is the first historical act'. In other words, even our so-called basic biological needs for food, shelter and the like, must be seen as specific, socially mediated contents, the principle of whose explanation is not our common physiological nature but the social relations of production, distribution and exchange. Though the idea of a 'biological essence' may seem, prima facie, a good deal more plausible than the spiritualised essence we are offered in classical liberal theory, Marx's attack on the 'human essence' is also an attack on this biological essence, the point being that just as there is no production in general so there is no biology in general. Even in regard to the so-called basic needs, he wants to argue that there is no separate, exclusively biological basis for them, and that this is true of any society, no matter how 'primitive'. If we fail to see this we remain trapped in a conceptual schema in which development is identified with the deployment of an abstract essence in a uniform time — precisely the schema that blurs the particular with the general and obliterates all knowledge of the actual. Even 'basic needs', then, should not be seen as mere forms or invest-ments, since they acquire their content through the medium and manner of their satisfaction. Hunger is certainly hunger, as Marx admits; biological drive is biological drive, but only in an abstract sense that has no concrete reference, and tells us nothing about the specifically human experience of it, since that experience is integral with the mode of its gratification. Only by looking at the cycle of activity and need, and the unity of production and consumption in their development, can we provide this kind of information; but this directs attention immediately to the role of social production in determining the development and expansion of needs. If we cling to the model of consumption determining production, and, in this more precise instance, of a biological essence determining that production, then we must accept that the explanation of this development must itself be biological. How, short of speculating upon some primary, biological type of need for 'progress' as such, can we ever hope to explain the expanded reproduction of needs? Yet the basic, primary biological needs are those which, precisely, are basic and primary. There can be no appeal, therefore, to the concept of a 'basic biological need' as the principle of the development of that which is, by definition, the basic and non-developed. If the 'need' for 'gorgeous apparel which scarcely keeps us warm', to which King Lear refers (see p. 17 above) is itself explained in biological terms, then what grounds remain for the distinction between it and the 'need for warmth'? The attempt to explain the particular development of human needs *wholly* in terms of biology must ultimately deny its initial postulate of a distinctively biological drive.

One wants to say, by contrast, and it is the essential message of Marx's attack on essentialism, that the basis for the explanation of needs in their determinateness is not to be found in individual biology but in the ensemble of social relations which give rise to a certain level and type of social production and mediate the consumption of its objects. It is only from the standpoint provided by this basis that we can begin to understand the specifically human capacity for enlargement and progressive variation of consumption. Abstracting from the particular mode of production, we see that what characterises human production, and allows us to demarcate between it and animal production is the degree to which it creates an external, objective patrimony (of material goods, knowledges, institutions, language and culture generally).[13] For while birds may build their nests, and ants and termites bequeath their heaps, there is nothing comparable in the extent of their objectification of themselves to that accomplished by human beings. Or, to put this slightly differently, if we want to draw distinctions between men and animals — and they are distinctions which progressively come to hold rather than having an original existence — then we can say that in contrast to men, animals produce practically nothing of any durability outside themselves, and if their production is cumulative, it is only very slowly so, and takes the restricted form of certain aptitudes towards determinate behaviour patterns, which comprise the stock, not of a social, but of an almost purely genetic patrimony, transmitted biologically as the *in*heritance of each member of the species. By and large it is specific to men to reproduce themselves, as Lucien Sève has put it, 'excentrically',[14] in the form of a durable and accumulating stock, or social patrimony, which becomes the external matrix of their behaviour, and to which, in turn, and dialectically, they react — in the experience of themselves as dependent upon objective production for the reproduction of their subjective selves. The reason for the ever widening gap between human and animal capacities (which might be expressed in terms of a process of 'hominisation' out of an original, undifferentiated animal state) is precisely that human beings are not restricted to a biological stock of inherited aptitudes; were they, *per impossibile*, to be so, then any difference would dissolve, for there is little or no difference between men and animals in the rate at which they extend this internal heritage. The point is that such a patrimony is not the only, or even the major source of human development, and the slow development in that sphere is in direct contrast to the very rapid development given to human beings in the form of their *social* patrimony. It is only because of this social accumulation that human beings escape the limits of individual biology and cease to have the kind of dependence upon nature that is found in the case of other animal species. Indeed, one might say that it is only because of this that the concept of 'human needs' acquires its interest and its problematic nature. For it is only because of this social accumulation that the tension between needs viewed as original, natural givens, and needs viewed as specific, historic and socally determined, arises in the first place.

3. The cognitive discourse and the question of 'true' needs

I have deliberately refrained in this and the preceding chapter from any discussion of the difficulties and confusions which the cognitive discourse introduces from the standpoint of any normative discourse based on assumptions about 'true' needs, and thus ultimately implying some theory of human nature. This is because my main concern throughout these chapters has been to justify my claim that historical materialism allows the question of needs to be posed for the first time in a genuinely open fashion when it exposes the closure upon it of any answers that are already given in terms of human needs.

But we are bound nonetheless to ponder both the adequacy of this discourse and to concern ourselves with the extent to which it can be reconciled with other elements in the Marxist conception and other views about human needs that are implicit to it, and at times, indeed, given explicit statement. And this will involve confronting a major problem that it appears to pose from the standpoint of Marx's condemnation of capitalist production and advocacy of socialism-communism. We have seen that it follows from the economic analysis of *Capital* that any account of needs which identifies these in actual consumption involves a denial of the facts of bourgeois society and is serving ideological purposes. The gap between needs (A) and needs (B), the 'wants of the masses', or, in short, the category of unfulfilled needs is an essential category in Marx's analysis. But to the extent that unfulfilled needs, like actual consumption, are themselves conceived as relative to a given stage of production and themselves theorised as always determinate, the question of their evaluation is left hanging. That is to say, from the standpoint of the cognitive discourse, any gap that Marx reveals between what the members of society need and what they actually consume must itself be seen as historic and relative, and not accountable in terms of any universal and essential human needs. In arguing that needs in both senses are historical and to be explained as the effects of particular forms of production with their particular relations of distribution, Marx appears to have sacrificed any grounds upon which to evaluate between forms of consumption. For we no longer have the concept of 'human nature' or of any defining set of 'truly human' needs by reference to which we can, as it were, take stock of the productive activity, with its particular effects on consumption, of any given 'society', any given mode of production.

Unlike the political economists who could argue that any actual consumption was a desirable and essentially 'human' consumption because it was the consumption dictated by 'human nature', Marx, who recognises and analyses the differences at the level of consumption rather than reading this off from a dumbly general 'human nature', is brought to the position either of equally confirming all differences in consumption (they are all equally the 'human' consumption of historically changing 'human nature') or of introducing a second discourse that is at odds with the stringent anti-essentialism of his cognitive arguments. Now in one sense, it is clearly absurd to suggest there is some kind of option here: Marx clearly damns capitalism and thinks of communism as alone a 'truly' human form of society. But in another sense, it is not so absurd, since Marx himself appears to opt for both alternatives and both are implied by different aspects of his critique of capitalism. From the standpoint of the first alternative, the critical dimension has to be confined to an assessment of particular modes of production in terms of the efficiency with which they are able to satisfy the needs they have in fact invoked; from the standpoint of the second alternative, it is extended to a critique of those evoked needs themselves. Now it may well be that the first line of critique necessarily implies the second. But if this is so, it is clear that the grounds upon which an anti-humanist Marxism privileges the 'scientificity' of the former over the 'humanism' of the latter are undermined. I have already suggested that Marx exposes the full dimensions of the question of needs precisely because he is inconsistent from the standpoint of adherence to the fact-value distinction which underlies the anti-humanist interpretation. But it is no accident that those who have aligned themselves exclusively with his cognitive discourse and have wanted to render all Marx's apparently normative claims consistent with this discourse, have felt obliged to insist that the latter be interpreted in terms, not of the greater humanity of socialism, but in terms of its greater efficiency. Or perhaps this point is better expressed by saying that this interpretation is one to which Marx's critique of capitalism is itself constantly tending. It is my own view that there is no single and univocal theory of needs underlying his critique, and that Marx himself is scarcely aware of the implications from the standpoint of the provision of an account of 'true' needs of his various lines of attack on capitalist production. I propose, therefore, in subsequent chapters to examine the 'anthropological' basis of these different lines of attack and their normative implications, even though this will be to discover a number of loose threads left trailing rather than any neatly woven fabric.

Notes

1   Or at least the *male* individual — the enlightenment of this new ideology tends to be confined to him alone.
2   K. Marx, *Grundrisse, op. cit.,* p. 221.
3   C. B. MacPherson, *The Political Theory of Possessive Individualism*, Oxford, O.U.F., p. 247f.
4   Or, as MacPherson has put it, 'at the point where labouring and appro-

priation became separable, full rationality went with appropriating rather than with labouring', *ibid.*, p. 234.

5   *Ibid.*, p. 245.

6   K. Marx, *Capital, op. cit.,* Vol. I pp. 283-85, 399-400, 407-8, 427-28, 429-30, 477-78, 535-38, 567-68, 619-20, 623-24, 688-90.

7   K. Marx, *Grundrisse, op. cit.,* p. 84.

8   *Ibid.*, p. 87.

9   And cf. *Grundrisse, op. cit.,* p. 400: '. . . increase of population is a *natural* force of labour, for which nothing is paid. From this standpoint we use the term *natural force* to refer to the *social force*. All *natural forces of social labour* are themselves historical products'. For a view of the formation of human society as a process of natural history, see S. Moscovici, *Society Against Nature*, Sussex, Harvester Press, 1976.

10 K. Marx, *Grundrisse, op. cit.,* p. 89.

11 E. Mandel, *Marxist Economic Theory, op. cit.*, p. 660.

12 L. Sève, *Man in Marxist Theory*, Sussex, Harvester Press, 1978, p. 213.

13 This is the central argument of the work by L. Sève cited in the previous note. See in particular Chap. II.

14 *Ibid.*, p. 234, and cf. p. 217f.

5 The Normative Discourse I: The Humanisms of the Economic Critique

I suggested at the end of the last chapter that Marx directs his criticisms of capitalist production from two apparently irreconcilable standpoints, the one appearing to preclude any judgment about the pattern of consumption and the historic needs to which, as the latest form of development of the productive forces, it has given rise, while the other directly condemns the pattern of consumption associated with capitalism. I also suggested that if this is so, it raises the question of the extent to which this critique is underpinned by antithetical value systems, or theories of 'true' need.

The criticism that is directed from the first standpoint can be summed up as an attack upon the *barriers to consumption that are imposed by capitalist relations of production*, and we can distinguish between three aspects of it: (a) capitalist production imposes a barrier upon consumption because it relies on a distribution of income that restricts the access of the mass of producers to the social wealth produced; (b) it imposes a barrier upon consumption because it is bound to the production of exchange-value and it can only realise exchange-value through the production of surplus-value; (c) it imposes a barrier on consumption because its allocation of social labour time is irrational, resulting in constant over and under production relative to existing needs. Now as they stand, neither this attack in general, nor any of its aspects taken in isolation, constitute an attack on the *nature* of the development of the productive forces, nor therefore upon what I have referred to as the 'ontology' of the consumption potentially permitted by that development. On the contrary, it is with this thrust of his critique that we must associate Marx's 'eulogistic' discourse (to be found throughout the *Grundrisse*[1]) on the 'spur' to development that is alone provided by capitalist production, on the 'universality' of the latter, its 'civilising influence', its revolutionisation of the 'encrusted satisfactions of present needs', and his general claim that the 'historical task and justification' of capital lies in its development of the productive forces of social labour.[2] So far from questioning its value from the standpoint of some theory of presupposed human needs, Marx 'commends' capitalism for the extent to which it breaks down natural limits on our consumption and encourages the emergence of an ever widening circle of 'wholly social' or artificial needs; for it is a *condition*, he tells us, of production founded on capital that there is:

... exploration of all nature in order to discover new, and useful qualities in things; universal exchange of the products of all alien climates and lands; new (artificial) preparation of natural objects, by which they are given new use values. The exploration of the earth in all directions, to discover new things of use as well as new useful qualities of the old; such as new qualities of them as raw materials, etc.; the development, hence, of the natural sciences to their highest point; likewise the discovery, creation and satisfaction of new needs arising from society itself; the cultivation of all the qualities of the social human being, production of the same in a form as rich as possible in needs, because rich in qualities and relations — production of this being as the most total and universal possible social product, for, in order to take gratification in a many-sided way, he must be capable of many pleasures (*genussfähug*), hence cultured to a high degree.[3]

Insofar, then, that there is an explicit commentary on the *nature* of consumption to be associated with the attack on capitalism's *barriers* to consumption, its judgment on that nature is positive, and positive, moreover, in the judgment that it passes on an *actual* consumption. For though one may feel that many of Marx's remarks (such as the one quoted above) on the 'civilising influence' of capital are inspired by his vision of the potential consumption it permits, and that this vision has blinded him to a more realistic appraisal of the consumption that in fact takes place under capitalism, there can be little doubt that as they stand these remarks are about the already realised achievements of capitalist production by way of the expansion of needs, and that they are devoid of negative commentary on that achievement. There is nothing in this discourse as it stands which suggests that we should view the consumption that takes place under the impetus of capitalist production, or the needs which are evoked in consequence, as an 'alien' consumption or as an 'alienation' of our 'true' needs, and to the extent that Marx thinks in terms of any 'false' consumption, it is not a false consumption he associates with the new and artificial needs that capitalism encourages and gratifies, but with areas of production (commercial and banking activities, for example)[4] which are essential to the reproduction of capitalist relations of production, but 'unnecessary' and redundant in principle (i.e., in a society based on a capitalistic development of the productive forces, and a capitalistic consumption, but which plans its allocation of social labour time directly with a view to the satisfaction of needs.)

We should note here, however, that while it is quite true that this line of attack implies no theory of 'true' needs based on essentialist assumptions (which is to say, invoking concepts of universal, transhistoric needs whose satisfaction is a precondition of a 'humane' existence), those anti-humanist interpreters who have aligned themselves exclusively with it and used it as a basis for arguing that Marx has expunged his critique of any kind of 'humanism' or that its connection with 'anthropology' is merely contingent, are surely mistaken. Indeed, were this line of attack not underpinned by some form of humanism, it would have no rationale at all. For why (to take the first of the barriers to consumption we have isolated) should it matter, if not for humanistic reasons, that capitalist relations of distribution restrict the effective demand of the masses? It is surely only from a humanist standpoint that it makes sense to speak of this as a 'barrier to consumption' since in itself an unequal distribution of income imposes no barrier to aggregate social consumption at all : what is lost to the consumption of the worker is 'compensated' for by the excessively luxurious consumption of the class of capital owners, or failing that, in the consumption of distinct sectors of the economy (armaments, space programmes, etc.) that are highly absorbent of a social value that exceeds the aggregate purchasing power exercised by the individual members of society. In other words, already implied in the idea that unequal distribution of social wealth is a barrier to consumption is the idea (a) that social wealth is wasted and 'falsely' spent in the luxurious consumption of the rich, and (b) that there are needs whose satisfaction is intrinsic to the well-being of the mass of the populace, and which are therefore in some sense 'truer'. In Marx's words : 'There are not too many necessities of life produced in proportion to the existing population. Quite the reverse. Too little is produced to decently and humanely satisfy the wants of the great mass.'[5] The humanism of the sentiment expressed here is clear enough, even though it would be an unwarranted assumption that it directly commits Marx to an essentialist position: we can interpret the wants to which it refers in terms of the historically developed and, relative to earlier epochs, fairly elaborate system of needs of the worker under capitalism; and the 'decency' and 'humanity' of their satisfaction can equally be regarded as relative. Such an interpretation would be consistent with the remark in the *German Ideology* that:

The positive expression 'human' corresponds to the definite conditions *pre-dominant* at a certain stage of production and to the way of satisfying needs determined by them, just as the negative expression 'inhuman' corresponds to the attempt, within the existing mode of production, to negate these predominant conditions and the way of satisfying needs prevailing under them, an attempt that this stage of production engenders afresh.[6]

Perhaps we can say, then, that the 'humanism' and the theory of needs to be associated with this line of attack on capitalism is one whose standard is set by the historic needs and new possibilities of gratification that capitalism has made possible. The concept of humanity that is invoked by it is itself relative and historic, and so likewise is the 'truth' of these needs and possibilities. And the basis of the criticism is, as already suggested, not the negative or alien nature of these needs and possibilities, but the contrast between the potential for satisfying these developed needs and the fact that the capitalist mode of production prevents its realisation.

It is also, arguably, in these terms that we should understand the second aspect of the attack on the barriers placed by capitalist production upon consumption, and which relates to the restriction it imposes on the expansion of the productive forces, and thus on consumption, as a result of its need to transform value (labour-time) into exchange-value, or, in other words, to incorporate it into the form of commodities that can sell, in the form of products distinct from value itself, distinct from the labour-time incorporated in them. For were this not necessary, this labour time becomes available to society in a form identical with itself, i.e., as free time. And the assumption is that this is free time devoted, or potentially devotable, precisely to the expansion of the prime productive force of society, namely, the working masses. It is free time for the development of the all round activities of the individual, time for the development of individuality.

This barrier, then, is not just a barrier to the consumption of the material wealth in fact produced by society, which, as we have seen is (wastage apart) consumed through the excessive consumption of the rich and specific sectors of production; it is a barrier to the production, and thus the consumption of wealth as such, since the wealth as such of society is to be measured by the aggregate labour-time of which it has avail. Capitalist society limits wealth/consumption by limiting its existence in the form of time/consumption of time. It is true, of course, that much of the 'free' time made available to a society that has freed itself from the need to realise value in the form of exchange-value, will become incorporated in material goods or services designed to further the all-round activities and development of individuals, and to that extent it will become 'necessary' labour-time rather than literally 'free', i.e., leisure time. But the point is that this expansion of necessary labour-time constitutes a quantitative and qualitative expansion of consumption (or, if preferred, expansion of the main productive force of society: its human agents) that is prohibited under a capitalist economy, and unmeasurable by any of the gages of productivity or of the 'value' of consumption that apply in capitalist society. It is, as Marx says, 'unmeasured by any previous yardstick'[7] and to that extent represents a transcendence of the law of value itself: for *to the extent* that the labour-time available to an individual is 'incorporated' in the development of his or her individuality, it ceases to be a *measure* of value; and were it to be argued that the 'value' of individuality were the socially average labour-time needed to produce it, that would presume what by definition is excluded — that we had a common measure of individuality, or that individuality were something common to different individuals. This, moreover, would involve mistakenly treating the 'development of individuality' as a finished product, rather than as an indefinitely expanding process — as the concept of an infinite potential for the development of life, even though in fact it comes to an end at death.

Now the humanist presuppositions of this second barrier are if anything even more obvious than in the case of the first, for the entire stress is on the potentiality for human development that capitalism has developed and now stands in the way of. But surely, it will be said, it then constitutes an attack directly upon the *nature* of consumption under capitalism, and it is underpinned not just by humanist but also by essentialist assumptions. For is it not the very *kinds* of activities, the very *forms* of consumption and the very *uses* of labour-time that are here subjected to criticism, and is this not a criticism that we can only make sense of on the assumption that there are other activities, forms of consumption and uses of time that are more appropriate to the fulfilment of human beings and most beneficial from the standpoint of their nature? In reply to this objection, however, it can be insisted that Marx regards the potential for individual development as itself a historic potential that has only come into being under the civilising influence of capitalism, and therefore could not feature among the needs of those living in earlier epochs. It is unmeasured by any previous yardstick, and transcends all earlier and limited possibilities of satisfaction. If its realisation is more appropriate and beneficial, it is so only relative to the developed 'nature' that is alone capable of enjoying its benefits. Having said that, however, it has to be recognised that when Marx gives us to believe, as he does at times, that this potential will be realised in *certain kinds of activity* (cultural, artistic, educational) rather than others, he certainly appears to be helping himself to assumptions about what constitutes a 'truly human' consumption that are strictly speaking disallowed by the argument for the merely relative 'truth' of (always developed) needs. In other words to the extent that Marx clearly does regard certain activities as more intrinsically human and thus, in a sense, 'measures' the development of communist needs by an existing yardstick, he introduces an essentialism that is difficult to reconcile with his arguments for the relativity of needs, and is at odds with his own (and his anti-humanist interpreters') conviction that he has expunged 'moral' questions about the assessment of needs from his account of their development. As we shall see, there are a number of other strands of his normative discourse of which this is equally true.

In fact I think that it has to be recognised that this tension is immanent to the third aspect of the attack on capitalism's barriers to consumption. The particular barrier here, it will be recalled, lies in the fact that capitalist production squanders social labour-time and is wasteful and destructive of value in its very attempt to satisfy an existing body of needs. This means, not only that it imposes a barrier to a potential consumption that it could have catered for with the production in which the social labour-time could have been incorporated, but also that it imposes a barrier to consumption in the sense that it may, and sometimes does, fail to produce the goods adequate to meet an already existing need equipped with the requisite purchasing power (and conversely that it produces goods for which there is no need, i.e., literally no need, not merely a lack of effective demand). In *Capital* III, this barrier is presented as the main deficiency of capitalism. The stress there falls less on the historic potentialities developed by capitalism which are so emphasised in the *Grundrisse*, but more on its inefficiency, its failure to 'meet' ('match', 'correspond' to) existing needs as a result of its subjection to a continual over and under production of goods relative to an existing social demand.

Now apart from the recognition of the production and consumption that could take place in the labour-time released for a society where production was controlled by the 'common mind', there is little in this line of argument that invites us to think of a radical qualitative difference in the consumption of such a society. The 'fault' of capitalism appears to lie entirely in the inefficiency with which it accommodates existing needs. In other words, it is this aspect of the attack upon the barriers to consumption that appears to adhere most closely to the relativist and non-essentialist account of needs that I have argued is the general implication of the economic critique. This, it should be stressed again, by no means warrants the anti-humanist *reductio ad absurdum* that M. Godelier suggests is the correct interpretation to be put upon Marx's positive 'evaluation' of socialist society as a 'higher' form:

But what does 'higher' mean here, what is the criterion on which this value-judgement is based?
The criterion is the fact that the *structure* of socialist relations of production *corresponds* functionally with the conditions of the rapid development of the new, gigantic, more and more socialised production forces created by capitalism (...) This correspondence is totally *independent* of any *a priori* idea of happiness, of 'true' liberty, of the essence of man, etc. Marx demonstrates the necessity and superiority of a new mode of production thus establishing a value-judgement without *starting* with an *a priori* criterion of rationality. This value-judgement is not a judgement of 'people'; it does not demonstrate any progress in 'morality' and 'victory' of ethical principles in socialist society. It is a judgement of

the properties of the structure, of the particular conditions of its appearance and functioning.[8]

I suppose it is just about possible that in his most puritanically anti-humanist frame of mind Marx might himself have been persuaded that this is what he 'demonstrates'. But if it is really what he demonstrates, one wonders why he took the trouble to do so. For why, we might ask, if it is not for humanistic reasons, does it matter that there is a 'functional correspondence' between socialist relations and socialist productive forces? Why is that desirable or 'superior' if not on account of what *human beings* can expect to gain from it? What possible reason could there be to be concerned one way or another with the equilibrium of a 'structure and its properties'? If that equilibrium is its own validation, and its superiority established independently of any judgement regarding its effects upon the human 'bearers' of the 'structure', then it is difficult to understand why Marx should have wanted to persuade *us* of the 'higher' status of socialism, or why Godelier in turn should bother with the question of what Marx 'demonstrates' as if some politics of socialism depended on it.

But even though it would be absurd to infer such anti-humanist conclusions on its basis, it is nonetheless true that it is this aspect of Marx's critical discourse which appears as it stands to be most freed of any evaluation of the nature of capitalist production and to exemplify most clearly the general critical standpoint of the attack on the barriers of capitalism.

On the other hand, if we look at the presuppositions upon which Marx bases his argument for the wastefulness of capitalist production and at the particular claims he makes in support of it, we discover themes that direct us to a rather different 'theory of needs' whose implications are difficult to reconcile with any strictly relativist position. For the charge that capitalism is inefficient in meeting needs is based on the supposition that there is a body of social needs that is pre-existent to its allocation of social labour-time. The question of the structure and nature of this presupposed body of needs was discussed in some detail in Chapter 3, where I attempted to demonstrate the manner and extent to which they are determined in their content by capitalist relations of production themselves. But I also argued that these determinations had to be seen as exercised within an area of 'free play' ultimately bounded by certain limit conditions accountable to the nature of the consumers themselves and imposing constraints on the quality and quantity of the use-values produced by any society.If we place it in this perspective, the attack upon capitalism's inefficiency in meeting a determinate body of presupposed needs is an attack on the waste it incurs in accommodating the constraints imposed upon the possibilities of its production as a result of the nature of those for whom it is producing, since these constraints limit the condition the very forms in which they can be conditioned by economic forces. Viewed in this light, it directs attention not so much to the role of capitalist production in developing needs and breaking down natural limits on consumption, but to the role of consumption in determining and limiting the forms that production can take, and capitalism is being criticised not so much for the 'internal' barriers it erects to the consumption potentially permitted by its development of the forces of production, but for the inefficiency with which it meets the 'external' barrier imposed by consumption itself. It is, in short, not so much the determination of exchange-value upon the kinds of use-value made available for consumption that it highlights, but the dependency of exchange-value upon use-value:

(capitalism's) first barrier, then, is *consumption itself* — the *need for it*...

capital as *production*, appears to encounter a barrier in the available magnitude of consumption — of *consumption capacity*. As a specific use-value, its quantity is irrelevant up to a certain point; then, however, at a certain level — since it satisfies only a specific need — it ceases to be required for consumption...

Use-value in itself does not have the boundlessness of value as such. Given objects can be consumed as objects of needs only up to a certain level. For example: no more than a certain amount of grain is consumed, etc.[9]

The argument of the *Grundrisse* here is expressed more adequately in a number of passages in *Capital III*. For example:

It continues to be a necessary requirement that the commodity represent use-value. But if the use-value of individual commodities depends on whether they themselves satisfy a particular need, then the use-value of the mass of the social product depends on whether it satisfies the quantitatively determined social needs for each particular kind of product in an adequate manner, and whether the labour therefore is proportionately distributed among the different spheres in keeping with these social needs which are quantitatively circumscribed (...) The social need, that is the use-value on a social scale, appears here as a determining factor for the amount of total social labour-time which is expended in various specific spheres of production. But it is merely the same law which is already applied in the case of single commodities, namely that the use-value of a commodity is the basis of its exchange-value and thus of its value (...). This quantitative limit to the quota of social labour-time available for the various spheres of production is but a more developed expression of the law of value in general, although the necessary labour-time assumes a different meaning here. Only just so much of it is necessary for the satisfaction of social needs. It is use-value which brings about this limitation.[10]

It is in the light, incidentally, of such remarks that we can understand Marx's comment that Ricardo is only 'exoterically concerned'[11] with the important category of use-value, and his remark (in the *Marginal Notes on A. Wagner*) that use-value plays a far more important part in my economics, than in economics hitherto'.[12] And we might also note that on the basis of this quote alone, L. Althusser must surely be wrong in suggesting that the only needs 'that play an economic part are those which can be satisfied economically: these needs are not defined by human nature in general but by their effectivity'.[13] It is true, of course, that Marx does give *a* definition of 'social need' in terms of effective demand. He writes, for example, that: 'The definite social wants are very elastic and changing. Their fixedness is only apparent. If the means of subsistence were cheaper, or money wages higher, the labourer would buy more of them, and a greater "social need" would arise for them.'[14] But the inverted commas are an index of his recognition that he is here identifying 'social need' with effective demand, and elsewhere when he uses the term, he qualifies it. Thus: 'For a commodity to be sold at its market-value (...) the total quantity of social labour used in producing the total mass of this commodity must correspond to the quantity of the social want for it, i.e. the effective social want.'[15]

The point here is that changes in demand, changes in 'social need' *in this sense*, presuppose the existence of needs conceived in another sense; needs in this sense are not the mere effects of changes in prices, but operate as an independent variable alongside changes in income level or changes in the prices of commodities in determining effective demand. In other words, there are a number of factors that can alter demand other than changes in income or price of goods. An anti-smoking campaign, for example, will effect the demand for cigarettes independently of changes in their price (and in doing so contributes to the specific dimensions assumed by the 'natural' consumption barrier upon their product-ion). Marx recognises the role played by independent factors of this kind:

Now, the difference between the quantity of the produced commodities and that quantity of them at which they are sold at market-value may be due to two reasons. Either the quantity itself changes, becoming too small or too large, so that reproduction would have taken place on a different scale than that which regulated the given market-value. In that case, the supply changes, although demand remained the same, and there was, therefore, relative over-production or under-production. Or else reproduction, and thus supply, remained the same while demand shrank or increased *which may be due to several reasons.*[16]

A little later on he points out that changes in demand relate not only to means of consumption but also to means of production. Thus a lowering in the price of cotton will lead to a greater demand for it on the part of the capitalist. But, he reminds us:

We must never forget that the demand for productive consumption, is under our assumption, a demand of the capitalist, whose essential purpose is the production of surplus-value, so that he produces a particular commodity to this sole end. Still, this does not hinder the capitalist, so long as he appears in the market as a buyer, say, of cotton, from representing the need for this cotton (...). But this does exert a considerable influence on the kind of buyer the capitalist is. His demand for cotton is substantially modified by the fact that it disguises his real need for making profit. The limits within which the need for commodities in the *market*, the demand, differs quantitatively from the *actual social need*, naturally vary considerably for different commodities; what I mean is the difference between the demanded quantity of commodities and the quantity which would have been in demand at other money-prices or other money or living conditions of the buyers.[17]

Here it is only possible to understand Marx as using the phrase 'actual social need' to indicate a level of consumption that would be established at a given point were it not the case that the level of demand is in fact determined by the logic of capital and a response to fluctuations in price and money capital available. The capitalist's 'real' need to make a profit is contrasted with a need, which would be reflected in a different level of demand, and which would be the result of determinations other than those of accumulation and valorisation.

In order to establish the inverted commas sense of 'social needs', the effective demand sense in which the concept represents that which is actually consumed, there must be recourse to a concept of social needs in the sense of a 'normal' level of consumption. Only against this norm can there be deviations in demand. The notion that the only sense of social needs is that of effective demand (*actual* consumption at a given point) would seem to gloss over the relation between the concept of neds as a norm sufficient for the reproduction of society and consumption in excess or below it, which is the result of changes in purchasing power. But furthermore — and this is the main point at issue in Marx's insistence upon the limitation imposed by use-value — it fails to acknowledge that this norm imposes itself as an ultimte limit on the possible extent of divergence from it. If more wheat is produced than is required to satisfy the norm, the price of bread falls and the effective demand and thus consumption of bread rises — *but only within certain limits.* A nation, as Marx says, can only consume a certain amount of the stuff (just as he points out in *Capital I* that the market may fail to 'stomach' all the linen thrown on it even though each piece of it contains nothing but socially necessary labour time).[18] In other words, the need, whether for wheat or for linen, is only elastic and manipulable within certain limits. When those are reached, the linen, or the bread will simply fail to sell, and the social labour time incorporated in it will be lost.

These limits, then, which express the point beyond which needs will not alter relative to changes in the price of goods or in income, can be said to be 'anthropological', accountable, that is to say, to the nature of the human beings who are served by production, and no analysis of economic production can deny them except at the cost of ceasing to be an analysis of human social production. Marx's insistence upon the limitation of consumption upon production, of use-value upon the possible forms taken by exchange-value, can be seen as the mark of his recognition of the undeniability of the anthropological element that must enter into any economic analysis, and it is this that renders his own analysis 'open' where that of the political economists is closed. From a social standpoint this means that Marx reveals the absurdity of defining a society's needs analytically in terms of its actual allocation of social labour time. For though it is true, of course, that all economic theory presupposes a body of needs, if it proceeds to define this body of needs in terms of effective demand, it produces a tautology — for the difference in effective demand must be associated with differences in the price of goods, these prices being a reflection, not a presupposition of, the allocation of social labour time.

Now if the argument that establishes the inefficiency of capitalist production includes arguments that only make sense in terms of the limits imposed by the nature of the consumers upon the possible historic variation of their consumption of certain use-values, then it clearly introduces a tension from the standpoint of a strictly relativist theory of needs and the associated notion of their limitless capacity for development. For as we have seen, the critique of capitalism's inefficiency is premised on the existence of presupposed needs which cannot be accounted for wholly as the effect of the development of the productive forces and the distribution of income, but are themselves such as to impose certain limits upon the possibilities of that development and distribution, limits ultimately referrable to the nature (the 'limits') of the consumers. Hitherto, these natural needs have emerged only in the form of references to the biological limits on, for example, a nation's consumption of wheat, or linen, and the attack has been more on capitalism's incapacity to assess these limits than directly upon the effects of this in human terms. Or rather, these effects are regarded as inhuman only in the sense that they preclude realisation of the historic potential for satisfaction that capitalism has brought into being, and their inhumanity is therefore relative to a historic stage of production. Nevertheless, when Marx invokes the concept of natural limits on consumption as part of his argument for the wastefulness of capitalist production he is invoking an essentialist concept of needs, and thus by implication a non-relative standpoint — a humanism based on the natural as opposed to historic needs of human beings — from which the effects of capitalism can be condemned.

It is from this standpoint, in fact, that Marx at times quite explicitly does condemn capitalist production:

Capital is reckless of the health or length of life of the labourer (. . .). To the outcry as to the physical and mental degradation, the premature death, the torture of overwork, it answers: 'ought these to trouble us since they increase our profits?'[19]

Modern industry, indeed, compels society under penalty of death to replace the detail-worker of today, crippled by life-long repetition of one and the same trivial operation, and thus reduced to the mere fragment of a man, by the fully developed individual fit for a variety of labours, ready to face any change of production and to whom the different social functions he performs are but so many modes of giving free scope to his natural and acquired powers.[20]

Can it be seriously doubted that remarks such as these are moral condemnations of capitalism based on some theory of absolute needs? Is it only because they are 'historically developed' that the workers suffer from the 'torture' of work and the degradation of their mental and physical faculties? Is the capitalist labour process only detrimental to them because they are themselves the 'product' of capitalist social relations? Are we to suppose that a mediaeval man would find the tasks he was required to undertake on a modern car assembly line less arduous or tedious than the contemporary worker? Are we to suppose that were the same car assembly line to be owned by the workers themselves that the mental and physical degradation accountable to the technical operations it required them to undertake would be any less than for those employed upon it under capitalist relations of exploitation? The answer, I suggest, is clearly no. It is not any historically developed set of social relations of production, nor any historical development of the workers employed under those relations that makes the performance of certain tasks in certain routines mentally and physically degrading. It is the nature of those tasks themselves; or, in other words, it is the physiological and psychological nature of those required to perform them. 'Degradation' here, refers us to the fact that by virtue of our membership of a particular biological species, we have physiological requirements, levels of patience and endurance and physical capacities that are a relatively permanent heritage, that will vary between individuals only within certain, fairly narrow, margins, and are subject to manipulation only up to a certain point.

This is not to deny that there is a specific degradation attributable precisely to exploitative and hierarchical relations of production, or that the anguish, apathy, frustration and sense of powerlessness that are commonly experienced by those employed under such relations, do not serve to 'overdetermine' the mental and physical suffering accountable to the intrinsic nature of the tasks they perform. But there is a distinction to be drawn between the two. And, in any case, if the 'specific' degradation accountable to exploitative and hierarchical relations is in any sense a common experience, it, too, bespeaks some relatively general and trans-historic features of human psychology. Even if Marx's critique were directed exclusively at the relations of private ownership of capitalist production, as the extreme anti-humanist interpretation of it tends to imply, and not at the nature and effects of that production in itself, it would still presume some 'theory' of the advantageous nature for those engaged in it of work performed under relations of common ownership, or, in other words, some theory of human needs in relation to work, some positing of value in this respect; for we have seen to what absurdities any attempt to attribute the benefits of socialism wholly to the 'structure' and its 'properties' is reduced. Besides, any attempt to present this interpretation as faithful to the spirit of Marx's critique (or, in other words, to render the terms of that critique wholly self-consistent) must proceed by denying both the letter and the spirit of that strand of it which is represented by the remarks we have quoted above, and which, I would argue, cannot be reconciled with the anti-essentialism of the cognitive discourse, since they clearly invite us to think in terms of certain relatively universal and transhistoric features of human nature. We must recognise, then, a certain kind of essentialism that runs as an undercurrent in Marx's critique of capitalism and in the positive evaluation of socialism and communism as 'higher' stages of human existence. For at the very least we must understand him to reject the physical and mental degradation, the premature death, the torture of over-work associated with the one and ideally removed from the other, and these features are not ones that can be thought without reference to the relatively permanent character of human beings.

But if we are obliged to acknowledge, not only that Marx happens to talk about human nature in an essentialist vein, but also that some such talk is an indispensable basis of any account of human society, how are we to reconcile this 'truth' about our needs with that other 'truth' about them for which Marx argues so convincingly, the truth, namely, of their always specific and 'historically developed' nature?

As a way of discussing this question, I propose in the next two chapters to look at two strands of Marx's anthropological commentary which reflect and reproduce the tension between these truths. The one concerns the distinction that is drawn in certain passages in the *Grundrisse* between historically developed 'natural' needs and 'wholly historic needs'; the other is a 'theory of personality' that I shall argue can be extracted from the section of the *Grundrisse* on pre-capitalist economic formations.

Notes

1 But see in particular, p.406f., p.525f.

2 *Capital, op. cit.*, p.259, and cf. Marx's attribution of Ricardo's 'importance' to his 'unconcern about "human beings"', and his having an eye solely for the development of the productive forces' (*ibid.*).

3 *Grundrisse, op. cit.*, p.409.

4 See, for example, *Capital, op. cit.,* Vol. II, pp.137-39, where Marx writes: '(circulation costs) are *faux frais* of commodity production in general, and they increase with the development of this production, especially capitalist production. They represent a part of the social wealth that must be sacrificed in the process of circulation', and cf., pp.134; 142; 152; 350.

5 *Capital, op. cit.*, Vol.III, p.257.

6 *The German Ideology, op. cit.*, p.474.

7 *Grundrisse, op. cit.*, p.488.

8 M. Godelier, 'Structure and Contradiction in *Capital*' in *Ideology in Social Science*, ed. R. Blackburn, Bungay, Fontana, 1972, p.354.

9 *Grundrisse, op. cit.*, pp.405-6.

10 *Capital, op. cit.*, Vol.I, p.202. On the different meaning of necessary labour-time which Marx refers to here, R. Rosdolsky comments in his excellent chapter on 'The Problem of Use-value' in *The Making of Marx's 'Capital'*, London, Pluto Press, 1977: 'Socially necessary labour-time is the labour-time required to produce any use-value under the conditions of production formal for a given society and with the average degrees of skill and intensity prevalent in that society ... We encounter this "Technological" meaning of the concept of socially necessary labour-time again and again in *Capital*, and in other of Marx's works. However, we also encounter

another meaning, according to which labour can only count as "socially necessary" if it corresponds to the aggregate requirements for society, for a particular use-value' (p.89). It is the same point that is made by Engels in his attack on Rodbertus in the Preface to Marx's *The Poverty of Philosophy*, London, Martin Lawrence, p.18: 'If he had investigated by what means and how labour creates value and therefore also determines and measures it, he would have arrived at socially necessary labour, necessary for the single product, both in relation to other products of the same kind, and also in relation to society's total demand'; and it is the same point that is brought out by C. Bettelheim *The Transition to Socialist Economy, op. cit.*, p.173 in reference to Marx's famous letter to Kugelmann: ' ... it is not enough for a product to be "sold" for the labour expended to produce it to be *wholly* socially necessary. For that, the total amount of social labour expended on producing the given article must correspond to the *social utility* of this article.'

11   *Grundrisse, op. cit.*, pp. 646-7.

12   *Marginal Notes on Adolph Wagner's 'Lehrbuch der politischen Okonomie'* in Marx-Engels *Werke* (MEW) Vol. 19, pp. 355-83. Translated by Athar Hussain in 'Theoretical Practice', No. 5, 1972.

13   L. Althusser, *Reading Capital*, London, New Left Books, 1970, p. 167. Nor is Althusser's claim here reconcilable with a number of other passages in *Capital*, where it is said, for example, that 'too few necessities of life' are produced under capitalism, and that there is a 'shortage of demand' for 'the very commodities which the mass of the people lack' (*Capital, op. cit.,* Vol. III, p. 257). If Althusser is correct, there is no concept in *Capital* of a 'need' for those commodities which Marx here speaks of, precisely, as 'lacked' or 'needed'. But perhaps, in defence of Althusser's claim, it will be said that in referring in this sense to 'lacked' or 'needed' commodities Marx is referring to needs that play *a* part, but not an *economic* part? This defence is scarcely acceptable, however, since the fact that such needs are not met and do not become effective is itself accountable to economic forces — to the unequal distribution of social wealth under capitalist relations of production. This inequality in distribution is the direct effect of the exploitation of labour upon which the capitalist mode of production depends. Can it be said, then, that the unfulfilled needs of the mass of socially developed persons play no economic role when the reproduction relations precisely depends on maintaining labour in a position in which it has no effective demand for the mass of the products it produces?

14   *Capital, op. cit.*, Vol. III, p. 188.

15   *Ibid.*, p. 192

16   *Ibid.*, p. 186.

17   *Ibid.*, p. 189.

18   *Capital, op. cit.,* Vol. I, p. 109.

19   *Ibid.*, pp. 256-7.

20   *Ibid.*, p. 458.

6   The Normative Discourse II: Historically Natural and Wholly Historic Needs

I think it will have to be admitted that the strand of his discourse about needs in which Marx speaks for a distinction between historically developed (natural) needs and 'wholly historic' needs is itself fairly ravelled, and about as confusing as it is enlightening.

We have already encountered a form of its expression in Chapter One in the notion of the historical 'suspension' of our 'natural necessities' as well as our 'former luxuries' and the transformation of what was previously superfluous into a historically created necessity.[1] As further expression of it, we can cite the following:

Capital's ceaseless striving towards the general form of wealth drives labour beyond the limits of its natural paltriness, and thus creates the material elements for the development of rich individuality which is itself as all-sided in its production as in its consumption, and whose labour also therefore appears no longer as labour, but as the development of activity itself; in which *natural necessity in its direct form* has disappeared; because a *historically created need has taken the place of the natural one*.[2]

But the distinction is perhaps most clearly indicated in Marx's discussion of the need for money, and I shall peg most of my own discussion upon that. Of the greed for money, he writes:

Money is therefore not only *an* object, but is *the* object of greed (*Bereicherungssucht*). It is essentially *auri sacra fames*. Greed as such, as a particular form of the drive, i.e. as distinct from the craving for a particular kind of wealth, e.g. for clothes, weapons, jewels, women, wine, etc., is possible only when general wealth, wealth as such, has become individualised in a particular thing, i.e. as soon as money is posited in its third quality (as independent commodity). Money is therefore not only the object but also the fountainhead of greed. The mania for possessions is possible without money; but greed itself is the product of a definite social development, not natural as opposed to *historical*.[3]

The distinction of which these quotations appear to speak is

111

between a natural albeit 'historically' *developed* need, and a historically *created*, and therefore 'non-natural' need, and we are invited to think, I suggest, of some kind of break in the chain of the development of a 'natural' need whereby it cedes its place to the 'wholly historic' need. Now clearly, this distinction betrween the 'historic-natural' and the 'non-natural-historic' is quite different from any distinction (such as, for example, that between needs (A) and needs (B)) that we have hitherto explicitly discussed and must be seen, I think, as an attempt to isolate *conceptually* two aspects in terms of which our needs as a whole can be thought, and must be understood. The one aspect is essentialist in the sense that it refers our needs to an abstract common 'natural' content of which they must be seen as the developed forms; the other aspect is relativist in that it presents needs as so many specific, historic contents that are ruptural rather than continuous with any historical development of their 'forms'.

The tension between these two aspects is a continuous presence in Marx's discussion of needs which the apparent innocence and simplicity of the notion of their 'historical development' serves to obscure. For if we pause to consider what it is that we are being told when we are told that our needs are 'historically developed' we are bound to discover the intrinsic ambiguity of that claim, and thus to confront the two conflicting aspects of the conceptualisation of needs that it embodies. In other words, the very notion of a 'developed' need invites us to question *of what it is* the development; and yet the claim about the historically developed nature of needs is intended and usually accepted as a claim to the effect that they cannot be viewed merely as developed forms of some essential content.

But in addition to the ambiguity of the notion of the 'historically developed' need, the distinction between 'historic-natural' and 'non-natural historic' introduces a further confusion. For it invites us to think not merely in terms of two different conceptual standpoints, or aspects, from which we can view our needs, but also in terms of some difference in kind between them, in terms, one might say, of an ontological difference between needs, rather than in terms of a conceptual difference of approach to one and the same need. There is a suggestion, at any rate in the passage on the need to labour, and even more so in the passage on the need for money, that we can distinguish between needs, which although historically developed, are 'natural' in the sense they refer us to a basis or common content in human biology-psychology, and needs which are literally historic 'creations', attributable entirely to social relations, and in this sense 'artificial' as opposed to natural. As examples of the objects of 'artificial' creations we are offered labour 'as the development of activity itself', and, of course, money. The case of labour is perhaps less convincing than that of money, not only because of the vagueness and difficulties of conceptualising the wholly historic activity that it becomes, but also, precisely, because we are still inclined to think of it as the result of a 'becoming', as in some sense the object of a developed, even if ruptural, form of a natural need. But the example of money does seem to be an unproblematic instance of the 'wholly historic' creation and certainly lends conviction to the 'ontological' distinction I am attributing to Marx. Indeed, it is not a distinction of which we need much convincing, since, it seems to me, it broadly corresponds to our own intuitions about our needs. It corresponds, that is to say, with our inclination to distinguish between a need that arises only with the appearance of an 'artificial' product such as money, and a general, natural need for food or relaxation, which though it is satisfied only specifically and in the consumption of particular products, is nonetheless not induced in us simply by virtue of its 'object' being produced. The very fact that we can all distinguish between the 'need' evoked by savoury smells coming from the kitchen and the need for nutrition as such, between the extreme hunger which will satisfy itself with anything to hand, and pace Marx, may do so with 'tooth and claw' even today, and the hunger for a joint of roast lamb or baked beans on toast, is significant here, for no similar distinction can be drawn in the case of the need for money: the need for money is always, definitionally, a need for a specific product.

But despite the force of this distinction between the ultimately 'natural' need and the 'wholly historic' need, I would suggest that it nonetheless introduces a confusion from the standpoint of the conceptual distinction between needs viewed as historical developments and needs viewed as historic contents. For if we accept the principle of that distinction, then even the 'natural' needs of the ontological distinction must be viewed from one conceptual standpoint(i.e., under their aspect as historic *contents*) as 'wholly historic', *sui generis* 'creations'. And when viewed from that particular conceptual standpoint, even so natural a need as the need for nutrition must always be understood as a specific hunger for a specific object consumed in a specific manner, and from that standpoint it is no different from any other 'non-natural' need, such as the need for money. But, then, conversely, any rigorous application of the conceptual distinction would have to examine the ontologically 'non-natural' needs from the conceptual standpoint of their historical development. In other words, from *that* standpoint we are invited to view so apparently a specific and wholly artificial need as the need for money as the developed form of a basic need or common content.

In fact, if we look at the account that Marx offers of the need for money, we find that, so far from adhering rigorously to any ontological distinction between the natural and the wholly historic need, it is in fact an account which is constantly viewing a supposedly 'created', non-historic need from the conceptual standpoint of its historical and 'natural' development.

I propose to look at this account in some detail, not only because of its intrinsic interest and the richness of its anthropological content, but also because of the light it sheds upon the different standpoints of the conceptual distinction, and thus, in turn upon the supposed confusion that is introduced from the standpoint of *that* distinction by the distinction between the natural and the artificial need.

The need for money has been presented hitherto as the prime instance of a wholly historic need and as such wholly without reference to any biological or psychological need and untheorisable as the development of such a need. But let us now consider that we are also told that it is the *form* of the general *auri sacra fames* or 'mania for possessions'. Indeed could Marx put the point more succinctly than by saying that monetary greed is a 'particular form of the drive'? And how else are we to interpret this 'drive' if not in terms of the abstract 'common content' of its forms, in terms of a 'basic' need whose forms would be, for example, greed for wealth in particulars x, greed for wealth in particulars y, greed for wealth in particulars z, ... greed as such, greed for money, the representative of all wealth? Interpreted thus, the drive is analogous to the 'hunger' which is 'hunger' despite the always specific content of any actual hunger, but in this case the drive appears to be psychological in character rather than directly biological. Moreover, viewed in this light, it would seem that the need for money is to be regarded in exactly the same way that Marx invites us to regard the specific need for a specific food, consumed in a specific manner, i.e., it is to be regarded as 'historic'.

But perhaps we should pause here to consider the nature of this 'drive' and the extent to which it is legitimate to speak of it as a general or 'basic' psychological need. The question is not easy to resolve, partly because of a laxity in Marx's language. Is the drive literally a drive for *gold* (or at least for a definable group of substances with certain common characteristics: they are tangible, not subject to decay, they are rare, they are aesthetically pleasing, they glitter, and so on)? Or is it, as Marx suggests by the phrase 'mania for possessions' a drive for wealth and possessions whose satisfaction is not confined to gold but is to be found in any number of different particulars (clothes, weapons, jewels, women, wine — and, of course, money)? If it is the more restricted need (which I shall speak of for short as the 'need for gold') then we have an instance of a relatively precise psychological drive to possess a certain type of object; if it is the less restricted need then we appear to have an instance of a need simply as neediness, sheer need to accumulate possessions, to own something, *n'importe quoi*, a pure proprietorialness, a need which might be said to be a general abstract psychological drive, but which is so general that we scarcely know what sense to make of it. Or rather, it might be said, we can make sense of it, but only in terms of a need to possess objects, not for their use-value, or aesthetic value, not as articles of consumption, but for their exchange-value, as articles for an always possible consumption. What Marx has in mind, it might be said, is not so much any 'natural' attraction to glitter, nor any need simply to possess regardless of the object, but is indeed precisely the need to possess objects themselves possessed of exchange-value, and since this is an already socially induced need, accountable entirely to a historic system of exchange relations, the reference to any general psychological drive is unnecessary to its explanation. But that suggestion only begs the question to which any consideration of the need for money as *a historically developed form of a drive* directly invites us — the question, namely, of what urges us to possess the objects possessed of exchange-value far in excess of any 'necessary' consumption of them. In other words, when he treats of the greed for money as a historical form of a drive, Marx is suggesting that its explanation cannot be given wholly in terms of the economic system in which it is the medium of exchange, but must be seen as the development of a non-specific 'mania for possessions', and furthermore that there is a psychological element which enters into the determination of the specific object, money, upon which the specific form of this mania is historically fixated.

Let us grant, then, that in talking about the 'mania for possessions' and about the *auri sacra fames* Marx is referring to a general psychological drive, and that we can distinguish between two aspects of it: (a) the need for gold regarded as a purely 'aesthetic' or 'naive' craving for glitter, and which enters into the explanation of the chosen repositories of exchange-value, and (b) the desire to accumulate wealth, a desire which enters into the explanation of the institution of all economic systems allowing for it. How do these two aspects relate to each other? Well, clearly it is no accident that our 'aesthetic' needs tend to be directed towards the objects most ideally suited to be repositories of exchange-value (gold, jewels, works of art, and so on), and the less subject to decay they are, the better they repay the aesthetic investment. But this cynical view of the matter must not be taken too far; certainly the drive to possess wealth has determined the content of our aesthetic needs, but then, too, it would be quite mistaken to neglect the determination exercised by the pure aesthetic need upon the objects that emerge as the carriers of exchange-value: such objects have intrinsic gratification as well as the gratification to be derived from the fact that they are representative of wealth: the brilliance of the diamond, the glitter of the gold, the pleasure of the painting, the taste of the wine: they, too, have had their part to play, and it is a part that is only accountable in terms of a psychology of needs.

How does all this relate to the need for money? In this respect that it is the commodity which satisfies both needs in one. It satisfies the *auri sacra fames* as a drive for a particular type of object (into which the natural quality of gold and silver enters as an aesthetic satisfaction), and the general drive for wealth as such, a drive which is never satisfied in any particular but is a hankering after that which is never converted and is infinitely convertible. Money is that seemingly impossible commodity which in its particularity satisfies that generality:

It is the *'précis de toutes les choses'*, in which their particular character is erased; it is general wealth in the form of a concise compendium, as opposed to its diffusion and fragmentation in the world of commodities. (. . .) Money (. . .) satisfies every need, in so far as it can be exchanged for the desired object of every need, regardless of their particularity. The commodity possesses this property only through the mediation of money. Money possessed it directly in relation to all commodities, hence in relation to the whole world of wealth, to wealth as such. With money, general wealth is *not only a form, but at the same time* the content itself. The concept of wealth, so to speak, is realised, *individualised* in a particular object.[4]

As this general representative of wealth it overcomes the negative aspect of hedonism by abstracting from it. Real hedonism involves consumption; the loss of gratification in the having of gratification still to come. Money, as an object in itself of pleasure and as the representative of all pleasures is precisely that cake which one can eat and always still have to eat; or, more eloquently, 'hedonism in the abstract presupposes an object which possesses all pleasures in potentiality. Abstract hedonism realises that function in money'.[5]

Money as the general form of wealth that can deny consumption of particular commodities, that permits wealth without the squandering of wealth, that is value incarnate untainted by the squalor of the natural commodity, is that alone wherein one can indulge the other aspect of this hedonism: the pleasures of miserliness. This is the asceticism that money permits, miserliness as the pleasure of a pure abstemiousness, that 'must sacrifice all relationship to the objects of particular needs, must abstain in order to satisfy the need of greed for money as such'.[6] It is the cult of money as self-denial, as 'economy and frugality, contempt for the mundane, temporal and fleeting pleasures; the chase after *eternal* treasure'.[7] Old Jacob placed his right hand on the younger and his left hand on his elder son, saying:

We consume among us too great an excess of wines from Spain, France, the Rhine, the Levant, the Islands; raisins from Spain, currants from the Levant, cambric from Hainault and the Netherlands, the silkenware of Italy, the sugar and tobacco of the West Indies, the spices of East India; all this is not necessary for us, but is paid for in *hard* money. If less of the foreign and more of the domestic product were sold, then the difference would have to come to us in the form of gold and silver, as *treasure*.[8]

Money, then, as treasure, is the simultaneous satisfaction of the specific need for the specific object of wealth and of the general drive, greed as such. The formation of the first need, I have suggested, cannot be understood without consideration of the psychology of our aesthetic appreciations, by which I mean to indicate our spontaneous approval of certain objects simply for themselves; elsewhere I have referred to such responses as 'naive' in order to stress that this is a form of response taken in abstraction (even if never found abstractly) from other forms of appreciation of the object (for its use-value, its exchange-value). Hence the object of this need cannot be any object: money today, as a concrete object, as opposed to a relation of exchange, still retains the aura of glitter, most obviously in the hierarchy of the coinage, but also symbolically in the mystico-magical cyphers of the banknote.

But of course, money, to be money and therefore to be that which uniquely satisfies the second drive, cannot exist only in the fixation of an entirely material, tangible form, as Midas learnt to his cost. The greed as such which is satisfied by money as medium of exchange, as that which permits the accumulation of wealth, is different in kind from greed for money as a particular object; and the satisfaction afforded by money as a particular object (the general form of wealth) is always different and 'impure' relative to the gratification *as such* of greed *as such* which money as medium of circulation, as the material representative of general wealth, permits.

The accumulation of money, for example, as a particular object and not as medium of exchange, can gratify the urge for ostentation or the need for security. Here we have the notion of wealth as 'an extraordinary thing, for use on Sundays only; to provide gifts for temples and their gods; to finance public works of art; finally as security in the case of extreme necessity, to buy arms, etc.'.[9] At the individual level, accumulation takes place for purposes of ornament or the proof of wealth. (Rothschild, Marx thinks he remembers, displays as his proper emblem two banknotes of £100,000 each mounted in a frame; but, Marx adds, 'the barbarian display of gold, etc., is only a more naive form of this modern one, since it takes place with less regard to gold as money. Here still the simple *glitter* . . . '[10]). Or else there is hoarding in order to bring wealth into safety from the caprices of the external world in a tangible form, which can be *buried* — the ultimate of securities (and anyone who has paused to consider the architecture of banks cannot but be struck by thoughts of the temple and the tomb).

On the other hand, mere accumulation of gold and silver, even when this takes place in the awareness of its role as money, is still not yet the satisfaction as such of the greed as such. In order for it to be so, money must be medium of circulation; it must be that which retains itself in the very consumption of itself. It is only money as circulating medium, as exchange-value, which prevents the diversion of greed as such into a particular greed which is satisfied either in the hoarding of money as mere object of contemplation, of security, of display, or else in the gratification of consumption as limitless waste, e.g., the gulping down of salads of pearls (though this also, of course, gratified, if only temporarily, an urge for ostentation, just as a modern counterpart — the infinite extension of the nuclear arsenal — also apparently affords for some a gratification of their need for security, though again, one fears, it will do so only temporarily).

But if it is only money posited in the form of exchange-value that, in pre-empting such diversions of it, represents and satisfies the pure drive, then the need for money is intrinsically contradictory. For though it is money alone that satisfies the particular and the general need, it can only function in both roles at once because it represents their opposition. The particular drive to accumulate money can only be satisfied provided its object is indeed money, and not mere natural gold and silver; but in order to retain itself as money, it must circulate; and in order, through the process of circulation, to be that which satisfies the general drive, and not to fall back, as a result of its exchange, into the particular satisfaction of a particular consumption, it must refuse both the inertia of the hoard and the waste of consumption:

Money in its final, completed character now appears in all directions as a contradiction, a contradiction which dissolves itself, drives towards its own dissolution. As the *general form of wealth*, the whole world of real riches stands opposite to it. It is their pure abstraction — hence, fixated as such, a mere conceit (. . .). On the other side, as *material representative of general wealth*, it is realised only by being thrown back into circulation, to disappear in exchange for the singular, particular, modes of wealth. It remains in circulation, as a medium of circulation; but for the accumulating individual, it is lost, and this disappearance is the only possible way to secure it as wealth. To dissolve the things accumulated in individual gratifications is to realise them (. . .). If I want to cling to it, it evaporates in my hand to become a mere phantom of real wealth. Further: the notion that to accumulate it is to increase it, since its own quantity is the measure of its value, turns out to be false. If the other riches do not also accumulate, then it loses its value in the measure in which it is accumulated. What appears as increase is in fact its decrease. Its independence is mere semblance; (. . .). It pretends to be the general commodity, but because of its natural particularity it is again a particular commodity, whose value depends both on supply and demand (. . .). And since it is incarnated in gold and silver, it becomes one-sided in every real form; so that when the one appears as money, the other appears as particular commodity, and vice-versa. As absolutely secure wealth, entirely independent of my individuality it is at the same time, because it is something completely insecure, the absolutely insecure, which can be separated from me by an accident.[11]

Here, as in so many passages already quoted, there can be little doubt of the psychological factors which Marx accepts as entering into the formation and particular character of the need for money. Or, to put this another way, though to a large extent the need for money must be explained as the result of the economic relations of a society in which money is the medium of exchange, and the need for money is therefore merely a need that must be gratified in order to gratify one's other needs, the need for money per se as that in which one gratifies the abstract hedonism of all pleasures *in potentia*, or the other aspect of that hedonism, the miserliness which is the fixation on the thing itself in deliberate denial of the pleasures it affords, cannot be explained in purely economic terms, but refer us to psychological determinations of a relatively universal and transhistoric kind: the mania for possessions and the *auri sacra fames* are present even in the absence of money relations, and enter into the formation of the particular need for money as opposed to the need for what money can buy; equally they play a role in determining the preferred concrete repository — gold and silver here in their aspect as glitter — of money relations; and finally, it is only if we take account of such psychological factors that we shall fully understand the 'magical' significance of money for the individual, the secrecy of our relations with it, the fetish of money, which still holds today, but is as old as the intimate and private gold sealed in the tomb of the Egyptian pharoah.

Let us now try to relate this account of the need for money to the distinction we discussed earlier between two different conceptual standpoints, demarcating not between two different kind of need, but between two different kinds of discourse about the same need. And let us see what light it sheds on the supposed confusion which is introduced from the standpoint of that demarcation by the description of certain needs as 'wholly historic' as opposed to others which are 'historic', but 'natural'.

It is clear that it is in regard to the need for money viewed from the second conceptual standpoint that the stress on the continuing and transhistoric element is relevant. It will be remembered that it was from this standpoint that the greed for money was viewed as a 'particular form of the drive', and the need for money was, it seemed, no less a 'historically developed form' of a need than was the so-called 'historic' but natural need. Much of the ensuing discussion of the need for gold was an attempt to explore the nature of the 'common element' by reference to which, within this particular conceptualisation, the need for money could be thought of as a mere form and not a specific, wholly autonomous content. And in the course of this discussion I investigated two aspects of this 'common element', this underlying and transhistoric psychological drive: its aspect as 'need for gold' (into which entered a pure aesthetic appreciation), and its aspect as 'mania for possessions', as pure proprietorialness, irrespective of the particular object of possession. Money, it emerged, *still regarded as a form of this drive*, was that object which satisfied both in one.

Of course, therein lies its difference: therein lies the importance of the first conceptual standpoint from which the need for money cannot be seen as a form but only and exclusively as a particular content, as that precise need which it is, and not the need which is an evolved or altered form of an earlier need. Before the existence of money there was no possible object that could satisfy both the need for wealth as a particular form of wealth and the need for wealth in general, for possession in general. One had to choose between wealth in gold, wealth in jewels, wealth in wine, and in so choosing forfeit wealth in *n'importe quoi*, sacrifice the mania for possession that is indifferent to its object. Hence to suggest that the need for money is but a form of the mania for possession, but one successor in a line of 'greed for x', 'greed for y', 'greed for z', is to overlook the break that it introduces into that line of succession, a break marked by the fact that 'with money, general wealth is not only a form, but at the same time the content itself', and 'the concept of wealth, so to speak, is realised, *individualised* in a particular object'.¹² From the first conceptual standpoint, then, money is a new object of an unprecedented need; it is indeed 'non-natural' as opposed to 'historic'. But it is only 'non-natural' by reference to the concepts of the 'natural' and the 'non-natural' that the conceptual distinction itself establishes : all needs are 'non-natural' when viewed from one standpoint, and all of them 'natural-historic' when viewed from the other.

We are now in a better position, perhaps, to see how the confusion about the 'non-natural' and the 'historic' needs relates to the ambiguity of the notion of a 'historically developed need'. If we interpret this as a claim about the specificity of needs, about their status as distinct contents rather than as evolved forms of an essential and transhistoric need, then we are inclined to identify 'historically developed' with 'non-natural'. But if we ask the question to which we are directly invited by any designation of needs as 'historically developed', the question, namely, of what it is that they are developments, then we are always referred to needs in their 'natural-historic' dimension. 'Historically developed' is ambiguous because it can be interpreted as instructing us to think of needs *not in their history*, or as instructing us to view them as the *outcome of a history*. But the ambiguity is itself instructive, and can be considered a kind of enlightenment. If we are to retain its insight, however, we must accept that the conceptual distinction it implies retains its force in the case of *any* need, and that it cannot be a distinction which allows us to distinguish between different types ('non-natural' as opposed to 'historic') needs. It is a distinction between a need viewed as content, where it is its specificity that counts, and whose explanation can never refer us to an anthropological history, but only to the nature of the individuals and socio-economic relations contemporaneous with its existence, and that same need viewed as a historical development — a conception in which it is the form of which the need is the development which counts, whose explanation will precisely refer us to the historical development of human beings, and therefore lead us into the consideration of the abstract biological and psychological needs that are the element common to all our specific needs, and by reference to which we are alone enabled to view them as particular developments. The abstract essentialism of the second standpoint is precisely that which has to be excised from the account conducted from the first standpoint. But any theory of needs which insists upon the one at the expense of the other will necessarily remain one-sided. But it is in this sense, too, that the 'theory of needs' is doomed as a theory if by theory is meant conceptual resolution, homogeneity of concepts, coherent systematisation. For this is a theory, if it deserves the name, whose theoretical statement is to the effect that all theorisation about needs must necessarily live in the field of forces created by the antithetical poles of relativism and essentialism.

Perhaps it will be objected at this point that even though the analysis of the complex determinations entering into the formation of specific needs directs attention to the presence of certain characteristically human biological and psychological 'drives', and even though Marx's critique of capitalism is at times quite explicitly rooted in some theory of 'human nature', none of this is really what one has in mind by a 'Marxist theory of needs'. For granted that there are these underlying themes to be excavated from the texts of the *Grundrisse* and *Capital*, they scarcely constitute any systematic 'humanism', nor are their critical and evaluative implications from the standpoint of the transition to a 'higher' form of society at all clear or mutually compatible. Indeed, they appear almost irreconcilable with the implications of the positive judgement on the potential productivity permitted by capitalism's development of the productive forces, since the realisation in a 'higher' society of that potential appears to be premised on the assumption of a human nature that has transcended all its purely 'natural' limitations.

I propose, therefore, in the next chapter, to look at an 'anthropological' discourse whose 'theory' of human nature is arguably both more explicit and more systematically worked out than anything I have hitherto investigated. I shall also raise the question of the relationship between this discourse and Marx's arguments against essentialism, and consider to what extent the two can, or should, be seen as complementary, and to what extent they are antithetical strands of his critique, implying different theories of 'true' need.

Notes

1 *Grundrisse, op. cit.*, p. 528.
2 *Ibid.*, p. 325 (my emphases).
3 *Ibid.*, p. 222.
4 *Ibid.*, p. 218.
5 *Ibid.*, p. 222.
6 *Ibid.*, p. 223.
7 *Ibid.*, p. 232.
8 *Ibid.*
9 *Ibid.*, p. 230.
10 *Ibid.*, 231.
11 *Ibid.*, p. 234
12 *Ibid.*, p. 218.

7 *The Normative Discourse III: the Loftier Satisfactions which are also Vulgar*

Throughout the *Grundrisse* Marx argues from a distinctive theory of personality, whose main theme is the double nature of human existence: the human personality is constituted at least as much in the excentric world of human productions, in the objective circumstances that confront the individual, as in the subjective self as psychological-biological entity; to be human is to live both an objective and a subjective 'mode of existence'. The theory finds its most explicit expression in the section of the *Grundrisse* devoted to economic formations preceding capitalism.[1] Marx cites three instances of such formations — the Asiatic, the Classical and the Germanic modes — and argues that the basis in all three cases is landed and agricultural production. Likewise, they all share a common aim: 'reproduction of the individual within the specific relations to the commune in which he is its basis'.[2] The aim, that is to say, is not wealth as such — not production of exchange-value, which is indifferent to the form of the use-value produced — but use-value as such, in the quantity and particularity that will allow a specific group of persons to meet the level of development of their needs and thus to reproduce themselves as persons within the specific social relations which bind them in their group and are the prerequisite of their production in that group.

Whatever the exact form of these social relations, they involve and rely upon a relation of the individual labourer to the conditions of his labour 'as his own',[3] as 'being his', as the 'inorganic nature of his subjectivity'. Initially this attitude of possession will have its exclusive object in the earth itself. In more developed conditions, it will include not only land but the animals which breed upon it, and the tools, implements, and so on, of labour employed in the production process.

This relation to the objective conditions of labour gives the individual an 'objective mode of existence' — an existence, says

125

Marx, which is 'presupposed to his activity, just as his skin, sense organs, are presupposed to his reproduction of them'. That is to say, just as the existence of the physical body in its given form is the precondition of its physical reproduction (a reproduction which includes the development of its sense organs, muscular powers and so on) so the objective conditions of labour are the preconditions of their reproduction and extension.

But this presupposed, proprietorial relationship of the indivdual is always immediately mediated by the individual's 'naturally arisen spontaneous, more or less historically developed and modified presence as a member of a commune', and is as much the result of, and presupposition of, a social existence as is language: 'an isolated individual could no more have *property* in land and soil than he could speak (though he could live off it as substance as do animals)'.[4] This social mediation of the individual's existence, which Marx points to here in respect of the ownership of the conditions of labour or of language — or, as he elsewhere suggests, of culture generally — clearly has complex properties. For while, on the one hand, it is impossible to think these aspects of individual existence as mere accretions to a core subjectivity, as if, in their absence, the individual would remain integral subject, sufficient unto his or herself, it is, on the other hand, also impossible to think of the individual as exhaustively given by these properties: a person is not his or her language, but neither is (s)he a person without it. This dialectic of ownership and being is what Marx describes as the *double existence* of the individual, who is 'subjectively as he himself and objectively in these natural, non-organic conditions of his existence'; and these non-organic conditions are themselves double: they have a subjective existence in the unity of the clan, tribe, community, and so on, and an objective existence in the material and implements of labour which form the object of the community's material appropriation. So, just as the individual's production is always mediated through his or her membership of the community, so the communal appropriation is always mediated by, and presupposes, the individual's relationship of ownership to the objective conditions of labour (a relationship which the community, in turn, itself mediates). This mutuality of dependence *is* the existence of the society and at the same time of the individuals comprising it, and the objective mode of its existence is as much essentially a part of the existence of the community and individual as is its subjective mode: 'They relate as proprietors to the natural conditions of their labour; but these conditions must also be constantly posited as real conditions and objective elements of the personality of the individual, by means of personal labour.'[5] This remains the case both in agricultural communities of the earliest kinds, and in the era of the craftsman and guild corporation system, where the community is based on the independence of working owners, and is thus posited as 'already made, derived and secondary'; here, too, though the instrument 'appears only as a means of individual labour, the art of really appropriating the instrument, of handling it as an instrument, appears as the worker's particular skill, which posits him as the owner of the instrument'.

In part, then, who one is in this objective mode of existence is given by one's constant use and handling of a particular set of tools in the pursuit of and development of a particular skill — for example, the fact of being a silversmith is a part of being the person who one is, and the skills, affinities, needs, aspirations, and so on appropriate to, and created in the course of one's labour as silversmith, are reproduced along with that labour just as is one's bodily existence.

Now this account of personality is provided at the point in the *Grundrisse* where Marx has revealed the essence of capitalist society as consisting (i) in its being a form of production characterised by the separation of the worker from the objective conditions of labour and (ii) as having as its end and purpose the production of wealth as such — of exchange-value rather than use-value directly. One of his concerns, therefore, has been to trace, from the vantage of knowledge reached about the capitalist mode of production, the diverse ways in which the relationship of separation can come about; for as he says, 'it is not the *unity* of organic and inorganic, but the *separation* that requires explanation'.

This separation is revealed as the gradual outcome of the development of the productive forces. This development is itself accountable to many and very diverse factors, and in the absence of such factors (as in the case of the Asiatic mode) relatively little progress or extension of the social patrimony will take place. But wherever there is development of the productive forces, it proceeds 'dialectically' (for example, a succession of good harvests may issue in increased population, thus in turn in increased labour force leading to increased productivity), and its result is a constant and progressive extension of society beyond the original basis of its reproduction. Up to a certain point, there is reproduction on that basis — and the limits can be more or less elastic depending on circumstances — but beyond these limits there is dissolution of the old basis, and production upon a new one.

The history of this progress of dissolution of reproductive bases, and thus of the limited forms of society reproduced upon them, is the history of social production whose outcome is capitalism — a mode of production in which the separation between workers and ownership of the objective conditions of labour is a complete one. And the account in the section on pre-capitalist formations illuminates what Marx means when he describes the worker under capitalism as having no objectivity, as being 'pure subjectivity, pure activity', as 'naked in his subjectivity', as 'objectless'. The worker is deprived of any objective mode of existence in the sense of an inorganic to which subjectively (s)he relates 'as to (her) his own', and the value creating possibility of her or his labour (her or his means of subjective reproduction) must objectify itself 'in an alien reality', in machines and material belonging to another — to capital, regarded as 'master over living labour capacity, as value endowed with its own might and will, confronting him in his abstract, objectless, purely subjective poverty'.[6]

The form of existence of the worker under capitalism, then, which is given in the 'connection-of-separation' from the objective conditions of labour, is a relation to him or herself, in his or her objective existence as 'not himself' or 'not herself' — but rather as the subjective property of another, in the form of the capitalist.

The personal ties of dependencies of association under earlier modes are present in the capitalist mode of production only in their having been extinguished: all personal ties are those of 'indifference', 'abstraction', 'generality'. Progressive exchange and the division of labour means that money, rather than any personal tie, becomes the social bond of capitalist society. Money as the individual of general wealth represents a 'general quality' as a 'merely social result'; possession of it is not the development of any particular aspect of its individual owner:

Wage labour on one side, *capital* on the other, are therefore only the forms of developed exchange and of money (as the incarnation of exchange-value). Money thereby directly and simultaneously becomes the *real community (Gemeinwesen)* since it is the general substance of survival for all, and at the same time the social product of all. But as we have seen, in money the community *(Gemeinwesen)* is at the same time a mere abstraction, a mere external, accidental thing for the individual, and at the same time merely a means for his satisfaction as an isolated individual. The community of antiquity presupposes a quite different relation to, and on the part of, the individual. The development of money in its third role therefore smashes the community. All production is object-ification *(Vergegenständlichung)* of the individual. In money (exchange-value), however, the individual is not objectified in his natural quality, but in a social quality (relation) which is, at the same time, external to him.[7]

This clearly suggests a quite general theory of needs according to which the direct gratification of needs (or 'objectification in one's natural quality') is replaced by an indirect gratification whereby the immediate satisfaction of needs is always an object-ification in a social quality. Thus, under an advanced exchange economy such as capitalism, or under any economy where money is still the dominant means of exchange, the direct need is necessarily mediated by the satisfaction of an abstract need (on the part of the worker to earn a wage, on the part of the capitalist to appropriate surplus-value), to which all members of that society are subject. This abstract need is really only one aspect of the need for money itself, and can be regarded both as the latest form of the 'need to objectify' and as an unprecedented ruptural need, dif-ferent in content from the content of all earlier objectifications, and breaking the line of their succession.

I shall delay discussion of this general theory, and for the time being merely point to some of its implications from the standpoint of capitalism and needs.

The social bond which binds the 'community' under capitalism, and finds its concrete expression in money, is at the same time the expression of the generality and abstraction from the particular which characterises the social production of capitalism. Labour itself is no longer a particular kind of labour, but labour in general. The individual enters the production process not qua possessor of a particular attribute or skill attached to his or her ownership of the means of using it, but qua possessor of a general abstraction —

labour capacity. This social labour, which in adult existence dominates the individual's life and represents the major expenditure of his or her time and energy, operates not as the central area in which to find the self and recognise one's own existence, not as that in which one can become oneself in inheriting possession of the social patrimony to whose existence and extension one contributes on a scale unknown to previous epochs — but rather as the preliminary condition of that minimal share in one's contribution which the wage allows.

Of course, as individual one does have particular attributes, skills, capacities, and these do in turn play their part in constituting one's specificity as a person, but these skills and capacities are not what gives one one's social character as a worker but appear peripheral to it. One's use of these skills is always mediated by the generality and abstraction of one's existence as wage-worker. The importance of this is clear in relation to the way we talk about the needs of the worker under capitalism. For it is clear that one works because one needs to — one needs to survive and reproduce oneself — and with the wage one receives in exchange for one's labour one is able to go out and procure those goods and services essential to that reproduction (which in one sense can be seen as one's physical reproduction, the replacement of one's energies in order to present oneself for work the next day, but in another sense is the totality of oneself and this includes the whole set of relations, objects, activities, on which one depends for reproduction of oneself as the person who one is). But it is also clear that under capitalism these forms of existence are such that in meeting their exigencies what one actually does is in abstraction from the gratification of any direct needs. One needs to eat, but the gratification of that need is necessarily mediated through the abstract need to earn a wage. And what one does to earn that wage is in abstraction and only indirectly relevant to the constitution of oneself and to the particular experiencing of the individuality and particularity of one's needs.

'Indirectly relevant' does not, of course, mean *ir*relevant: what one does, and how one does it, have very relevant psychological and biological effects in constituting one's individuality; it means only that in most cases these effects themselves pass through the mediation of the need to earn a wage. In this sense, part of one's existence is itself an abstraction. That is to say, if we take Marx's thesis of the constitution of the self through the objective mode of existence as a general thesis, applicable to the formation of personality under every mode of production, then capitalism is that mode of existence which confronts the individual with an abstract, undifferentiated general mode of objective existence, whose character is precisely antithetical to the development of individuality, but which is nonetheless the mode of existence in which the individual has to find himself/herself. It will enter into the formation of personality in the form of an abstraction from personality. The individual is 'found' in the very fact of not being so found.

That view of the matter is, of course, too general, and stands in need of much qualification in the face of claims that many workers under capitalism do derive direct gratification from their work, so that in this sense their social production effects the production of needs it is able directly to gratify. Where this happens, however, it is arguably the case that there is a correlative degree of control over the tasks performed; and also that their nature (intellectual, creative, dependent on a high degree of skill, and so on) is such as to make it least possible to intervene to separate the worker from assimilation of his or her productions, or to deprive him or her of the knowledges, capacities and creations which are the outcome of the work. The contradictory tendencies of the development of the capitalist labour-process could be seen in the light of this relationship of the worker to his/her productions: on the one hand, the need to exert overall control over the labour-process leads to attempts to break the proprietorial relationship between the worker and his or her work — hence rationalisation of jobs, 'de-skilling', automation, and so on. On the other hand, the detrimental effects on profit that result from job dissatisfaction in highly 'rationalised' labour-processes that finds its expression in sabotage, rapid turnover of labour force, loss of 'corporate spirit', general ennui, and so on, have forced management into adopting various techniques of neo-Fordism (attempts, albeit very compromised ones, to re-enrich tasks, often by providing the grounds for a more 'proprietorial' relationship to them: one works on an entire product instead of upon a single component, or in clerical work some 'extension of self' is allowed through the introduction of personal responsibilities towards the consumer, and so on.) There is now an extensive literature about the labour-process and

a number of empirical and theoretical accounts of these contradictory forces and their effects, so I shall not go into the point in
any more detail here.[8] But I think it is clear enough, that if one
would argue for this view of the constitution of the self through
one's objective modes of existence, the apparent exceptions to the
general form of its effects under capitalism can equally, and
perhaps more readily, be comprehended as confirmations of the
thesis.

Now a second point can be made. For if it is the case that in a
sense the worker is 'deprived' of what in earlier epochs was the
main and central ground of 'individualisation', this ground now
presenting itself in the form of an absence of possibilities for
individualisation, then we might expect the direct, concrete
'extension of the self', or 'discovery of the self in objectification'
to be displaced from the centre onto the periphery. That is to say,
if the individual, qua being human, has a need to objectify,
individuate and come to feel his or her own particularity, then we
might expect this need to seek some outlet to compensate for the
blockage it encounters in its traditional and 'rightful' terrain. And
there is, indeed, a way of regarding the existence of most people
under capitalist relations that is perfectly consistent with this
expectation. It might be argued that this is an existence which is
precisely characterised by the displacement of production by
consumption as the main area in which the individual 'develops'
the self. For if we cannot 'express' ourselves at work, at least we
may try to do so to some extent at home — through our possessions, our leisure pursuits, our gardens and do-it-yourself, 'our'
clubs and teams, and, most importantly, through our friends, our
lovers, our children and our pets: the intensity of the 'personal'
and 'personalising' investment in these activities and relations that
typifies contemporary society is a poignant testimony to the
importance of their role as 'natural extensions' of the self.

On the other hand, we might expect that if this displacement
from production to consumption is genuinely a 'displacement'
from the standpoint of living a properly 'human' life, i.e., if we
can speak of it in terms of the 'loss of its proper object', then we
might expect it to have contradictory properties. And again, we
might think of these in terms of a tension between an urge towards
'privatisation' and an urge towards 'sociality'. Instancing the
former we might cite all the tendencies which allow and promote

individualisation in areas peripheral to work, the very 'nuclear-ness' of the family, monogamy, emphasis on private space and private possession (all of which have an economic function, but their analysis is not exhaustively given in this); as instances of the latter, we might cite the proliferation of groups, societies, clubs and so on which form in the pursuit of every type of religious, cultural, recreative and sporting activity — and all of which allow for and respond to a need for a 'sense of self in the community', a comraderie, or individuation through identification of the self as 'belonging'. In many cases these take on a quite chauvinist character, suggestive of ways in which analysis of such phenom-ena as racism, sexism, nationalism, and so on, would need to take this factor into consideration. Indeed, it would seem to be a factor in the formation of political consciousness itself; here the notion of class *membership* is significant, and reflective of the 'proprietor-ial' attitude that the individual can adopt towards the unity of the class in which (s)he finds her or himself. (Intellectuals are again perhaps something of an exception here, there being little con-nection between their class origin and the class with whose interests they come to identify, if, indeed, they identify with any, and little coherence even at the level of their intellectual pursuits. But this relative absence of a class unity in which intellectuals partake is perhaps no more than what might be expected of a group whose pursuits in themselves allow a good measure of immediate individualisation. The absence of forms of objective unity that can mediately bind social groupings can be linked to the degree of objective existence that the individuals of those group-ings find immediately).

To sum up, then, we have a theory which seems to find a good deal of empirical support, to the effect that to be human is to exist in a given society and to develop oneself as person in and through the objective conditions of one's existence, so that it is literally impossible to exist as a person in the absence of this objective mode of existence. Applied to capitalism (or any advanced monetary exchange economy) we find that this is characterised by a deprivation of the inorganic to which the person can relate to 'as to his own', as to 'an extension of his body', and that this deprivation returns in the form of an abstract dimension of personal existence. And this is true not only of the wage worker but to a greater or lesser degree applies to all individual existence under a generalised system of exchange-relations. The capitalist equally, for example, mediates his or her gratification of his or her concrete existence through the abstract need to accumulate value; and one could in principle theorise the forms of existence of individuality under capitalism in a way that would expose the nature and degree of penetration of this abstract dimension of existence in respect of the various classes and groupings composing society and the manifold functions performed in its reproduction. It is a society which is characterised precisely by the fact that most individuals are preempted of 'direct extension' of themselves objectively. What the individual is in his or her objective mode is given by the fact of this separation from objectification: he or she is pure 'subjectivity'.

But the time has come to look a little more critically at this theory and to return it within the framework of the tension between the cognitive and normative discourses. I have suggested in previous chapters that there is a normative current in Marx's critique of capitalism whose essentialist implications are inconsistent with the relativism of needs and absence of any absolute criteria for assessing patterns of consumption that the cognitive discourse argues for, and that this current is associated with a 'theory of need' that refers us to general, transhistoric features of human biology and psychology that define and *limit* our possibilities of happiness and gratification, whereas the 'theory of need' which is associated with the cognitive discourse refers us to an infinite development of needs that is freed of any natural presuppositions or limits.

How does the 'theory of personality' examined above relate to this tension? I suggest that it relates to it precisely by reflecting it. But then, on the other hand, it only reflects it because of a difference in interpretation it permits, and because it is ambivalent itself in its evaluative thrust.

On the one hand, the pejorative language of 'nudity', 'objectlessness', 'loss of self', and so on invites us to think of the mediate and non-direct relationship of the producer to the objective conditions of production as an impoverishment. Interpreted thus, this theory has obvious similarities to the theory of alienation, if it is not, indeed, no more than a more sophisticated and elaborated version of it. Yet, on the other hand, it could equally be argued that to speak of the 'objectlessness' of the worker under capitalism is not necessarily to imply that this is an alienation or impoverishment in itself, but only to describe the particular grounds of the formation of personality that characterise a particular historical period. It does not follow automatically from this 'theory of personality' that the loss of extension of self in the inorganic is either to be regretted or approved. It follows only that *if* the individual personality is formed at least as much through what objectivity presents to subjectivity as through what subjectivity brings to objectivity, *then* the separation between the subject and object will itself be the defining objectivity that the individual confronts under capitalism. When interpreted in this sense, the theory of personality stands as a wholly general and unbiased theory about the role of the 'proprietorial' attitude or 'regard' to the objective conditions of existence in constituting the individual. This 'proprietorial' attitude is not so much consciously experienced (as it is, of course, in the case of legal ownership of property) but something that is realised spontaneously and unconsciously in the very process of 'appropriation' of the conditions of existence as *presuppositions* of the self.

As we have seen, this relating to objective conditions as an extension of the self can take very different and paradoxical forms. Thus under slavery and serfdom, the individual slave and serf are themselves regarded by their owner or master as part of the inorganic conditions of their respective reproduction of themselves — as mere 'things' or chattels, precisely as non-persons. On the other hand, if this proprietorial regard is a fundamental and universal response, then slave or serf will equally relate to the conditions of their slavery and serfdom as to themselves — they will relate to themselves as 'things' or 'chattels' — and this relation of their subjectivity to their objective conditions will be characterised by a subsumption of their subjectivity within the objectivity of an existence 'only for others'.[9] The very objectivity of an existence 'only for others' will paradoxically be in the mode of sensing themselves as 'not persons'. As we have seen, the relationship acquires a similarly paradoxical, though antithetical, form for the wage-worker under capitalism, who appropriates the self as a person in the objective mode of existence only to discover that it is a totally objectless person. He or she is at the opposite pole from the slave, totally not thing, wholly person. But it is precisely this absence of any specific extension of the self in objectivity, or the non-specificity of the objective mode of existence, that Marx regards as the prior condition of the *unlimited* development of the self and the all round expansion of needs that alone becomes possible when one is freed from all presupposed, natural limitations. That same capitalist production which casts its agents into the void of objectlessness, is also that which drives labour 'beyond the limits of natural paltriness',[10] and in comparison with which all earlier stages of production appear as 'mere local developments of humanity and as nature idolatry' because nature:

... ceases to be recognised as a power for itself and the theoretical discovery of its autonomous laws appears merely as a ruse so as to subjugate it under human needs, whether as an object of consumption or as a means of production. In accord with this tendency, capital drives beyond the national barriers and prejudices as much as beyond nature worship, as well as all traditional, confined, complacent, encrusted satisfactions of present needs, and reproductions of old ways of life . . .[11]

It is on the self-same ground, then, of the 'theory of personality' to be extracted from his notes on pre-capitalist formations that Marx opposes to the language of 'nudity', 'objectlessness' and 'alienation', a language (equally larded with evaluative terms) of the 'paltry', 'limited', 'encrusted', 'merely local', 'confined' and 'complacent'. Instead of the implied regret for capitalism's destruction of personal ties, and of the *immediate* relationship between the individual and the objective conditions of the formation of the self, there is a eulogy on its civilising influence in breaking down the presupposed limits to consumption. The value of capitalist production lies in the fact of its expansion of consumption, in the 'all-sided' development it permits, in its refusal to be satisfied with any simple reproduction or merely sluggish development of needs. We should note that the development of money is itself included in this commendation since it wreaks havoc with that particularity which characterised both the objects and the manner of satisfaction of earlier epochs — a particularity which from the standpoint of the other evaluative bias of the theory of personality seemed essential to the 'fullness' and 'plenitude of self' of the individuals, and without which one would remain as pure 'nakedness', whose objective self returned only in the form of an 'abstract, general personality', but which from the standpoint of this bias now appears as a limit on personality. On this point we might cite the following:

> Since he exchanges his use-value for the general form of wealth the worker becomes co-participant in general wealth up to the limits of his equivalent — a quantitative limit which of course turns into a qualitative one as in every exchange. *But is bound neither to particular objects, nor to a particular manner of satisfaction.* The sphere of his consumption is not qualitatively restricted, only quantitatively. This distinguishes him from the slave, serf, etc.[12]

(Though we might also note in passing, how inconsistent this comment is with the implications of his arguments for the restriction imposed by use-value upon exchange-value. For clearly the worker under capitalism *is* qualitatively restricted as a consumer by natural exigencies. If one chooses to expend one's share of general wealth entirely on plastic gnomes and visits to the zoo, one will simply not survive.)

Now if it is true that the 'theory of personality' is the common ground for these apparently antithetical accounts of need, and the apparently antithetical judgements upon 'true' need that they imply, I think it is clear that this theory cannot be regarded as incorporating any negative judgement upon the 'loss of humanity' that is entailed by the loss of reproduction of one's self in one's specificity. On the contrary, it has to be seen precisely as the theory that supports and confirms the discourse about the all-sided development that an all-sided and non-specific extension of self in one's objectification of self makes possible. Whereas interpreted in one sense it appeared to reflect some recognition of the 'natural' limits and presuppositions of any satisfaction of needs, and to insist on their importance from the standpoint of that satisfaction, interpreted in another way, it overrules any theory of true need that pays deference to such limits and presuppositions. Hence at the very point at which Marx explicitly recognises this duality of value-systems he wants to transcend it on the basis of this same theory of personality:

> In bourgeois economics — and in the epoch of production to which it corresponds — this complete working-out of the human content appears as a complete emptying-out, this universal objectification as total alienation, and the tearing-down of all limited, one-sided aims as a

sacrifice of the human end-in-itself to an entirely external end. This is why the childish world of antiquity *appears on the one side as loftier*. On the other side, *it really is loftier* in all matters where closed shapes, forms and given limits are sought for. It is satisfaction from a limited standpoint; while the modern gives no satisfaction; or where it appears satisfied with itself, it is *vulgar*.[13]

Earlier we have been told that although the 'old' way of looking at things, which took the human being as the aim of production, regardless of his/her limited national, religious and political character, seems to be loftier when contrasted with the modern world, where production appears as the aim of mankind, and wealth as the aim of production, in fact:

When the limited bourgeois form is stripped away, what is wealth other than the universality of individual needs, capacities, pleasures, productive forces, etc. created through universal exchange? The full development of human mastery over the forces of nature, those of so-called nature as well as of humanity's own nature? The absolute working-out of all his creative potentialities with *no presupposition other than the previous* historic development, which makes this totality of development (. . .) the end in itself, not measured by a predetermined yardstick? Where he does not reproduce himself in his specificity, but produces his totality? Strives not to remain something he has become, but is in the absolute movement of becoming?[14]

In other words, the very idea of 'objectlessness' as 'alienation' has itself to be seen as an alienation — as the endowing of a mere 'appearance' with the form of reality; and so far from privileging the human being as an already existing, presupposed individual over the unrealised and only potential individual, it is the latter who must be seen to be the *real* and actual aim of production. The 'loftier' view *is* loftier insofar as it values the human being as an existing plenitude, and insists that a failure to satisfy that specific plenitude will necessarily involve a deprivation: it says, in effect, what matters is who we are now, not what we become. But it is lowliness itself to a view that sees emancipation from all erstwhile realisations of self as the condition of self-realisation. When capitalism, in separating the individual from the objective conditions of existence, deprives the individual of the 'realisation of self' in the specific, definite extension of his or her personality that is his or her objective mode of existence, this can be regarded either as a genuine deprivation, or as an emancipation — since the individual is now freed from a given form of self-reproduction and in principle in a position to posit what personality (s)he will become through her (his) objective mode of existence. 'Object-lessness' permits an infinitely varied objectification. Regarded as deprivation, objectlessness must necessarily be a loss from the standpoint literally of self-fulfilment; regarded as emancipation, it becomes the condition of that same fulfilment through a many-sided consumption. Of course, this is only so in principle since in fact under capitalism the person is in a position to posit his/her objective mode of existence only as far as the wage will stretch. But the point of the stress on the civilising influence of capitalist production is that capitalism develops the productive forces to a point where both needs and the technical possibilities for their satisfaction have been expanded and sophisticated in a way that would permit each individual this many-sided gratification *in fact* once the fetter of capitalist relations of production had been removed and those relations replaced by relations of communism.

We can characterise this deprivation/emancipation dialectic in terms of the antithetical utopias they seem to imply: 'regressive-nostalgic', on the one hand, 'productivist-scientific', on the other. On the one hand the ideal appears to be a Rousseauesque[15] community of small-holders and craftsmen, each living the full-ness of their personality in the specificity of the trade they ply, their crafts and skills, their limited stock of possessions and so on. In the other case, the ideal is an existence 'unmeasured by any predetermined yardstick', but characterised by an indefinite ex-pansion of the productive forces, an unparalleled development and application of science, a seemingly limitless consumption.

Now there can be no doubt that Marx's vision of communism is cast in the latter mould, for he was, as we know, the most damning critic of all nostalgic forms of utopian socialism. Or, to put this otherwise, though Marx reveals the antithetical value-systems, or 'theories of need' which underlly these different utopias, and shows himself to be aware of the intrinsic tension of a 'loftier' view which is also the 'vulgar' view — and never more clearly, I suggest, than in these sections of the *Grundrisse* which I have been discussing — his final option is clear enough.

As far as this concerns the 'theory of personality', this means, I think, that it would be mistaken to endow it straightforwardly with the pejorative force of the theory of alienation. In other words, if the theory of alienation is a theory of the necessary loss of self in the forcible separation of the self from the objective conditions of existence, which then confront the self as a wholly alien objectivity, which it relates to only as 'not its own', then it must be the condition of objectlessness itself which must be seen to constitute alienation. Yet objectlessness will also characterise the individual under communism to the extent that 'rich development of individuality' will depend on the absence of any pre-found, definite (and limited) self-objectification. The political implications of any identification of objectlessness with alienation are therefore nostalgic-regressive, and the only theory of 'alienation' whose implications are consistent with Marx's 'productivist-scientific' view of communism is one that associates alienation, not with objectlessness as such, but with the historic exigence for all needs, all exploitation of the infinite potential of one's objectlessness, to proceed via the detour of the need for money. Viewed in this light, the concept is the concept of the mediated (and in fact always unequal) access to the world of consumption opened up by capitalist productivity, and has nothing to do with the 'alien' nature of that world itself, or its objectifications.

We have reached the position, then, it seems, that the dominant value-system within which Marx is operating, the theory of 'true' need that so to speak triumphs in the last analysis in his work, is one that has freed itself from any value-system that can pass judgment upon the developed needs themselves of capitalist production, as opposed to upon the relations in which that production takes place. In other words, it would appear to be incompatible with the value-system underlying the second of the two aspects of the critique of capitalism between which I earlier distinguished.

Throughout this discussion, I have tended to underplay the fact that it is the value-system underlying the first aspect of his critique that emerges as dominant. The reason for this is that I have wanted to concentrate upon another fact, namely, the extent to which Marx is inconsistent in his employment of this value-system. I have suggested that in the very economic analyses that appear to support and confirm his predominant value-system he is involved in recourse to arguments underwitten by the 'subordinate' system. In the following chapter, I shall concentrate rather upon the fact that these value-systems *do* exist in a relationship of dominance-subordination, and I shall relate to the dominant system in a more critical light, questioning both the coherence of the grounds upon which it is presented as dominant, and the acceptability of its political and psychological implications. In a sense, then, I shall be abandoning the terrain of the Marxist texts themselves, where as I have tried to show, the two value systems are inextricably enmeshed, in order to relate to them in themselves, and in a separation that my text will impose on them.

Notes

1   *Grundrisse, op. cit.*, p. 471-14.
2   *Ibid.*, p.472.
3   *Ibid.*, p. 485. '. . . these different forms of the commune or tribe members' relation to the tribe's land and soil — to the earth where it has settled — depend partly on the natural inclinations of the tribe, and partly on economic conditions in which it relates as proprietors to the land and soil in reality, i.e. in which it appropriates its fruits through labour, the latter will itself depend on climate, physical make-up of the land and soil, the physically determined mode of its exploitation, the relation with hostile tribes or neighbour tribes, and the modifications which migrations, historical experiences, etc. introduce . . .' (p. 486).
   The discussion of this section of the *Grundrisse* provides a fertile field for further study both in the light it sheds on the distinction between 'property' and 'possession', and on the concept of forms of property, not in the sense of legal forms, but in the sense of the relations of production presupposed and formalised in legal forms. It is clear that legal forms do not have a direct correlation with (i.e. are not direct expressions of) these non-legal forms of property relations — witness the history of Roman Law (and cf. what Marx has to say about the category of legal possession in the 1857 Introduction). See E. Balibar's comments p. 241 in *Reading Capital, op. cit.*, and the many references in the *Grundrisse* to the 'dialectical inversion' of the property right that allows the semblance of equal exchange in the capitalist mode of production (p. 456f.; 460; 469).
4   *Ibid.*, p. 485.
5   *Ibid.*, p. 476.
6   *Ibid.*, pp. 456-71, and cf. pp. 295-7.
7   *Ibid.*, p. 226; cf. p. 157.
8   See, for example, A. Gramsci, 'Americanism and Fordism' in *Prison Notebooks*, London, Lawrence and Wishart, 1971; A. Gorz (ed.), *The Division of Labour*, Sussex, Harvester Press, 1976; H. Braverman, *Labour and Monopoly Capitalism*, N.Y., Monthly Review Press, 1974; A. Sohn-Rethel, 'The Dual Economics of Transition', *Bulletin* of the CSE, 2: 2, 1972; CSE Brighton Labour Process Group, 'The Production Process of Capital and the Capitalist Labour Process', *Capital and Class* 1, 1977; M. Bosquet, 'The Prison

Factory', *New Left Review*, No. 73, 1972; M. Hales, 'Management Science and the Second Industrial Revolution', *Radical Science Journal*, No. 1, 1973; E. P. Thompson, 'Time, Work Discipline and Industrial Capitalism' in *Past and Present* 1967; C. Goodey, 'Factory Committees and the Dictatorship of the Proletariat', *Critique*, No. 3, 1974.

9 One of the very few genuinely Marxist films ever made, Tomás Gutiérrez Alea's *The Last Supper*, precisely captures this relationship of the slaves to themselves as chattels, and the bitterness and difficulties of its transformation.

10 *Grundrisse, op. cit.,* p. 325.

11 *Ibid.,* pp. 409-10.

12 *Ibid.,* p. 283.

13 *Ibid.,* p. 488.

14 *Ibid.,* pp. 487-8.

15 Though here, of course, I am thinking not so much of the Rousseau of the *Social Contract* as of the Rousseau of the *Discourse on Inequality*.

8   Beyond a Simple Pleasure Principle:
Marx, Rousseau, Freud

1.   Marxism, utopianism and psychological 'monism'

I propose in this chapter to abstract entirely from the economic analysis of needs in order to concentrate upon a number of psychological questions that are raised by talk about 'self-fulfilment', 'development of individuality', and by the concept itself of the '*satisfaction* of needs'. I shall discuss these questions in the context of the tension between the 'regressive' and 'progressive' dimensions of fulfilment that were outlined at the end of the last chapter, and thus in terms of its implied oppositions between needs as limitations upon the possibility of self-fulfilment and self-fulfilment as conditional upon the transcendence of all limits upon gratification.

Though this tension is a constant, if submerged, presence in Marx's economic analysis and in the various 'anthropological' discourses we have examined, there is no doubt that he gives no place to a concept of 'needs as limits' in his vision of communist society. For this, as we have seen, he characterises in terms of a 'presuppositionless' development of needs and an infinite capacity for gratification, and speaks disdainfully by contrast of the 'complacency' of a limited and 'encrusted' mode of satisfaction. He thus in some sense clearly thinks of an authentic self-fulfilment as involving an indefinite expansion of wants, a continual transcendence of the self-satisfaction of the moment, an almost rapacious furthering of new forms of gratification. I want to question the coherence of this view from a number of differing standpoints.

As a way into the discussion, we might begin by questioning why it is that Marx so clearly thinks that 'progress' for the individual consists in the development of new needs. Now one answer to this, I think, is that he does so because it directly reflects his positive judgement upon the development of the productive forces of science and technology. Or, in other words, one is given the impression that from the standpoint of the value-system that underlies Marx's belief in the progressive nature of an infinite development of needs, there can be no questioning of the 'humanity' of the productions of science and technology since human progress is the direct reflection and complement of their achievements. This in turn suggests that the only framework for thinking the 'development', 'enrichment' and 'elaboration' of needs is provided by the concepts in which Marx thinks the nature or essence of scientific progress — the 'development of the productive forces', the 'increase in productivity', the 'expansion of wealth'; and that the expansion of needs and rich development of individuality is unthinkable except in terms of a more highly evolved science and technology. Does this mean, then, that Marx conceives of human development and enrichment as the direct effect of scientific activity — so that an (always historic) human nature is 'read off' from scientific development, whose confirmation it is, and the whole question of the extent to which scientific progress takes place in the interest of human needs, and is subordinated to them, is precluded, for scientific development simply *is* the development of what human beings need? In short, does Marx de-essentialise human nature only because he conceives of scientific progress as essentially beneficial? Is the rejection of an essentialist anthropology compensated for by the adoption of an essentialist theory of science?

Whatever answers we give to these questions, there is no doubt that the 'productivist' discourse invites us to pose them and to accept their rhetorical force. This is not to deny, as I have said, that even in this discourse Marx offers a 'dialectical' conception of the relationship between human needs and scientific progress, or, of course, to neglect the extent to which the essentialism of science is off-set by many explicit and implicit themes that we find alongside it. Nor is it to deny the definite achievements of science in furthering human emancipation and in securing and extending the pleasures of life. It is only to argue that the dialectic becomes vacuous if it is maintained in isolation from any independent consideration of what constitutes emancipation and pleasure. Marx of course chooses to stress the *control* that science and technology permit in furthering the satisfaction of human needs rather than the aspect I have highlighted and from which human needs are seen as the effects of scientific progress and its human reflection, but unless this is backed up by a theory of needs and interests that can be satisfied through that control, the force of his argument is lost, and there is no reason to privilege the aspect that he does.

We can look at this same issue in the light of Marx's utopianism, or, if preferred, his essentially optimistic vision of the future society. On what does Marx ground this optimism? Certainly not in any optimism about human nature, for if he is to remain faithful to the principles upon which he rejects the credos of the socialist utopians, his own utopianism must be grounded in the rejection of any theory of human nature whether optimistic or pessimistic. In other words, his optimism is not premised on the belief that human nature is essentially good, but rather upon the belief that human nature is not essentially anything, and that if the future is rosy it is not so much because man will therein realise his essential nature but because of the developed man who is 'achieved' through the development of the productive forces and by virtue of the benefits that scientific progress can bestow. This means that there is none of the distrust of scientific rationality in Marx's 'utopia' that we can associate with a Rousseauesque idealisation of an age before 'iron and corn' had ruined humanity, or with a Fourieresque pseudo-science of 'harmonisations', or with a Thoreauesque conception of self-sufficient individuals of limited technical means bent on the 'return to nature', or even with a Marcusian ideal of a society in which the forces of the 'playful' Id triumph over the repressive Ego of labour. This is not to deny, of course, that there are many interpreters of the Marxist vision of post-capitalist society (among whom, of course, are to be numbered Marcuse himself and other thinkers in the tradition of the Frankfurt school) who have wanted to question the automatic concurrence of scientific with human interests, and who would insist that the question of the compatibility of scientific and human values was a question that Marx himself never ceased to pose.

Now it seems to me that Marx *does* indeed pose that question repeatedly, but that he does so in and through the inconsistency of his differing strands of thought; whereas too often his interpreters have been over favourable to him on this score, and have wanted to regard the fact that the question is raised at all as itself a form of resolution to it. In this respect they have paid too little attention to the problem of integrating Marx's 'humanist' themes with the 'productivist' discourse, and have relied on what are little more than slogans ('abolition of the division of labour', the overcoming of 'alienation') to cement the two together. Here a failure to examine the credentials of the theory of alienation or to consider what, if any, psychological implications it has for the possibilities of human happiness and development of self, goes along with a too willing acceptance of Marx's dicta about the capacities of science to overcome the presumed grounds of that alienation (division of labour, stultifying work routines, and so on). But if we remove the comforting umbrella of the theory of alienation, which seems to provide such an all-encompassing knowledge of human needs, we immediately confront the void of our actual ignorance about the possibilities and limitations of human satisfaction in work (or at play, come to that). And our confidence must immediately be undermined in the notion that the abolition of the division of labour or extensive automation, whether or not they are practically achievable, will allow the required satisfaction. Or perhaps this point is better expressed in terms of the possibility of *conflict* between the satisfaction of needs of which the development of science and technology is the enabling condition, and needs whose satisfaction is preempted by that very development. Marx in the *Grundrisse* emphasises the role of automation, for example, in releasing the free time that is an essential condition of the development of rich individuality. But is it a purely nostalgic and romantic need that is expressed in the anxiety that the vision of an automated world tends to arouse? And even if it is nostalgic, is it any the less a need? Is it any less authentic? Might it not express some limits or presuppositions of which we ought to take account?

I am under no illusions as to the extent to which it will be deemed a heresy to broach these questions by anyone who regards Marxism as having exposed the illogic of even posing them. We have been told over and over again by these Marxists that it is not technology as such, not the machine as such, not automation as such that is 'alienating', but the use to which these are put and the social relations in which they are employed. But in the absence of a more profound psychology of needs than we currently possess, can we be sure of that claim? Indeed, if alienation is anything more than a synonym for capitalist exploitation, then it would seem to be a concept in a psychological theory about work relations that would precisely have to face that kind of question. For it then becomes a theory about the more or less 'human' nature of differing forms of human objectification (including objectification in machinery, computers and electronic systems). I do not want to prejudice the answer to this kind of question, but only to raise it as an instance of what I have in mind in speaking of the possible conflict between human needs and scientific rationality, and as a way of questioning Marx's optimism on that question.·

Perhaps, too, we should relate the question of a possible conflict in needs to one of the main themes of Marx's account of communist society: the abolition of the division of labour. Now Marx himself clearly never questions for a moment that the abolition of the division of labour is a precondition of the full satisfaction of needs and the development of individuality; but if we view it in the light of the 'regressive-progressive' tension we invite a somewhat different appraisal of its role, for this tension might be said to be the expression of a possible conflict at the level of the development of individuality between specialisation in one's tasks and occupations, on the one hand, and unlimited diversification of them, on the other, between, one might say, the pleasures of concentration and the pleasures that distract it. Here, it should be stressed, I am concerned only with the question of the break-down of the *technical* division of labour which Marx appears to envisage in communist society, and to commend from the standpoint of the development of individuality; I am not here challenging the necessity of the abolition of a hierarchical social division of labour based on a privileging of 'mental' over 'manual' labour and on that divorce between the conception and execution of tasks which is designed to facilitate the exploitation of the great mass of workers. But the overcoming of a social division of labour of this kind is consistent with individuals devoting themselves exclusively to a particular branch of productive activity, whereas Marx appears to assume that a further condition of the development of rich individuality is diversification in the very kinds of activity that any individual undertakes over a given period, and I am suggesting that it is this assumption that bears further examination in the light of the opposition between a 'regressive' and 'progressive' interpretation of self-fulfilment. We have seen that the 'regressive' interpretation tends to a view of self-fulment as dependent upon the extension of self in a certain, necessarily limited and specified occupation enabling an inorganic reproduction through the 'presupposition' of the skills and use of instruments essential to the pursuit of that occupation, while the 'progressive' interpretation presents personal fulfilment as dependent upon the transcendence of the 'paltry' and merely 'local' self who is trapped within the confines of a simple self-reproduction based on attachment to a specialised pursuit. Now if this 'regressive-progressive' tension is worthy of any serious consideration at all as a framework in which to think about the relationship between a person's activities and that person's self-fulfilment, then it would follow that so, too, is a view of the role of the division of labour as not only detracting from, but also contributing to human self-fulfilment. Likewise, it suggests that we would have to reconsider the 'need' for its abolition from the standpoint of the development of individuality. We would then be thinking within a framework of contradictory tendencies, a framework within which it makes sense, for example, to query the extent to which the 'all round' individual is the 'fulfilled' individual, and to pose questions of 'industrial' psychology about the relationship between human satisfaction and the division of labour.

It is clear, however, that once one places oneself within such a framework of thinking one adopts a conceptual framework that regards the psychological determinations that enter into the formation of needs, and exert their influence upon reactions to objective circumstances, as themselves complex and contradictory in tendency. One is then no longer thinking within what might be termed a 'monist' perspective upon human psychology — one is no longer assuming that the subjective aspect that enters into the formation of the individual's response to the objective conditions of existence can be thought of in terms of psychological forces that are univocal and self-consistent.

It has, it seems to me, been a tendency of commentary on Marx's 'utopian' themes to adopt such a 'monist' perspective, and this has led to an evasion of real and important psychological issues of which Marxism must take much fuller acount if it is to expand on the range of its pertinence to the contemporary political situation. These are issues, however, which Marxism as it stands is simply not conceptually equipped to accommodate. The refusal to recognise this fact, and the need it implies for Marxism to enter into a more serious engagement with psychology, is based on a naive overestimation of Marxism's powers as 'total' science that must prove damaging in the end to Marxism itself, and will encourage psychologists themselves in the view that a Marxism so assured of its own self-sufficiency can have little to contribute to *their* field of study.

While considerations of the kind outlined above could only be introduced in the light of the adoption of a non 'monist' perspective, they are also presented as arguments for rejecting that perspective. I now want to suggest that they can be pressed further, and that to the extent that they imply that some conflict in needs, some antithesis of possibilities of gratification, may be the condition itself of satisfaction and self-fulfilment, they directly invite us to consider placing the 'regressive-progressive' tension within the context of some wider and more fundamental theory of the contradictory nature of human needs, and to consider the possibility that we possess 'negative' or 'irrational' drives or needs that operate against our best interests and the fulfilment of our 'true' needs. Marx, it would seem, never put to himself the question of 'recalcitrant' or 'deviant' psychological forces of this kind, but tended rather to regard all evil in human affairs as attributable to social relations and institutions that themselves record a history (or pre-history) of class struggle. But that might well seem evasive to one who would question why it is that human society has developed through oppression, brutality and class struggle, and not on the basis of a peaceful and egalitarian collectivity. (Is one to assume that class struggle is the condition of development, whereas peaceful coexistence can only lead to stagnation?) Besides, to the extent that Marx, however inconsistently with his rejection of essentialism and his stress on the always historic and relative character of 'human nature', does clearly recognise transhistoric determinations of an anthropological kind, both physiological and psychological, there is no reason *a priori* why he should disallow the possibility of determinations both at odds with each other and working against the realisation of a truly communist society. Indeed, there is one determining psychological drive of this kind which Marx appears to recognise, namely the 'mania for possessions' which we discussed in Chapter 6, which must strike us as directly incompatible with the collectivist and non-self-aggrandising spirit we associate with the communist vision. Now, it would, of course, be naive to suggest that the defenders of the Marxist conception of communism do not have a ready answer to this kind of problem, for they will tell us that it is not only the relations of ownership but the very nature of individuals that are transformed in the process of development of a communist society, and that this proceeds correlatively with the eradication of a merely bourgeois greed and possessiveness. Such a response, however, is a prime instance of what I have described elsewhere as a refusal to regard Marxism as anything other than a series of readymade solutions; for what is at issue here, I suggest, is precisely the problematic nature of these alleged 'solutions'. In the first place, there is the problem of the 'dialectic' between alteration in social relations and alteration in human nature. (To what extent are communist relations of ownership responsible for effecting the desired change in human nature? To what extent is that change in nature a precondition of the alteration in social relations?) But secondly, and more relevantly to our particular concern here, to the extent that Marx invites us to conceive the 'mania for possessions' as a transhistoric drive that can take various 'forms', he clearly does not see it as wholly specific to bourgeois society (even though the particular form it assumes in bourgeois society — 'greed as such' — is also a specific 'content'). The question, therefore, as to whether this drive survives the transformation of capitalist society is clearly not automatically ruled out of court. And presumably, too, we should link this 'need for possessions' to the 'proprietorial' attitude towards one's objective conditions of existence that is such a central element in the 'theory of personality' which I have argued can be extracted from the account of pre-capitalist formations. This proprietorial 'regard' or 'attitude' is clearly not conceived by Marx as necessarily a 'selfish' or privatised affective response, nor does it have anything to do with legal ownership, for it characterises the individuals' relationship to the objective conditions of existence even in a primitive communistic society where all these conditions are collectively owned: it is the attitude which mediates his or her existence as a member of the communality. And, of course, it is in terms of the 'proprietorial' attitude that Marx speaks of the individual's participation in such incontrovertibly social-collective 'property' as language, custom, religion, culture and so on.

But wherever there has been a development and expansion of human society, so, too, it would seem, there has been an increase in the extent to which this 'proprietorial' regard can only, so to speak, find its satisfaction in privatised ways, requiring the endorsement of legal relations of possession. The sphere of satisfaction (once the earth itself) for this proprietorial attitude has been increasingly narrowed to the point where, for most individuals today, it cannot even be gratified in the ownership of the instruments and skills of a particular craft or occupation, but must be displaced onto an area of consumption, finding its most immediate outlet in private possessions. Even one's possession of such collective property as language and culture might be said today to have acquired a privatised form in the sense that in any class society they cease to be a common, homogeneous possession and come to represent a quite heterogeneous set of objective conditions to which any individual will only have a delimited and partial access.

Now presumably under relations of communist production, where labour is directly social, this proprietorial regard will be restored to its rightful field of application and no longer need to seek its main outlet in the area of individual consumption: it will be directly gratified in the productive activities of the individual. However, since this individual is also the all-round individual and no longer attached to any particular pursuit that he or she relates to as an inorganic self to be reproduced alongside the organic, or, in other words, since the objective conditions of existence to which one relates 'as to one's own' are *non-specific*, then there is no definite and 'presupposed' dimension of the self to which one relates as to one's particular self. Under communism, where Marx suggests that every activity undertaken by the individual is productive activity in the sense that it contributes to the production of individuality, then the distinction between the area of consumption and the area of production is eroded: in a communist society the private consumption of the individual, as opposed to his or her contribution to social production, is thought of as itself a contribution to production, since the aim of social production has become the development of individuality that takes place through this 'consumption'. And yet it is precisely because the possibilities of self-objectification through this 'consumption' (self-production) are conceived of as non-specific, as unlimited and undefined, that it is legitimate to query the extent to which it encompasses the satisfaction of a 'mania for possessions' and private ownership in the ordinary sense. Can the communist art lover, for example, be permitted to develop a rich individuality through the collection of works of art? Is the possibility of 'cultivating one's own garden' a condition itself of being 'individual' in any but a purely biological sense? To what extent is it practically desirable — desirable, that is to say, simply from the standpoint of accommodating needs for specific objects — for collective ownership to replace private ownership, and what might be the effects of a more collective ownership upon the possibilities of self-development? It is clear that from the standpoint of the saving of the labour-time of production (and thus of the expansion of new needs) that collective ownership of a wide range of goods that are typically privately owned in contemporary societies would be desirable, but the potential development of needs it permits may well be in conflict with the actual existing needs of individuals and with the actual process of their self-development. Even if it is supposed that individuals will have transcended any purely proprietorial urge to possess for the sake of possessing, it will nonetheless remain the case that the need for any use-value will be spatially and temporally specific — it will be a need to have the use of the object at a given time and place. Indeed, we might think of this specificity as a mark of its authenticity: it is part of the wastefulness of a capitalist mode of consumption that we 'need' to own goods in order to guarantee the fulfilment of our authentic but only occasional-specific need to use them. Collective ownership of a number of such goods could obviously circumvent a great deal of this waste, but it would introduce the problem of coincident and therefore conflicting authentic needs for goods held in common.

But my concern here is not to speculate upon the practical problems that would challenge any society that wanted to economise on social labour time by expanding on the range of collectively owned goods, or upon the various options that might be open to it (I would be sympathetic, in fact, to anyone who thought such speculation at the present time was altogether too academic to be worthy of much consideration). My concern has merely been to place consideration of the concepts of 'self-development' and 'rich individuality' in the context of a general psychology of needs that is at least prepared to pose the question of the role played in individuation by certain 'needs' (eg. to accumulate possessions, for privacy, for ostentation and self-display, and so on) that exponents of the communist future have tended to dismiss in too cavalier a fashion as the mere transient products of a bourgeois existence. Here again, it is the question of the limits placed by human biology and psychology upon the breaking down of the limits upon human satisfaction and self-development.

2. The psychology of satisfaction: correctives to a 'monist' conception

Most of my remarks in the preceding section have been concerned with potential conflicts in needs arising at the level of the allocation of work and distribution of goods in a communist society. But I have hinted that discussion of such possible conflicts might need to be placed in the context of wider and more fundamental tensions characterising the psychology of subjective human reactions to the objective conditions of human existence. In the absence of any explicit recognition by Marx of the kind of problems that might beset a communist society, let alone of any underlying psychological factors that might contribute to their formation, it would be pointless to speculate on what 'line' he might have taken in regard to them. By and large, it would seem, most of his remarks on socialist and communist society tend to the view that all conflict and contradiction in the satisfaction of needs would have been eradicated, since human nature has hitherto been divided against itself only within, and as a result of, a contradictory order of social production and distribution; the complement of this view is what I have referred to as a 'monist' conception of our psychical nature and a notion of human happiness as a simple and harmonious state that is disturbed only by external interference rather than being itself intrinsically complex and turbulent.

By and large, most commentators have also tended to accept this conception without much further question, and if there has been a reluctance on their part to speculate on the presence of relatively universal and transhistoric psychological determinations on human life, there has been an even greater reluctance to

entertain the idea that these may be complex and even contradictory in character. We shall see some of the ways in which this
reluctance as tended to affect the various 'reconciliations'
between Marx and Freud that some have attempted to effect.
Likewise, the question of psychic conflict at the very level of what
constitutes human happiness has never, it seems to me, received
the attention from socialist thinkers that it deserves. Even S.
Timpanaro,[1] who is almost alone in insisting that Marxism must
encompass a pessimistic dimension, and that it must recognise
limitations upon the possibilities of human happiness, confines his
pessimism to biological factors pre-emptive of satisfaction (ill-
ness, old-age, death) and neither raises the issue of psychologically
pre-emptive factors, nor, it would seem, does he consider the
possibility that happiness may itself be a complex, and, so to speak,
tension-ridden, experience.

In one sense, this reluctance of Marxism to entertain the
possibility of any kind of dualist conception of human psychology
is rather curious (though, perhaps, to be linked to its fear of
contradictions), given that this conception has been so pervasive
and permanent a framework of our reflections about ourselves
and our societies. Would the debates of Plato and Aristotle, of the
Stoics and Epicureans, have had much meaning, or even have
taken place, in the absence of the recognition of the opposing
motives governing our actions and our quest for happiness?
Indeed, the universal and transhistoric antitheses of art and
philosophy, which from time immemorial have opposed reason to
passion, Dionysus to Apollo, classicism to romanticism, thought to
sentiment (and, of course, art and philosophy to 'reality' and
'reality' to art and philosophy) have been an age-long sympton of
this recognition, even if it is only comparatively recently that
psychoanalysis has rendered some of its terms (and our various
inversions, simplifications and denials of them) more explicit to
us.

In another sense, of course, this tendency in Marxism is not so
curious, since it might be said to be the direct reflection of the
'revolution' it has effected in our understanding of ourselves (and
of our reflections upon ourselves); for the message of this
'revolution' is, as we know, to the effect that our 'nature',
including its 'conflicts' and its various tensions, is itself the
product of our social institutions and attributable in the last

analysis not to anthropology but to economic determinants.

Yet, as we have seen, that conception may be too simple to accommodate all, or even most, of what Marx himself has to say on the subject of human needs. And since, moreover, in expanding some of what he has to say, we have in turn encountered a type of dualism in the 'regressive-progressive' tension discussed above, it is not altogether obvious that Marxism has rendered all such psychological discussion redundant. More importantly, the issues it raises seem central to an understanding both of the nature of the various societies in the world today attempting to implement a socialist economy and of the various and often very conflicting feelings such societies elicit in us. For example, I would suggest that some of the unease with which sympathetic socialists in the West regard the achievements of Soviet and Chinese societies relates to what is felt to be an insensitive and counter-productive attempt to 'harmonise' needs and thus to simplify and crush the expression of what could prove fruitful tensions were their existence not regarded as a potential danger to the fabric of society. Such tensions are germane, I believe, to an individual's experience of 'being in society' and will have variously benign or malign effects for both the individual and society depending on the extent to which they are allowed a public as opposed to private existence.

There are a number of reasons, then, why one might want to query the adequacy of the 'monist' psychological conception, and I propose to do so in what follows via discussion of two rather different conceptions, both of which, however, I shall argue, have relevance to the dualism of the 'regressive-progressive' tension. The one is that provided by Rousseau's distinction between *amour propre* and *amour de soi*; the other, upon which I shall dwell at more length, is Freud's theory of the two principles of mental functioning (pleasure principle and reality principle) and his later, but related distinction between Eros and Thanatos.

3.   *Amour propre* and *amour de soi*

At the point where Rousseau appeals to the distinction between *amour propre* and *amour de soi*,[2] his main concern is to invert the Hobbesian conception of an intrinsically wicked human nature, and to argue that Hobbes has confused a care for our own self-preservation, in itself a natural and unprejudicial concern, with the gratification of 'a multitude of passions which are the work of society' and flow from that *amour propre* which society alone instils and which is absent from the state of nature.In a footnote on the two motivations, he writes:

Amour propre must not be confused with love of self: for they differ both in themselves and in their effects. Love of self is a natural feeling which leads every animal to look to its own preservation, and which, guided in man by reason and modified by compassion, creates humanity and virtue. *Amour propre* is a purely relative and factitious feeling, which arises in the state of society, leads each individual to make more of himself than of any other, causes all mutual damage men inflict one on another, and is the real source of the 'sense of honour'.[3]

Abstracting from the framework within which the distinction is drawn, with its mistaken assumption that it makes sense to speak of a pre-social human existence, I suggest we can treat this as a psychological theory of conflicting tendencies characterising the individual's relation to self and others. The distinction it makes has been described as between 'forms of practical reason which aim at the satisfaction of desires (self-love) and those which serve to increase self-esteem (vanity)'.[4] Of course, increase in self-esteem also represents a desire to think well of oneself, and in that sense *amour propre*, too, must be recognised as aiming at the satisfaction of desire. The two are therefore perhaps better differentiated on the basis of the mode of gratification of their desires — those of self-love being in principle gratifiable autonomously of others, those of *amour propre* having a logical dependence on the existence of others as potentially approbatory. Even interpreted in this light, however, there remains an ambiguity in the notion of self-esteem, which can either take the form of self-appraisal in despite of what others think, or, as is more common, perhaps, can be the effect of others thinking well of one. But even those who esteem themselves the more on account of their indifference to what their neighbours think, are clearly manifesting a desire that *others* should approve or admire them precisely on account of this very indifference, so that their motivation is not an exception to the 'other dependency' of the mode of its gratification, but rather only explicable in terms of that.[5]

As far as Rousseau is concerned, it is clear that he has in mind a distinction primarily between instincts of self-preservation, which he takes to be common to all animals, and a vanity that is the distinctive feature of the human animal, which is satisfiable only through *comparison* of one's achievements with those of others, and which constantly urges one on to emulation. Rousseau, of course, chooses to stress the factitious and divisive character of *amour propre*, but the love of honour was seen by Aristotle, and by the Greeks in general, as among the more laudable of human motives. (It is this antithesis of values which Nietzsche exploits with such fine irony in *The Genealogy of Morals*.)[6]

Rousseau regarded *amour propre*, then, as the mark of man's distinction from the beast, for while animals clearly share our propensity for self-preservation, they lack our spirit of emulation, our zeal for distinction, to which the desire for self-esteem of *amour propre* is intrinsic. Clearly, this distinction must ultimately be referred to our *self-consciousness*, which alone permits the process of comparison and contrast essential to *amour propre*, and which is arguably the fundamental feature delineating between the human and other animal species. Thus, while Rousseau regards *amour propre* as expressed originally in and through the contemplation of our superiority to the animal kingdom, he is more concerned with the role played by its developed form within human society itself, where its invidious operations, though defining of humanity, are also regarded as its potential ruin. Commenting on this divisive character of *amour propre*, Andrew Collier has made the point[7] that while self-love is not intrinsically damaging, since it will only be in conditions of scarcity that my satisfaction of desires must proceed at the expense of yours, *amour propre* by contrast is intrinsically scarce, and intrinsically in conflict with that of others, since my vanity can only be satisfied at the expense of injuring yours.

From the standpoint of the 'regressive-progressive' dichotomy, I suggest that the motive of self-love is that which we would associate with a limitation of needs, the merely 'local' self-reproduction of ourselves, whereas self-esteem or vanity seems to beget infinite wants, and is more concerned with a progressive differentiation of the self than with the preservtion of the self in its sameness. *Amour propre*, it would seem, is that motive which urges the individual beyond the confines of an established 'plenitude' of existence; it is the need to emulate that leads to the constant striving to become more than what one already is; it is the differentiation of the self that can only take place in comparison and contrast with others, and is therefore necessarily *extrovert*. *Amour de soi*, on the other hand, is essentially introvert, for it is a genuinely selfish urge, a 'looking to one's own interests' that is logically detached from any concern for the interests of others, and only proceeds at their expense contingently, in situations where the preservation of self can only proceed at the cost of damage to the other's self-preservation. Clearly, historically we have never been freed from such contingency, for it has precisely been a history of class struggle, and therefore of division between the interests of self-interested groups. But in a society of abundance, characterised by an egalitarian distribution of social wealth, the logic of *amour de soi* would suggest that any one person's is compatible with every other's, and vice versa.

What, then, of *amour propre*? Are we to presume that in such a society it disappears and no longer retains its function of differentiation of the self? That it plays no part in the development of one's rich individuality? Yet it seemed the principle of the expansion of one's needs that is so central to this conception of 'rich individuality'; it seemed to be that which pushed one beyond the stasis of who one is towards the infinite development of the one whom one is always yet to become. Perhaps it will be said that in a classless society of abundance, self-esteem will be stripped of its negative aspect of factitious competitiveness. It will cease to be a divisive force and become a positive virtue. Everyone, it might be said, in a communist society, will esteem themselves, but no one will do so at the expense of anyone else. But one can object to this line of argument on two grounds. On the one hand, if the argument is premised on the acceptance of the essential duality of human motives expressed in the distinction between *amour de soi* and *amour propre*, then its conclusion is invalid since it rests on the covert introduction of a concept of *amour propre* that is other than that of its original premise. On the other hand, if the argument is based on the concealed premise of the transformability of human nature that would be required for *amour propre* to assume this different form, then it only succeeds by way of denying as part of that same premise the existence of *amour propre*, since *amour propre* is the concept of that aspect of human nature which makes such a transformation highly questionable, if not impossible.

But let us approach the issue under a different aspect; let us consider how close this communistic ideal of a non-self-aggrandising, non-competitive *amour propre* is to endorsing certain effects that are traditionally associated with *amour propre*, and are possibly no more desirable or less destructive than those deriving from its more overtly aggressive and invidious forms of expression. Here I have in mind the urge to altruistic acts and acts of self-denial that are at odds with the egoism of *amour de soi*. After all, are not bourgeois morality, and the Christian ethic generally, premised on the approval of *amour propre* in its aspect as altruism? It is the need to repress our selfish urges that it encourages, Christ being the epitomy of this self-renunciation, of one who sacrifices *amour de soi*, and, careless of self-preservation, dies on the cross in order to teach others the virtues of self-sacrifice and to enjoy the esteem that alone accrues to the truly humbled and the truly martyred. Inveighing against the slave ethics of this form of *amour propre*, Nietzsche writes:

All truly noble morality grows out of triumphant self-affirmation. Slave ethics, on the other hand, begins by saying *no* to an 'outside', an 'other', a non-self, and *no* is its first creative act. This reversal of direction of the evaluating look, this invariable looking outward instead of inward, is a fundamental feature of rancour. Slave ethics requires for its inception a sphere different from and hostile to its own. Physiologically speaking, it requires an outside stimulus in order to act at all; all its action is reaction.[8]

One does not necessarily have to join in Nietzche's whole-hearted celebration of 'aristocratic' over Christian values, of Rome over Israel, of the nobility of self-enjoyment over the debased meekness of asceticism, to accept that the potentially self-sacrificial nature of a 'selfless' *amour propre* may be as compromised and compromising as are its more candidly invidious forms. Indeed, it might even be argued that in our ordinary social intercourse, where manifestations of ostentation, enjoyment of our own self-esteem, pride in our achievement, and so on, are generally disapproved (so that in order to approve ourselves and gratify *amour propre* we shall need to dissimulate our possession of it or of the pleasure we derive from it), this *amour propre* provides a breeding ground for dishonesty and hypocrisy in our dealings with others. For if vanity or self-esteem is intrinsic in some form to human beings then a constant encouragement to suppress this desire and to value expressions of modesty and humility over expressions of pride and self-satisfaction entails a constant inner conflict within the individual and a certain but equally constant measure of dissimulation in the individual's dealings with others. I am not myself convinced of the overall social or psychological benefits of a more candid expression of *amour propre*, though I would not deny the suffering incurred through the more covert mode of its gratification; but it is clear that there are arguments to be made on both sides. And it is, I think, equally clear that whatever the exact complexion one would put upon the *amour propre* supposed to characterise a communist society, one would not automatically free it of such tensions or of the dialectic of gain and loss to the individual and society to which hitherto it has given rise.

Indeed, of such tensions, as of the general tension between *amour de soi* and *amour propre*, we might say that they obey Plato's 'universal law ... that opposites are generated always from one another, and that there is a process of generation from one to the other'.[9] For is it not for reasons of vanity that *amour de soi* despises *amour propre*, and is it not ultimately for reasons of self-preservation, in this world or the next, that *amour propre* transcends and denies *amour de soi*? Or to put this another way: when *amour propre* divides itself against itself in the form of a morality of altruism, it opposes self-sacrifice and self-denial to the competitive self-affirmation that is its other aspect (its factitious aspect stressed by Rousseau), so that within the circle of its extroversion it repeats the original distinction between *amour propre* and *amour de soi*. Likewise, when *amour de soi* rejects the factitious spirit of *amour propre*, it reasserts the values of *amour propre* in the moment of its denial, for it precisely esteems a self that has freed itself from competitive emulation. The opposing moral discourses to which they give rise are both motivated by vanity, for it is only vanity that could motivate the desire to be rid of it. (One might note in this connection the propensity to preserve a measure of self-esteem by insisting upon a self-sufficiency that can prove damaging to the aims of *amour de soi*; it is often those in most need of the various state benefits to which they are entitled who refuse to avail themselves of them on the grounds that they need no one's charity.)

Must one then conclude that vanity is an essential aspect of human motivation and can only be deprived of gratification at the expense of human happiness? In response to this question, A. O. Lovejoy has suggested[10] that the proposal to extirpate motives arising from self-esteem and emulation would be some-what analogous to a proposal, in physical therapeutics, of total excision of the heart or the liver, though he does recognise that, like those organs, such motives can give rise to grave disorders of feeling and behaviour, so that:

If it were at all feasible to eliminate the underlying affective and appetitive components, and if in doing so we should not at the same time be eliminating the psychic sources of much that is generally regarded as most valuable in human experience and behaviour, then the radical programme of complete extirpation would be the right programme. But such extirpation is not feasible, and, if it were, would destroy the springs of action in man which differentiate him from the creatures below him in the scale of being, give rise to his most admirable achievements, and are the conditions of the possibility of civilised social life.

The question of the role and necessity of motives of vanity cannot, I suggest, be detached from our original question regarding the extent to which human happiness requires a denial of what one is in the interests of that which one might become; from the question, that is, of the dependency of satisfaction upon the dynamic creativity that can only proceed at the cost of the simple reproduction of the pleasures of sameness. For if that denial and that dynamic are essential components of human happiness, and if *amour propre* is its presupposition and the main form of its expression, then the latter must indeed be regarded as an indispensable feature of any society that pursues the goal of human fulfilment and well-being. Even Rousseau, for all his horror at the ruinous effects of *amour propre*, must perforce recognise its creativity ('O fureur de se distinguer, que ne pouvez-vous point!') and that without it there would have been no art and science, and no humanity to ruin. This is a theme that Nietzsche, too, flings in the teeth of his own derision of the hypocrisies of *amour propre*:

This secret violation of the self, this artist's cruelty, this urge to impose on recalcitrant matter a form, a will, a distinction, a feeling of contradiction and contempt, this sinister task of a soul divided against itself, which makes itself suffer for the pleasure of suffering, this most energetic 'bad conscience' — has it not given birth to a wealth of strange beauty and affirmation? Has it not given birth to beauty itself? Would beauty exist if ugliness had not taken cognisance of itself, not said to itself, 'I am ugly'?[11]

This theme also finds an echo in Marx's contempt for the 'vulgarity' of a quiescent self-satisfaction.

If, then, it is of its nature irremovable, and if it is the vanity of vanities to want to expunge such vanity from human affairs, then those who would argue for a transformation of human nature wherein it would be eradicated, must needs examine their own motives. And in any case, as I have suggested, were such a transformation possible one might question its desirability. As far as Marx's own conception of communist society is concerned, this is no doubt too vaguely sketched for one to insist upon the pertinence to it of Rousseau's distinction. But I think it remains the case that, despite the stress on 'rich individuality', we are frequently presented with visions of a future society whose perfection is associated with the altruism rather than the egoism of its members, and where the immediate concern for self is valued less than its 'sacrifice' to the well-being of society as a whole. In the light of such visions, we must ask how far the communist 'ethic' is still imbued with the bourgeois-Christian ethic of self-denial and self-transcendence. Marx and Engels inveigh against Stirner in the *German Ideology* precisely on the grounds of the essentially bourgeois nature of his egoism. But bourgeois thought was itself also dominated by moral disapprobation of egoism, and Stirner's views were a scandalous affront to its values. Of course, I am well aware that it can be argued that in the self-same moment that they expose the ground for the production of bourgeois morality, Marx and Engels expose the ground for the antitheses and simple inversions (between egoism and altruism) in which that morality moves and thinks — and thereby transcend the very terms of those inversions. And it is this form of argument that is produced by those who assure us that we cannot judge the nature of communist society because of its 'nature' it will have broken with the limited-bourgeois conceptual framework of moral thinking in which, alas, our present judgements are necessarily entrammelled.[12] On the basis of such arguments, Marx is allowed to avoid all moral dilemmas of the kind that find expression in the antitheses of reason and passion, *amour propre* and *amour de soi*, egoism and altruism, self-sacrifice and self-affirmation, since it is made a matter of *fiat* that in a classless society of abundance there will no longer exist the kind of scarcity nor the kind of divisive psychological motives that systems of morality serve to express, disguise and justify in class society. But a simple denial of the relevance of moral issues may be thought to be more of an evasion than a resolution of them.[13] Is it in fact possible to contemplate a society in which questions of morality will not enter into decisions about the distribution of social wealth? Do they not do so the moment we think in terms of 'equality' or 'inequality' of individuals? And if they do so enter, is that not because of the existence even in a classless society of abundance of antithetical and conflicting needs that it is recognised will require some arbitration between them? And these are conflicts that will exist not only between the individual and society, between the divisive *amour propre* of the particular will and the virtuous, civic-collective *amour de soi* of the General Will, but also within the individual, too, as the conditions of the possibility of happiness.

4.   The Freudian Perspective

...dissatisfaction, which results from the replacement of the pleasure principle by the reality principle, is itself a part of reality.[14]

Today there is much talk, most of it by Marxists rather than Freudians, of 'integrating' Marxism with psychoanalysis, of 'reconciling' the two bodies of thought and of their 'unification' into a single theory. I believe in fact that such talk is misguided in principle, since to the extent that our only possible relationship at the present time is to Marxism and psychoanalysis in the forms in which they have already developed and currently exist, it is not so much a question of their 'reconciliation' as of the differences between them, and of what these differences imply for the distinctness of the two respective theories. In other words, I believe that what psychoanalysis can bring to Marxism, and vice-versa, is a clarification of their respective theories (and thus of both the richness and the limitations of their approaches to what at the most general, and therefore banal, level, can be said to be the object common to both: human society). It is this clarification of their differences, of their comparative explanatory powers and their limits, rather than any blurring of distinctions, or attempts to overcome them, that it seems to me ought to be regarded as the proper aim at the present time of any discussion of the relations between Marxism and Freudianism.

In stating this, I do not mean to imply that nothing is to be gained from a confrontation of Marxism and psychoanalysis, and even less that there is nothing in common in their aims and perspectives. Indeed, were it not for this common ground between them, the question of their 'integration' would scarcely have arisen in the first place. But it does seem to me that to speak of a 'unification' in this cae is not very helpful, since the condition of any unification properly so-called would be a radical transformation of both theories as we currently know them. And this brings me more nearly to my main concern here, which is with the nature of the 'reconciliations' between Marxism and Freudianism that we have been offered, and with the grounds upon which they are made. In discussing these reconciliations, I shall be arguing upon two separate but related fronts. In the first place, I want to suggest that the form these reconciliations have taken has been determined aforehand by the fact that they have been conducted from a standpoint that privileges Marxism, and thus uses the adaptability of psychoanalysis to Marxism, rather than the adaptability of Marxism to psychoanalysis, as the criterion of success. Secondly, I want to suggest that reconciliations that proceed along these lines, and whose underlying motivation is to reveal the compatibility of a re-modelled Freudianism with an unmodified Marxism, involve a denial or evasion of what is arguably most valuable in the Freudian perspective, or of that, at any rate, which it would well re-pay Marxism to approach in a more self-critical light and to consider more fully.

One way of putting these points, though it is over-simple as it stands, is in terms of the 'monist' conception of the human mind that I earlier suggested was a feature of socialist thought and to be associated with its inclination to portray the emancipated society of the future as one in which the individual will be freed from all conflicts and tensions at the level of needs and their satisfaction. Although those adopting this conception rightly suppose that the forces of social liberation in which Marx placed his trust (development of the productive forces, abolition of private property and of the division of labour) are not in themselves enough to guarantee the psychological emancipation of the individual, and that in some sense Freud has shown us why this is so, they yet suppose that psychological liberation must be equated with the deliverance from psychic conflict and that therefore Freudian theory — if it is to supplement or complement Marxist theory — must in turn have shown us how this deliverance can be achieved. The tendency is thus to think that the psychological liberation of the individual under communist society must be explained on the basis of the disappearance of the duality of Id and Ego, and of the opposition between Pleasure Principle and Reality Principle, that is taken to be the mechanism of repression under capitalist society. Or to put this otherwise: if it is assumed beforehand that human gratification is not the product of tensions, but their eradication, then it is clear that the dualistic framework of Freudian thought must be related to as a problem to be resolved or overcome in order for it to be rendered consistent with the (supposedly) Marxist vision of communism, rather than as itself an enlightenment and a form of resolution. We do in fact find Marxists who (if they do not reject psychoanalysis outright) tend to consider Marxism to be reconciled, or reconcilable, only with a Freudianism that no longer retains its essential dualism; or, more exactly, who argue that historical materialism is consistent only with a 'corrected' or 'de-ideologised' version of psychoanalysis, according to which the dualistic framework which Freud himself (mistakenly) thought to be applicable to human society in general is recognised as having only historical application and therefore to be theorising what are contingent rather than necessary features of human existence.

There are three issues, then, bound up together here. The first concerns the possible 'hypocrisy' (by the scare-quotes I intend to suggest its unconscious nature) of those who would 'integrate' Marx and Freud in this fashion; the second concerns the interpretation of Freud's thought upon which they base the supposed resolutions of Freud's dualism — and I shall argue that this is mistaken, and furthermore that were it not for this misinterpretation there would be no motive to construct those resolutions in the first place; the third concerns the *a priori* convictions about human gratification which underlie the attempts at integration — convictions, I shall argue, which ought to be seen to be disproved, or at the very least undermined, by anyone accepting (as the 'integrators' professedly do) that Freud has revealed new and important truths about human psychology.

As a way into discussing these almost inseparable issues, let me simply begin by questioning the coherence of those who, persuaded by the force of Freud's arguments concerning the existence of the Unconscious and convinced of their relevance to Marxism and of the extent to which they complement the latter's insights upon the nature of society and the formation of our conscious selves, hope to integrate Marxism with psychoanalysis on the basis of a retrieval of the 'scientific' elements of the latter, a process they more or less identify with 'historicising' Freud's thought. Though, as we shall see, the integration can take quite antithetical forms, the integrators share a common theme, namely, that Freud, rather like the bourgeois economists pilloried by Marx, eternalised bourgeois society (or at any rate class society), reading the psychological conflicts of its members as general to all mankind, and regarding the causes to which he attributed them as immutable laws of nature. Freud, it is said, failed to perceive the specific and historic nature of the psychological processes he discovered because he was himself the victim of the reigning ideologies of his own historical epoch. But once we, from the vantage of a Marxist perspective, have understood his eternal-isation of specific and historical features, we can accept his account of the formation of repression without being committed to his pessimism: there is no longer any reason why the progress of civilisation must necessarily be viewed as in one way or another involving denial of a complete and genuine gratification. I say 'in one way or another' because, as I earlier suggested, we encounter two different lines of interpretation here: *either* the Id is taken to be the locus of our 'true' needs and it is thus supposed that the process of de-repression must correspond to a process of subordin-ation of Ego to Id, of Reality Principle to Pleasure Principle, *or else* it is the Ego that is regarded as the locus of 'true' need and human happiness must therefore depend on the denial or eradication of the needs deriving from the Id.

Thus, H. Marcuse, adopting the first line of interpretation (and offering, it must be said, what is probably the most thoughtful and thought-provoking 'reconciliation' of a Freudian with a Marxist perspective), has attempted to historicise and 'de-pessimise' the contrast between Pleasure Principle and Reality Principle on the grounds that this does not express a necessary duality or conflict in human nature, but rather the historical fact that civilisation hitherto has progressed as domination. He claims, that is to say, that Freud's analysis of the repressive instincts under the impact of the Reality Principle *does* generalise from a specific form of reality to reality pure and simple, but that this does not in itself vitiate against the truth of the generalisation — that a repressive organisation of the instincts underlies all historical forms hitherto of the Reality Principle in civilisation. But he goes on to argue that though this has always hitherto been the case, it is mistaken to regard it as a necessary feature of all human society, and that the scarcity that has up till now rendered repression a necessary condition of existence no longer justifies its continuance in a world of material abundance, where scarcity is no longer an obstacle to the full satisfaction of needs.[15] Hence Marcuse is led to account for the continuation of repression in terms of a redundant or 'surplus' repression necessitated by the continuance of social domination: its cause is not so much the struggle for existence as the interest in prolonging the struggle — the interest in domination. With the end of social domination, therefore, there will no longer be any obstacle to the release of the forces of the Id, and Marcuse speculates upon a future society in which the energies of the libido, currently diverted into labour and maintained in a state of repression because of the organisation of work, are channelled into their rightful areas of sensual, playful and artistic gratification.[16]

Now this is in many ways an over-simplified version of Marcuse's argument and may even be open to the charge of caricature. It is, in fact, my own opinion that Marcuse's position is arguably more complex than I have portrayed it as being. But I would also maintain that if we allow it to be more complex, then we shall have to allow that it is that much more ambivalent in the claims it is making. Is Marcuse arguing ultimately for an absorption of Reality Principle into Pleasure Principle, or for a synthesis between them, wherein each remains the principle of a distinct set of needs? But whatever position we attribute to him on this issue, to the extent that a dominant theme in his work is the 'truer' nature of the desires of the Id, and the desirability of an undivided service in the interests of the Pleasure Principle, it would seem to exemplify that pattern of motivation which I am calling in question: the whole effort to free Freud of his a-historicity by showing that the tension between Pleasure Principle and Reality

Principle is a merely transient and contingent feature of human existence takes place under the conviction that a permanent state of tension between the two is incompatible with any optimistic view of human society. And wherever there is a tendency to characterise the possibility of happiness as dependent upon the gratification of the desires of the Id, there is also a tendency to think that the only Reality Principle consonant with that gratification is one whose demands have completely converged with those of the Pleasure Principle, to which it no longer stands in any relationship of distinctness or opposition.

Now it is, of course, precisely this privileging of the supposedly more 'natural' Id, and the subordination of social to instinctual demands that it appears to recommend, that other would-be integrators of Marx and Freud have found so difficult to accept. For they are quick to point out that this Marcusian optimism has little in common with that of Marx, which stemmed rather from his faith in the ability of culture, especially scientific culture, to rectify its own negativity and to promote an increasingly non-natural gratification precisely through the control over nature that society affords to us. It is further argued that when interpreted correctly, Freud's distinction between Pleasure Principle and Reality Principle both shares in and serves to confirm this Marxist optimism.[17] After all, does not Freud initially present the distinction as a principle of explanation of human survival and growth? Does he not suggest that to remain fixated upon the hallucinatory gratifications of the Pleasure Principle would prove disastrous from the standpoint of this survival and growth, which can be ensured only through obedience to the Reality Principle? (Compare in this respect the discussion of the Freudian distinction between wishing and needing in Chapter 3). Viewed in this light, the Pleasure Principle is the psychic principle of a merely fantastic gratification, the Reality Principle the principle of real satisfaction, and the opposition between the two can scarcely be interpreted as an opposition between a body of 'real' needs deriving from the Id, and the 'false' or repressive needs of the adapting Ego. Indeed, so far from presenting the Pleasure Principle as more authentic, or encouraging the view that we should privilege it as such, it suggests that it is the Reality Principle that we should regard as more essential to human well-being. For does it not deflect us from the suicidal pleasure of the

Pleasure Principle and redirect us towards the real and substantial gratification of our needs? And does it not follow, then, that so far from being repressive of our needs, the Reality Principle is essentially de-repressive, since it does not repress the desires they provoke, but rather our fantasy that these have already been satisfied?

Hoisting one's banner, then, to the other horn of the Freudian dilemma, one can achieve a 'reconciliation' between his views and those of Marx that is quite antithetical to that of Marcuse,[18] for now it is the Reality Principle rather than the Pleasure Principle that is the essential force of liberation and demystification. The stress here is laid on the function of the Reality Principle is releasing the individual and society from a merely fantastic and illusory pleasure, the cost of which is the denial of real needs in favour of the false gratifications of a mystified existence. Here it is the dominance of the Reality Principle that is seen to be in the interests of human happiness, whereas the Pleasure Principle is that which reigns in the 'mad' society of capitalism, where 'false consciousness' encourages the pursuit of illusory and irrational goals. It is the Pleasure Principle that is repressive in its effects since it represses real satisfactions and displaces them onto hallucinatory gratifications.

Now this interpretation is, in many respects, closer to Freud's own conception of the matter than its Marcusian antithesis. But it equally departs from Freud if it is allowed to become the grounds for privileging one aspect of the Pleasure Principle-Reality Principle relationship, since it must then portray that relationship as an essentially negative opposition whose transcendence is a condition of a full and 'truly' human satisfaction of needs; and this, I shall argue, is not part of Freud's argument, and indeed amounts again to a denial of the 'dialectic' of human happiness of which his account of the relationship between Pleasure Principle and Reality Principle might be said to be the expression. It is an argument moreover, which, like its antithesis, appears to be grounded in some false dichotomy between 'nature' and 'culture' which is foreign to both Marx and Freud; for what is in fact an inner conflict between different kinds of instinctual demands, both of which have origins in 'nature' or biology, and both of which undergo specific cultural transformation, is interpreted as a simple conflict between biology and society, nature and culture, in which 'nature' (whether identified with the needs of the Id or with those of the Ego) must be allowed to emerge triumphant over the false manipulations of culture. But even if one were to accept the coherence of the notion that human beings are possessed of a body of 'real' needs associated with their 'nature' rather than the manipulations of culture, there seems no *a priori* reason to suppose that these will all be of a kind and mutually consistent. In any case, there seem to be no grounds for privileging nature qua nature, and the temptation to do so reflects the incoherence of an optimism about society that, having denied all social grounds for its optimism, must turn to nature to justify its continued faith in humanity.

Now it is true that Freud is at times (for example, in *Civilisation and its Discontents*) guilty of placing some such evaluative load upon his distinction. But it seems to me that to the extent that he does so, he is at odds with his own theory. The issues here are in any case very complex, and I propose to postpone discussion of them till later, since I believe that the problems that they raise are somewhat different from those with which I am primarily concerned here. They involve, that is to say, questions about the 'ideological' light in which Freud at times viewed his 'scientific' discoveries rather than questions directly relating to the content of the latter as originally presented and theorised, and it is that which I now want to discuss.

No one, I believe, who reads Freud's account of the relationship between Id and Ego, Pleasure Principle and Reality Principle, in an unprejudiced fashion could possibly suppose (whether or not they accept that account) that he is arguing *either* that the two are in opposition, *or* that either of them would 'disappear' or become wholly subsumed within each other in some future, more 'human' society. It is true that he argues that the aim of psychoanalysis is to allow Ego to be where Id was; but even were this to be achievable in practice, it would be the achievement of a synthesis of desires deriving from two distinct mental regions both of which would still retain their distinction even in their 'harmonisation', since the whole point of distinguishing between Id and Ego is to distinguish between two different types of instinctual needs both of which, it is Freud's opinion, must compromise on each other as the condition of a full satisfaction. In other words, so far from regarding either Id and Ego as the privileged source of our potential happiness, Freud insists upon the idea that psychic well-being is itself only accomplished through the reconciliation of the two. It is therefore mistaken to interpret Freud's slogan as suggesting the annihilation of the Id (all Ego, no Id . . .), for it is on the contrary a slogan about the desirability of their effective synthesis — where synthesis means synthesis, and not an Hegelian identity in which all differences have disappeared.

It is only if we interpret his slogan in this way that it remains compatible with his actual account of the relationship between Pleasure Principle and Reality Principle. Equally, however, it is only if we reject that account, or over-simplify it, that we shall be moved to effect a 'reconciliation' through subordination of one to the other. For nothing of what Freud says (unless it be when offering some personal evaluation of the message of his theory, rather than when presenting that theory as such — see below) suggests that we should view either Id or Ego as repositories of our 'truer' or more 'authentic' needs, and the only reason for supposing that he does rests on a reduction of that dualism to the age-old classic pre-Freudian (and, in fact, pre-Marxist) dualism of nature versus culture, biology versus society, head versus heart and reason versus passion.

What Freud, by contrast, is concerned to stress is not so much the opposition between the two as their complicity, and he portrays the tension between them as arising out of the represent-ation by the Ego of the exigencies of reality, which it would have the Id pay heed to the better to accommodate its wishes:

The relation to the external world has become the decisive factor for the Ego; it has taken on the task of representing the external world to the Id — fortunately for the Id, which could not escape destruction, if, in its blind efforts for the satisfaction of its instincts, it disregarded that supreme external power . . . In that way it has dethroned the pleasure principle which dominates the course of events in the Id without any restriction and has replaced it by the reality principle, which promises more certainty and greater success.[19]

So far, then, from presenting Id and Ego as locked in combat, Freud depicts the latter as engaged in a constant striving to further the ends of the former by forcing it into a more realistic relation-ship with the conditions of its satisfaction. On this view of their relationship, they are both equally in the business of securing our well-being, and both functioning as components of our gratif-ication. Seen in this light, we must discount the idea that the concepts of Id and Ego, Pleasure Principle and Reality Principle, are concepts that themselves prejudge the content of human gratification on the basis of some division of the latter into its 'real' and 'false', or more or less 'human' components, and regard them as explanatory concepts designed to account theoretically for the processes whereby that gratification is achieved. It is even more important to discount the idea that they are concepts of different bits of extra-psychic reality (nature-culture) that are supposedly incorporated mentally, and between which the mind divides — so that Id becomes the concept of a 'natural' or 'biological' region, and the Ego the concept of its 'social-cultural' region. (Or else, on the interpretation which privileges the 'reality' of the Ego, the Ego is regarded as the concept of our 'natural' selves as opposed to the 'perversions' to which they are subjected by the Id.) And if that conception is mistaken, it further follows that it would be wrong to regard these concepts as direct descendents of the dualism of head and heart (or of reason and passion). For though it is true that Freud himself tells us, 'adopting a popular mode of expression', that 'Ego stands for reason and good sense while the Id stands for the untamed passions',[20] he also makes it clear that he regards the very *rationality* of the Ego as consisting in its preparedness, indeed its eagerness, to heed the 'passions' of the Id and to accommodate them with as little compromise as possible. In other words, the 'popular mode of expression' is unfortunate if it is taken to suggest that Freud regards the Ego as the adherent of a puritan ethic counselling the pleasures of asceticism over those of an unbridled sensuality, for as it is portrayed by him elsewhere, there is nothing anti-hedonistic or anti-sensual about the Ego; on the contrary, its 'realism' is associated with its more 'diplomatic' — and hence potentially more fruitful — manner of going about the gratification of our passions.

But if Id and Ego are complicit in this fashion, and there is nothing intrinsically repressive about the Ego, why is it that the synthesis, which is in the interests of both, and which each, in a sense, has as its interest, is so continually thwarted? Why has psychoanalysis got such a job on its hands in the first place? In answering this question, we are bound to introduce a certain qualification into our presentation of Freud's account. For hitherto, I have been referring to it as if it were uncomplicatedly 'dualistic', whereas, of course, it is to the *third* mental region, which he theorises under the name of Super-Ego, that Freud refers us for the answer to this question. In its role as 'conscience', Super-Ego 'watches over' every attempted synthesis of Id and Ego, and in so doing undermines the very possibility of such a synthesis. For, as if the Ego did not have enough on its hands in bringing the wishes of the Id to their gratification via the detour of reality, the Super-Ego must further complicate its task by suggesting that, after all, gratification is not what it wants, or what it can only have at the cost of that deprivation of happiness which is known as guilt. In its function as prohibition and renunciation of pleasure, the Super-Ego is therefore constantly thwarting the very aims of the synthesis of Ego and Id by questioning its desirability, and the Ego

... is observed at every step it takes by the strict Super-Ego, which lays down definite standards for its conduct, without taking any account of its difficulties from the direction of the Id and the external world, and which, if those standards are not obeyed, punishes it with intense feelings of inferiority and guilt. Thus the Ego, driven by the Id, confined by the Super-Ego, repulsed by reality, struggles to master its economic task of bringing about harmony among the forces and influences working in and upon it ... if the Ego is obliged to admit its weakness, it breaks out in anxiety — realistic anxiety regarding the external world, moral anxiety regarding the Super-Ego and neurotic anxiety regarding the strength of the passions of the Id.[21]

But rather than protract this account of Freud's metapsychology, I shall here simply reiterate my point that far from licencing an account of the Ego as essentially repressive, it in fact gives the lie to this view, and the very idea that the 'repressed' person is the 'neurotic' person (and its macroscopic reflection in the notion that 'repressed' societies are 'neurotic' societies) must be reconsidered in the light of Freud's account of neurosis as the result of the *collapse* of the Ego in the face of the demands upon it, rather than as a result of its successful repression of them.

Though I have suggested that the recognition of the third mental region constituted by Super-Ego is at odds with my presentation of Freud's account of the mind as 'dualistic' and invites what is in fact a 'triadic' conception, it might still be argued that from the standpoint of its implications for the construction of any future and more humane society it is the essential dualism of the Freudian perspective that should be stressed, since the repression which Freud associates with the Super-Ego is the contingent effect of specific social circumstances that are in principle removable. In other words, it might be said that at least as regards the formation of the Super-Ego Freud is open to charges of eternalising features of society that are merely historical, since he argues for its permanence on the assumption that the form of the family in bourgeois society, and its particular educational and authoritarian social institutions, are necessary to civilisation as such. But even this argument seems somewhat dubiously based: we can certainly envisage the dissolution of the family as we know it; and it is to be hoped that we might eventually experience a society in which education and work could proceed independently of institutional forms of the kind that reinforce Super-Ego; but whether we can envisage a society in which the child has ceased to be dependent on the nurture and protection of the adult (which is the grounds itself of the discipline that becomes internalised in the form of Super-Ego) would seem to be a different matter, since that does seem precisely to be biologically rather than socially determined. In this connection, we should note that Freud places almost all the responsibility for the formation of Super-Ego upon the fact of that biological dependency, regarding reinforcement through social institutions as a secondary affair that would have little effect were we not already possessed of the basic and 'rudimentary' Super-Ego that is instilled parentally.

In any case, I think one must challenge the underlying assumption of any argument that would persuade us of the contingency of Super-Ego — the assumption, namely, that we would all be better off were we freed from the promptings of conscience and the pangs of guilt. We must certainly distinguish between neurotic and healthy guilt (the former to be associated with over-estimation of the control we exert over reality), but (as John Mepham has put it to me):[22] what would happen if the child (or adult) felt no guilt at killing the father? So far, then, from assuming that the removal of the function of Super-Ego is a condition of human emancipation, we should regard the latter as an agency which, like the Ego, is necessary to harmonisation and realisation of satisfaction since it mitigates the ruthlessness of the Ego-Id pursuit of pleasure, so making it possible to relate to the *real other* (who poses less of a threat to our happiness than we had imagined, but whose substantial existence as a condition of genuine gratification must be the more respected).

In conclusion, then, I would argue that any attempt to reconcile Marx with Freud on the basis of the triumph of Pleasure Principle over Reality Principle, or on the contrary principle of the triumph of Reality Principle over Pleasure Principle, can only proceed by way of simplifying or undermining the framework for under-standing mental functioning that it was Freud's specific con-tribution to have proposed and elaborated. It must therefore call in question the acceptance of psychoanalytic theory that sup-posedly motivates the original exercise of 'integration'. I would further argue that there may be good reasons, when it comes to a 'reconciliation' of psychoanalysis with Marxism, for Marxists to think in terms of entertaining a conceptual framework that presents the possibility of human happiness as essentially depend-ent upon an interplay of conflicting forces, rather than in terms of removing the complex tensions which the Freudian perspective introduces into the theorisation of human needs and their satis-faction. With neither of these claims do I intend to endorse everything that Freud says, or every aspect of its presentation; but equally I do not think that the Freudian conceptual framework must automatically be viewed in a pessimistic light by socialists and thus denied or circumvented in order that an optimistic view of human potentialities be preserved. An optimism that is too impatient with considerations of what in human psychology may limit, complicate and even exert itself as counter-productive in the pursuit of happiness, is not only unrealistic but inhumane. Here, as always where what is at issue is the possible transform-ation of our needs and the expansion of the sources of self-fulfilment, the prior condition is a more adequate understanding of why we possess the needs that we do, and of why we may feel that self-fulfilment is dependent upon resisting attempts to alter its existing sources. Freudian theory, at the very least, I suggest, sheds some light upon the complexity that we have seen to characterise human affective attitudes to the objective world of human productions.

5. Freud's pessimism

It remains to say a word or two about the 'pessimism' with which

Freud himself invests, or is alleged to have invested, his theory of mental functioning. I have presented Freud's distinction between Reality Principle and Pleasure Principle as a primarily 'neutral' piece of theorisation which does not incorporate any evaluation of its own theoretical content. But there is no doubt that Freud himself 'compromises' on the neutrality of this picture by the later thesis (elaborated in *Beyond the Pleasure Principle*) of the opposition between Eros and Thanatos (a distinction between the life preserving sexual instincts, and the Death instinct, or instinct for inertia and freedom from excitation by external stimuli). For the distinction between Pleasure Principle and Reality Principle is then seen to have relevance not only to the satisfaction of 'ego-instincts' (the instinct for self-preservation: the need for food, and so on) but to the satisfaction of the sexual, as opposed to the Death instinct, the former being associated with the Reality Principle, the latter with the Pleasure Principle. In short, to work in the service of the Pleasure Principle is no longer merely to pursue hallucinatory gratification of our somatic needs, but to work in the service of the Death instinct. Furthermore, although the latter is initially described in terms of the 'urge for repetition', or the urge to 'free the mental apparatus from excitation and to return to the quiescence of the inorganic'[23] — as the urge to satisfy needs without the disturbance of the system of real satisfaction — it is later specified (in *Civilisation and its Discontents*) as the harmful instinct of aggression, and by that time has come to be regarded by Freud as an inevitable, but quite definitely evil force. Indeed, it is his belief in the instinct of aggression that leads him to accuse the socialists of 'idealistic misconceptions of human nature',[24] for while he claims that he has no economic criticism of the communist system, he argues that the psychological premises on which it is based are untenable:

In abolishing private property we deprive the human love of aggression of one of its instruments, certainly a strong one, though certainly not the strongest; but we have in no way altered the differences in power and influence which are misused by aggressiveness, nor have we altered anything in its nature. Aggressiveness was not created by property. It reigned almost without limit in primitive times, when property was still very scanty, and it already shows itself in the nursery almost before property has given up its primal, anal form; it forms the basis of every relation of affection and love among people (with the single exception, perhaps, of the mother's relation to her male child). If we do away with personal rights over material wealth, there still remains the prerogative in the field of sexual relationships, which is bound to become the source of the strongest dislike and the most violent hostility among men who in other respects are on an equal footing. If we were to remove this factor, too, by allowing complete freedom of sexual life, and thus abolishing the family, the germ-cell of civilisation, we cannot, it is true, easily foresee what new paths the development of civilisation could take; but one thing we can expect, and that is that this indestructible feature of human nature will follow it there.[25]

Freud, of course, has himself come under heavy attack from the 'socialists' for such sentiments, on the grounds that the attribution to 'human nature' of an aggressive instinct is a classic instance of Freud naturalising and eternalising behaviour that is in fact socially induced and historically relative. Now there is no doubt in my mind that Freud is too glib and dogmatic in his claims about our 'destructive' instinct, and significant in this respect is the incoherence of his arguments for it. In the passage cited above, for example, he seems to want to argue both that aggression is socially induced by private property and the family, and that it is also an inevitable psychological 'given'. He himself, it would seem, also lacks confidence in his claims, for he recognises in *Civilisation and its Discontents*[26] that the existence of an aggressive instinct is not empirically established but 'is merely based on theoretical grounds' and hence 'not entirely proof against theoretical objections';[27] and I think this lack of confidence can be linked to the vacuity of his claim in the final lines of the passage cited above. For it seems clear that Freud is here reluctant to pursue the issue any further precisely because he has himself ceded so much to theoretical *objections* to the aggressive instinct (i.e., objections to the effect that it is accountable to private property and the family) that he is no longer sure of the theoretical grounds for claiming it to be an *instinct*: a petulant 'well, it will be there anyway!' is brought in to fill the void that he himself has exposed in his theory, and the curtain is brought down on the matter just at the point where he has prompted the question whether this 'indestructible feature of human nature' must necessarily take destructive forms in the hypothetical society that he has granted will have removed the main causes of destructiveness. (Another, and perhaps more fruitful way of posing this question is in terms of what we are going to count as 'destructive' and why, and how much 'destruct-iveness' we can tolerate. The mistake — and it seems to be shared in this argument by both the 'socialists' and Freud — surely lies in thinking that the empirical discovery of aggression in the nursery must imply the inevitability of its maturation into the aggression that is manifested today in the overkill capacity of the nuclear arsenal, or, inversely, that one can only disprove that inevitability on condition that one can 'disprove' the existence of nursery aggression).

But it is not only in respect of his theorisation of the aggressive instinct that Freud is less than coherent in his pessimism, for, on the one hand, while he bemoans the 'repressive' effect of a civilisation that he claims is premised on the sense of guilt induced through renunciation of our instinctual life,[28] and views culture as a series of curbs and prohibitions upon our most immediate and spontaneous urges — to the point even of speculating that some civilisations, or even possibly 'the whole of mankind', have become 'neurotic'[29] — he does also, on the other hand, quite clearly regard at least one component of our instinctual life, namely the aggressive instinct, that is curbed by this 'repressive' civilisation, as a decidedly negative influence.[30]

On the whole, then, I think one would have to accept that despite the expressions of regret about the renunciations incurred through obedience to the Reality Principle, and the reference to the 'bitterness' of the experience of life that constrains us to obey it, Freud never really suggests that we might fare better if we heeded only the dictates of the Pleasure Principle. For this he always characterises as an essentially conservative principle whose counsel of inertia would in the end prove disastrous, since its 'repetitious' and merely 'fantastic' gratifications would literally prove the kiss of death.

So even though it is true that Freud is inclined to introduce an evaluative bias into his thesis of the principles of mental function-ing and the respective regions of their governance, he was never really tempted in the way that some of his Marxist interpreters have been to abandon the thesis of their interplay in favour of a 'monist' conception. And this is a dialectical conception that I have already suggested Marxism might do better to retain than attempt to dismantle, and which I think has relevance also to Marx's own discourses about human needs.

We might, in this connection, for example, consider the kind of insights that the supposition of conflicting instinctual responses allows on the nature of pleasure itself, and upon the tensions we experience in relation to our pleasures.

Freud expresses the conflict between Eros and Thanatos in terms of the double nature of our strivings for happiness, which, on the one hand aim at the absence of pain and unpleasure, and on the other, at the experiencing of intense feelings of pleasure. It is the latter, alone, he thinks, which constitute happiness in the true sense, and hence we have the paradox that happiness is at loggerheads with the Pleasure Principle:

What we call happiness in the strict sense comes from the (preferably sudden) satisfaction of needs which have been dammed up to a high degree, and it is from its nature only possible by an episodic phenomenon. When any situation that is desired by the Pleasure Principle is prolonged, it only produces a feeling of mild contentment. We are so made that we can derive intense enjoyment only from a contrast and very little from a state of things.[31]

Stripped of the psychological terminology, this appears to be the age-old problem of hedonism, which the Stoics and Epicureans had explored so fully long before: whether to suffer the slings and arrows that always lie in wait upon intense pleasure, or to take refuge in the *ataraxia* of painless contentment. Freud himself, it would seem, thinks we are 'so made' that happiness lies in the first option, and it is true, in fact, that few have followed the admonitions of the philosophers and found their happiness in the tranquility of indifference to the pleasures of the 'ordinary mortal'. But it is equally true, I think, that very few have been motivated *only* by the desires for the pleasures of the moment, however intense, knowing as they do that such happiness is usually only bought at the price of vulnerability to an equally intense unhappiness (the ecstasy of a great love, for example, that entails such intolerable suffering on the loss of its object). In other words, whether we accept that it is intense pleasure that alone constitutes 'true' happiness, or happiness in a narrow sense, it is clear enough that in a broad sense happiness is a complex affair, riven by conflict between the extremes of a fleeting but utter and ungovernable joy and a prolonged but mild and governed contentment.

And if this is the case, then it suggests a number of questions of relevance to the Marxist account of self-fulfilment and the development of 'rich individuality' in communist society. For example, assuming that rich individuality is associated with the acquisition of happiness, is this the happiness of mild contentment, or does it encompass the ecstasy that derives 'only from a contrast and very little from a state of things'? And if it can include this latter enjoyment, does this mean that the edge of lack is essential to the true satisfaction of needs, that happiness is as much to do with lacking as with having, that potential pleasure counts for as much, if not more than actual gratification, and that the substance of human happiness lies as much in the need to be satisfied as in the satisfaction of needs?

When posed in so bald a fashion, such questions may appear to advance us little. But in a sense, that is precisely the point of making them, for my aim in the discussion of this chapter has not so much been to provide a psychology for Marxism, as to draw attention to the vacuity of any discourse about 'self-fulfilment' and 'rich individuality' that insists always on the transcendent nature of those concepts relative to any understanding that we currently bring to them, and thereby excuses itself of the need to relate the terminology of Marxist 'utopian' thought either to our ordinary intuitions about ourselves, or to a psychology that has arisen on the basis of a study of actual human experience and affectivity.

When viewed in that light, I would want to argue that such questions do deserve attention, and that Marxist commentators have been over-hasty in dismissing their relevance, and too ready to assume that there would be no place in a 'truly human' society for psychical conflict issuing in contradictory patterns of need. It is, of course, precisely that assumption that inspires those bland utopian visions of a future existence of such perfect harmony that most ordinary mortals would draw back in alarm from the portals of its paradise, regarding flight as the more truly human course:

... Why does the painting of any paradise or utopia, in heaven or on earth, awaken such longings for ... escape? The white-robed, harp-playing heaven of our sabbath schools, and the lady-like, tea table elysium represented in Mr. Spencer's *Data of Ethics*, as the final consummation of progress are simply on a par in this respect ... *tedium vitae* is the only sentiment they awaken in our breast.[32]

This is a sentiment to which some of Dante's readers may have succumbed, however guiltily, as they progress from the excitements of Hell to the beatific tranquillity of Paradise, and which is succinctly expressed in Goethe's claim that 'nothing is harder to bear than a succession of fair days',[33] and which finds numerous echoes elsewhere in literature.

Now Marx's utopian vision is clearly not quite that of Mr Spencer, but his expositors have not served him well to the extent that they tend to close down the gap between the two. As we have seen, there are at least two strands of thought intertwined in Marx's dicta about human needs, and one of these — which I have characterised as the 'progressive' discourse, and which I have also argued is predominant — would seem to espouse a much more dynamic conception of human fulfilment than the harmonious contentment of the communist utopia sometimes ascribed to him would suggest. In fact, the idea of an unlimited expansion of needs is clearly much more in line with the energetic strivings of Eros than with the retreat to the comforts of a mere self-preservation that is counselled by Thanatos. But equally, the other and subordinate strand in his thought — the theory of the reproduction of self through a presupposed existence — would seem closer in conception to Freud's portrayal of the Death instinct, for it would seem that it is in terms of the promptings of this, rather than of Eros, that we might understand the non-dynamic, simple reproduction of needs which the 'regressive' discourse asks us to contemplate.

One cannot help, in fact, being struck by the correspondence between this Freudian dualism and the antithetical strands of Marx's discourse about needs. It is a correspondence which I have also suggested holds to some degree in the case of Rousseau's dualism of *amour propre* and *amour de soi.*[34] But I would not want to push the parallels too far, nor would I want to make any exaggerated claims about the enlightenment they introduce. My main purpose in citing them, and in dwelling at the length I have upon the comparison between the Rousseauesque and the Freudian 'models' of psychic conflict, is to bring out the duality that lies at the heart of Marx's forays into psychology, and to lend conviction to my original claim that Marx is far from consistent on the matter and that his supposed 'solutions' to the question of human needs serve to expose more fully the complex dimensions of that question.

6.   Freud and Marx — a difference in project

It remains to comment briefly, by way of a footnote to this chapter, on a point which I think is pertinent both to the particular comparison that I have drawn between Freud's and Marx's views on human society, and to any attempt to compare them. This concerns the difference in the enterprise in which they were respectively engaged. For insofar as Freud indulges in speculation about the nature of civilisation in general, I think it has to be accepted that, whatever opinion one holds of his views on that issue, he was motivated by a desire to explain why it had taken the form that it had, and that from that standpoint an explanation in terms of class struggle would not have satisfied him, the fact that civilisation had proceeded on a basis of class exploitation being itself regarded as an explanandum.

In other words, it should be recognised that Freud was engaged in an enquiry more fundamental than that of Marx, an enquiry into the psychological determinants upon the very form itself of human development, and as such unsatisfiable by any appeal to the effects of that form upon human psychology. If it is true that history hitherto has been the history of class struggle, it is only true because history has been the history of an ever-expanding consumption and objectification. Now if what is sought is some explanation of the initial motives for such expansion and object-ification, then it might well be argued that explanations in terms of the fact that it has always taken place through the vehicle of class struggle are not in themselves sufficient. Moreover, it is not even as if the fact that human objectification has always proceeded on that basis can be adequately explained in terms of external constraints. It is true that there are some thinkers (Marcuse, for example, and also Sartre) who would put a great deal of weight on scarcity as the explanation of class struggle, thus assuming that had nature proved more bountiful the expansion of consumption could have proceeded undivisively since the satis-factions of one group would never have required deprivations on the part of another (an assumption, incidentally, from which it would appear to follow that in a society of abundance the abolition of classes will not be a political but a scientific achieve-ment). But this appeal to scarcity is quite counter to the Marxist account of the matter, where division into classes is attributed to the forceful appropriation by one social grouping of the *surplus* product, and therefore, more fundamentally, to the fact that human.labour can, and, save for certain peripheral exceptions, has always been able to do more than reproduce itself. In other words, it is not the scarcity of social wealth but the unequal distribution of the aggregate social wealth at any given epoch that is reflected in class society, so that to understand that history is a history of class struggle is to understand that it is a history of exploitation, of the elitist appropriation of the surplus of others' labour. But that, of course, implies that the responsibility lies not with nature but with man; and that in turn prompts questions as to why human development has proceeded on an exploitative basis and not via an egalitarian distribution of an ever-expanding, if always (from the standpoint of a subsequent epoch) 'limited' wealth. What is it in human beings that both seeks this dominance over others and is prepared to submit to it?

Whatever we think of the Freudian 'solutions' to such questions, we must admit, I think, that it was these that concerned him, and that Marxist solutions in terms of the evil effects on human nature of bourgeois society would not have satisfied an urge to discover why human society developed its bourgeois form. It is these kinds of question that Marxists today need to confront with more courage and less fears about their heresy. When the motor of history is ticking over quietly in unison with the machinery of its oppression and potential destruction, and a significant element of the authentic force of social emancipation is pouring scorn on the credos of its theoretical mouthpiece, and resisting their implement- ation, the time has perhaps come to think more critically about the faith and to be less self-critical about doing so. Nor can this mean shifting the whole burden of explanation on to the concept of 'ideology' viewed as an essentially objective force of mystification pre-empting the proletariat from realising its task and destiny. The world is certainly deceptive to the beholder, and Marx and other thinkers have enormously advanced our understanding of the ways in which it is; less attention has been paid to what it is about the beholder subjectively that allows, encourages and may even prefer deception. Why is a world that is so 'clearly' intoler- able in so many respects so extensively tolerated? Any answer to this question must begin, I suggest, by querying the correctness of formulating it in that manner. For perhaps part of the answer to it lies in the fact that it is no longer so *clearly* intolerable. Traditionally the struggle of the workers has been a struggle against the material conditions of their existence with the emphasis upon the deprivation of material needs, and social revolution has tended to come in answer to extremes of poverty and oppression and non-fulfilment of the most basic 'physical' wants. Today, however, in an advanced industrial country such as Britain, the relatively high material standard of living enjoyed by the majority of workers has reduced the urgency of their 'need' for revolution and blurred its clarity. The deprivations that are suffered are arguably just as great and the oppression just as brutal, but they are less tangible and for that very reason less obviously felt. If you are deprived of food, you feel the pangs of hunger; if you are deprived of love, or of opportunities for creative activity, or of the space and time that are preconditions of any self-development, you do not so much feel the loss as lose the power to feel — you become the victim of a vicious regress, caught up in a process that numbs sensitivity in the very act of depriving it. If we accept, then, as I do, that contemporary 'advanced' society deprives the mass of people of such 'immaterial' sources of gratification in equal or even greater measure than it deprives them of fulfilment of material needs, then this poses specific problems for the standpoint of social revolution. One of the most daunting of these, I suggest, lies in the fact that psychological deprivation of this kind is felt less urgently the more extensive it becomes, since it is part of the process of deprivation that one loses the power to feel that anything is urgent. In this sense, non-fulfilment of these psychological needs tends to be self-sustaining and self-perpetuating: it breeds not indignation, but apathy, and a sense of the futility of any political initiative. If, in the face of this process, the Left continues to retreat to the safety of orthodoxy, and to confine itself to appeals to 'the dictatorship of the proletariat', it will do little, I suspect, to reverse it.

Notes

1 S. Timpanaro, *On Materialism*, London, New Left Books, 1975; see especially Chap. 1, and cf. Chap. 11 of *The Freudian Slip* by the same author, London, New Left Books, 1976.

2 J.-J. Rousseau, *Discourse on Inequality*, London, Everyman, 1973, p. 66.

3 *Ibid.*

4   See A. Collier, 'On the Production of Moral Ideology', *Radical Philosophy*, No. 9, 1974.

5   On this 'ambiguity', see the interesting comments of A. O. Lovejoy, *Reflections on Human Nature*, Baltimore, John Hopkins, 1961, p. 110f., and his discussion of what he terms the human trait of 'approbativeness' (susceptibility to pleasure in the judgements of others) and its various manifestations, *ibid.*, pp. 65-245.

6   F. Nietzsche, *The Genealogy of Morals*, New York, Doubleday, 1956, p. 147f.

7   A. Collier, *art. cit.*

8   F. Nietzsche, *op. cit.*, p. 171.

9   Plato, *Phaedo*, XV, 71.

10 A. O. Lovejoy, *op. cit.*, p. 127.

11 F. Nietzsche, *op. cit.*, p. 221.

12 This is a form of argument that it also employed in the *Critique of the Gotha Programme*, on which see Chap. 9.

13 Cf. on this point the very persuasive comments of C. Castoriadis, *The Crossroads in the Labyrinth*, Sussex, Harvester Press, (forthcoming), Chapter on 'Value, Equality, Justice and Politics'.

14 S. Freud, *Two Principles of Mental Functioning*, Standard Edition, *op. cit.*, Vol. 12, p. 225.

15 H. Marcuse, *Eros and Civilisation*, London, Abacus, 1972, see especially Part I and Part II, Chap. 6. Cf. J.-P. Sartre, who also attributes the existence of class to a 'world too poor for the satisfaction of human needs without constant constraint, renunciation and delay' and thus regards Marxism itself as only relevant to the understanding of such a world and as itself transcended with the transcendence of the world of scarcity (*The Problem of Method*, London, Methuen, p. 34).

16 H. Marcuse, *op. cit.*, Part II, especially Chap. 9.

17 See, for example, A. Collier, *art. cit.*

18 This is the shift of emphasis I find implied in an interesting article by D. Ingleby (a re-worked version of which, entitled 'Psychoanalysis and Ideology' is shortly to appear in *Towards a Critical Development Psychology*, ed. J. M. Broughton.) It should be said, however, that Ingleby's argument is primarily directed against the possibility of any 'integration' of Freudianism *as it stands* with Marxism, since he regards the former as thought within and reproducing the ideological perspective on nature and culture, and on the relations between individual and society, that is the subject of Marx's critique.

19 S. Freud, 'Dissection of the Personality', *New Introductory Lectures*, Pelican Freud Library, Harmondsworth, Penguin, 1973, p. 108.

20 *Ibid.*

21 *Ibid.*, pp. 110-11.

22 Commenting on an earlier draft of this chapter, in which I myself had tended to under-play the importance and necessity of the Super-Ego.

23 S. Freud, *Beyond the Pleasure Principle*, Standard Edition, *op. cit.*, Vol. 18, p. 36; cf. p. 18f.

24 S. Freud, *Civilisation and its Discontents*, Standard Edition, *op. cit.*, Vol. 21, p. 113.

25   *Ibid.*, pp. 113–14.

26   *Ibid.*, pp. 121–22.

27   Not, perhaps, that one should place too much weight on this argument, inconsistency of this kind being so typical of Freud; or rather, what is typical is the mild hypocrisy with which the qualification or counter-argument is offered, since Freud himself has no real doubts as to the correctness of his claim. In marked contrast, I think, is the integrity of his hesitations in *The Interpretation of Dreams*.

28   This, of course, is the theme developed by H. Marcuse, whose view of the relation between Pleasure Principle and Reality Principle is no doubt closer to that of this Freudian perspective upon it than is that of the antithetical interpreation. Accepting the negativity of Freud's judgement on the Reality Principle, Marcuse rejects only the assumption that it is necessary. He then, of course, has to confront the problem posed to his theory of the liberating and essentially humane forces of the Id by the supposition of the Death instinct — which he does by absorbing it into Eros. But whether or not we are prepared to accept Freud's hypothesis of a separate instinct of aggression, or even to accept that our instinctual life is characterised as much by a conservative urge for quiescence (for the inertia of the inorganic) as by the progressive urge of Eros, there can be no doubt that Freud would not have allowed the dominance of the Pleasure Principle, associated as it always is with the mere freedom from unpleasure prompted by the Death instinct, to be incontrovertibly desirable from the standpoint of humanity. Any attempt, therefore, to reconcile Freudianism with an optimistic conception of human potentialities on the basis of the triumph of Pleasure Principle must do violence to Freud's conception of the latter. For if it would retain the distinction between the two, the negative, inertial, aspect of the Pleasure Principle must be discounted in favour of its 'truer' and more creative representative, the mental forces of fantasy (which, incidentally, must be allowed a much more substantial capacity for objective change than the notion of hallucinatory pleasure suggests); alternatively, if the dominance of the Pleasure Principle is actually conceived in terms of the emergence of a different 'non-repressive' Reality Principle, then Pleasure Principle and Reality Principle are in effect identified, and the original Freudian duality is spirited out of existence.

29   We should note, however, that even this remark is pretty tentative, and off-set by others elsewhere about the superiority of 'real change in the relations of human beings to possessions' over the commands of ethical systems, and by Freud's ultimate refusal to express an opinion one way or the other upon the value of human civilisation — and that in 1931, when its prospects scarcely looked very rosy. Given its even less rosy prospects today, and the submissive posture it seems for the most part prepared to adopt to the possibility of the final holocaust, one cannot escape the depressing thought that, were he alive today, he might have fewer qualms in committing himself to a definite opinion. What is certain is that anyone who is tempted at the present time to indulge in general speculations about the nature and course of civilisation must find the Freudian conception of the Death instinct almost too painfully apt and importunate. Less speculatively, and

even more distressingly, E. P. Thompson has recently found it necessary to invoke the concept of 'exterminism' (see 'Notes on Exterminism, the Last Stage of Civilisation', New Left Review, 1980, No. 121).

30   S. Freud, *Civilisation and its Discontents*, *op. cit.*, p. 145.

31   *Ibid.*, p. 76.

32   W. James, 'The Dilemma of Determinism' in the *Will to Believe and other Essays on Popular Philosophy*, New York, Longman, 1897, p. 167.

33   Goethe, *Weimar*, 1810–12 — the lines are cited by Freud himself in *Civilisation and its Discontents* (p. 76), though he adds that Goethe may be exaggerating.

34   A dualism which arguably can itself be translated into psychoanalytic terms, for it would appear to be quite close in conception to Freud's distinction between primary and secondary narcissism.

9 The Suppression and Emergence of a Politics of Human Needs

1. 'Distribution according to needs...': solution or problem?

Here, by way of conclusion, I propose to raise again the issue of the relationship between production and consumption, for I see it as representing the point from which almost all the issues discussed in this book diverge, and upon which they ultimately reconverge. I shall proceed in the first instance by addressing myself to a statement that no work purporting to deal with Marx on the question of human needs can reasonably fail to consider:

In a higher stage of communist society, after the enslaving subordination of the individual to the division of labour, and therewith also the antithesis between mental and manual labour have vanished; after labour has become not only the means of life but life's prime want; after the productive forces have also increased with the all-round development of the individual, and all the springs of co-operative wealth flow more abundantly — only then can the narrow horizon of bourgeois rights be crossed in its entirety and society inscribe on its banners: From each according to his ability, to each according to his needs![1]

Possibly the most famous of all Marx's statements about communist society, this is also arguably the most evasive, confused and problematic of any of the claims he makes about human needs. Indeed, the unsympathetic reader is likely to accuse it outright of circularity on the grounds that the very conditions which Marx assumes to be *prior* to any distribution according to needs themselves constitute a series of institutions that have already determined which needs there shall be distribution in accordance with, and therefore themselves comprise 'distribution according to needs'. How, in fact, can 'needs' themselves be the principle determining distribution unless some principles for determining what is to count as a need have already been decided upon?

Of course, Marx *is* assuming some such decisions to have been made (and thereby assuming certain principles as already involved in the determination of needs) when he assumes the abolition of the division of labour, the disappearance of the mental-manual antithesis, the establishment of labour as life's 'prime want', the increase in the development of the productive forces responsible for 'abundance' and the all-round development of the individual, to be the conditions of a 'higher' stage of existence. But in arguing that these conditions are the *presuppositions* of a full satisfaction of needs, Marx suggests that it is only a society that has transcended the need to evaluate its needs or to determine them in any fashion that can allow for any full satisfaction of needs. He is here assuming, then, that the superior 'value' of the higher stage of communist society lies precisely in the fact that it will no longer be constrained by the need to adopt any policy upon needs, since the needs of its individuals will do the job for it. Here we encounter, in highly condensed form, that same tension which runs right through Marx's account between the fact that he must make certain implicit judgements upon human needs, and his reluctance to be involved in any such judgements. In arguing that all the achievements (the abolition of the division of labour, and so on) that themselves incorporate a policy on human needs and are underpinned by certain judgements about what is 'good' for society, are mere *pre-conditions* of the satisfaction of needs, Marx is enabled to evade the question of the policy of needs to be pursued by any fully realised communist society, and to avoid any evaluation of *what it is* that society should harness and distribute its social wealth in accordance with. It looks, then, as if one crosses the 'narrow horizon of bourgeois right' only when one has avoided the constraint of any political decisions whatsoever. But at that point, one wonders if one is still in the terrain of *human* society — of that society whose distinguishing characteristic it is, as Marx himself often enough insists, to be *political*. One writer, commenting on the 'solution' offered in this passage from the *Critique of the Gotha Programme*, has profound doubts on the matter:

We may well ask whether this 'solution' of the problem does not amount, in large measure, to a suppression of the conditions under which such a problem will exist, and whether Marx's 'answer' does not in truth state that the only way in which the question of justice (or in other words of politics) can be resolved is through the creation of conditions under which that question will no longer be posed. Is not the apparently 'impregnable' character of Marx's answer accountable precisely to its *mythical* content? When he aims to 'cross the narrow horizon of bourgeois right in its entirety', is he not really aiming to escape from right as such (as indeed he expressly states on several occasions), and to dissolve the law away altogether onto the actual behaviours of individuals, to eliminate any gap between private and public and between the society which institutes and society as instituted, and to return to some (supernatural) 'naturality' of man by which, having escaped from the bonds of 'abstraction', he would become immediately a concrete universal, or, in Marx's own phrase, 'total man'?[2]

Yet, 'mythical' as it may be, Marx's solution has all too often been accepted precisely as a solution, and indeed heralded as one of the most enlightened statements ever made on the subject of social justice. And for that reason alone it would seem mistaken to dismiss it over-hastily. Moreover, there is surely something quite correct and enlightened about Marx's view of what does constitute an equitable society, and why it does, even if there is something profoundly mystifying about the notion that this can be achieved through a 'distribution according to needs'.

Where Marx is enlightened, of course (though he is not alone in being so[3]), is in seeing that a truly just or equitable society cannot be a society that treats its members as equal. Or rather, a just society only treats its members as socially equal when it treats them as naturally unequal. All societies that have not yet crossed the horizon of bourgeois right (and these include first stage communism, or socialism) are, on this criterion, less that equitable, since in treating of individuals as naturally equal they deny them social equality. Marx's basic argument, then, is that any society which distributes its social wealth in proportion to the labour contributed by each individual will be guilty of an unfair distribution since individuals are unequal in their capacities and differ in their needs. Now the injustice of capitalist society is, of course, doubly compounded in this respect, for although the principle of the 'fair and equal' exchange between the labourer and the capitalist appears to accord with the principle 'to each according to his labour' the wage that is paid to the labourer in this 'fair and equal' exchange in fact conceals an appropriation of the latter's labouring capacity. Capitalist society is therefore based not only on an unfair principle of social distribution, but upon an unfair application of that self-same principle. But even socialist society, while it constitutes an undeniable advance in justice, since individuals would in fact under socialist relations be paid or rewarded in accordance with their labour capacity, yet remains unfair precisely to the extent that it continues to base its distribution of wealth upon that principle. Hence the necessity to replace this proportionality (between the labour in-put and the return for it) by a dis-proportionality (whereby each contributes whatever (s)he is able and receives 'in return' whatever (s)he may need). In other words, the equitable society is one in which there is no longer any commensurability between 'what is put in' and 'what is got back': the 'in return' is precisely not a commensurate 'return' and there is no longer any calculus of in-puts and rewards.

So far, then, so good: if one accepts that there are natural inequalities between individuals one is bound to accept Marx's claim that any distribution of social wealth that overrides these natural inequalities, and therefore treats individuals as if they were equal, is bound to be less than fair and equitable. But is one bound to accept that questions of 'right' are no longer relevant where proportionality has ceded to disproportionality? What is it that underlies the attempt to correct the inequalities of the proportional distribution unless it be a concept of the rights of individuals? And this concept, it would seem, is not something quite other than the bourgeois concept: one would only insist that distribution according to need must replace distribution according to labour if one was already inspired by the conviction that individuals had a right to be treated equally — which is precisely what the bourgeois principle, *as a principle*, and in distinction to any application of it, insists. Distribution according to needs is not the abolition or transcendence of this right, but its concrete realisation, since persons unequal in their capacities and needs are rendered equivalent through the difference in their respective share of the total social wealth.

But it is at this point, of course, that we confront the major problem in Marx's 'solution'. For this fundamental belief in the equality that should be achieved, and can only be achieved, on the basis of treating persons unequally in terms of the proportion between labour in-put and rewards, presumes a common agreement as to what constitutes the 'natural' inequalities between persons, and some 'measure' by reference to which they can be judged 'unequal'. And here Marx's argument appears to be quite circular, for you 'distribute according to needs' in order to *correct* the 'natural' inequalities that a merely egalitarian distribution leaves intact; but then the only concept we are offered with which to understand and assess these 'natural inequalities' is the concept of a difference in needs, that difference being determined not relative to any common agreement as to what constitutes needs, but simply reflecting a difference in the 'nature' of the individuals. The point, here, is that it is only if it has been determined *socially, institutionally*, what constitutes a natural inequality, that it becomes meaningful to speak of 'differences' between individuals relative to it, and that there is anything 'in accordance' with which distribution is made and the equalisation of individuals effected. But if it is left to the individuals themselves to 'judge' of their needs, then they can judge what they like, and there is no guarantee at all that distribution according to what individuals judge to be their needs will be an equitable distribution. Even if it were conceded that individuals had some common agreement about what constituted the 'natural' differences that in turn constituted the differences in their needs, this would still presume that needs were natural properties that differed naturally between individuals; and that, of course, is a presumption that we would be a little reluctant to ascribe to Marx. In other words, is Marx here flying in the face of all his own arguments about the 'historic' nature of our needs, about their socially instituted content, about the dominance of the role of production in developing needs, in order to tell us that, after all, under communism, 'needs' are pre-found as natural givens marking the differences between persons, each of whom will be the autonomous possessor of his or her needs, and all of whose needs conjointly will determine, rather than flow from, the process of production and its sytem of distribution?

However 'good' the intention of Marx's dictum about 'distribution according to need', and however much one may applaud the spirit in which it is offered, there can be little doubt of its incoherence from the standpoint of his own rigorously anti-essentialist position on the nature and formation of needs, and his own insistence on the 'historically developed' and socially, rather than individually, determined character of human needs. Here again, one might quote C. Castoriadis:

Do we not find ourselves supposing these 'needs' to be fixed, definite, or else supposing that their development takes place in accordance with a naturality (an 'all-round development') which requires no commentary? Are we not taking them to be by definition indisputable, mutually compatible, *good*? But are needs in fact *physei* or *nomou*, natural or instituted? If they are *nomou* (as, trivialities apart, they are), if every need is socially instituted, then what does it mean, even with reference to the 'means of consumption', to say 'to *each* according to *his* needs'? . . . Contemporary societies — American, French, Russian, Chinese — create, in the breasts of the off-spring of the dominant classes, the 'need' for a private plane, a villa in Saint-Tropez, a *dacha* . . . : to each according to their needs?[4]

Well, no, of course not; and Castoriadis is somewhat disingenuous in his suggestion that Marx intends his claim to have meaning for any but a classless society. But this should not obscure the fact that it leaves the main point unresolved: *what* needs? And there is, of course, a parallel incoherence in the notion of 'from each according to his capacities' for the capacity to labour is, as Marx is himself the first to insist, in every importantly differentiating sense, socially and not genetically determined. Differences in physical strength, patience, endurance and so on between individuals are as nothing compared to the difference in 'capacity' that results from the social organisation of work, and the technologies in which labour power is harnessed. Does it indeed make sense to talk of 'from each according to his capacities' in a society where any individual capacity is a function of the collective capacity for labour, and where what each can perform is dependent upon what every other collectively and co-operatively performs? In other words, any individual's labouring capacity, so far from being a natural, pre-given capacity, will depend almost entirely on the nature of the labour-process in which that individual is engaged, and it is this labour process and its technology that fixes the capacity of any individual contributing to it. But if the capacities of any individual are primarily socially determined, then the contribution of each individual must itself become a social rather than an individual decision. It will be the task of society itself to determine what individuals both in general, and as particular individuals, should be expected to do. One individual is 'naturally' capable of keeping pace with the speed at which the assembly line happens to have been fixed, while her companion is equally 'naturally' incapable of doing so, and both of them, of course, are contributing according to their capacities. But the real and important capacity has been fixed elsewhere — by whoever fixed the assembly line speed in the first place — and unless we are to assume that everything is fine with our two workers busily contributing as they are according to their capacities, then something has to be done about this other 'capacity' and about the existence of the assembly line in the first place, and to be done collectively by society as a whole. In reducing differences in labour capacity to natural differences between individuals, Marx in effect evades all the really crucial *political* questions about what it is *reasonable* to expect individuals to do in the way of work, about what organisations of the labour process are most conducive from the standpoint of the double aim of producing 'in abundance' and avoiding 'mental and physical degradation', about what human beings need, as opposed to what they are capable of, in relation to their work. (In this connection we should note that any genuine distribution according to needs would appear to involve a distribution according to what each individual needs in regard to work — the 'prime need' — but how is that to be reconciled with a contribution not according to what one might need to do, but according to what one is capable of doing?)

There is no doubt, then, that in these appeals[5] to 'distribution according to need' and 'from each according to his capacities', Marx only 'solves' the question of political justice by refusing to allow it to exist as a political question. By treating 'needs' and 'capacities' as natural, as an original, predetermined property of individuals, and by allowing them to decide *for* society what that society shall be like, Marx naturalises politics itself: the whole burden of political decision is handed back to Nature, where our 'nature' will decide what we need, and what we do will be determined by what 'nature' can do.

Yet, and at risk of repetition, it must be stressed how contrary this naturalism of needs and capacities is to the whole force of Marx's exposure of the errors of political economy and its associated 'theories of man'. For who was it, if not Marx himself, who showed us that individuals do not inherit their needs (except to a minimal degree, and even then only in the most abstract conception) in the form of a natural, biological patrimony, but acquire their needs (including the content of their 'basic' physiological and psychological needs) excentrically, and independently of their wills, through their encounter with the objective social patrimony into which they are born and through which they live out their lives? And, who, if not Marx, has shown us that an individual's capacity for work is only indirectly related to a given, physiological constitution, and is primarily to be thought in terms of the productivity of labour brought about by a given level of development of the productive forces in its unity with a particular form of social relations? In other words, as Marx himself constantly insists, one's capacity for labour is no less socially acquired than are one's needs, and it is on pain of mouthing the most 'dumb generalities' about either that one reduces them without residue to their basis in the individual, and fails to take account of the way in which social institutions have always operated upon natural 'givens' so as to create the distinctive, cultural existence that is human existence.

So, unless all this Marxist insight in quite irrelevant (or a piece of blindness) when it comes to an understanding of communist existence, then it must be acknowledged that it is communist relations of production and the institutions of a communist society that will to a very large extent determine the content of needs and capacities, neither of which can therefore be viewed as original in-puts existing prior to the institution of communist relations, these latter being regarded simply as the appropriate response to them. Just as we cannot theorise the presupposed needs of capitalist production in wholly anthropological or wholly economic terms, so likewise, it would seem, we cannot refer the explanation of the needs that are presupposed by communist production either exclusively to 'nature' or exclusively to a 'prior production'. At the very most, the notion of 'from each according to his capacities' and 'to each according to his needs' might fit a primitive communist society where needs had not expanded beyond the need for food, shelter, clothing of the crudest kind, where individuals differed in their needs only in respect of genetically determined differences in size, sex, number of off-spring dependent upon them, and where, in the absence of any technological development, labour capacity was simply a matter of physical strength and stamina, and could therefore be regarded as a natural endowment that differed naturally between individuals. But such a society, it is clear, would be a simple-reproductive society, which allowed very little individuation (precisely because the limits of variation of *natural* differences are very restricted), which would be unlikely to afford much in the way of leisure or free time, and which would know no expansion of needs. A far cry, one might think, from the 'unheard of development of the productive forces', the 'rich development of individuality' and the 'needs unmeasured by any previous yardstick' that characterise scientific communism.

2.   'Life's prime want'

In this connection, let us pause for a moment to consider Marx's claim that labour becomes 'life's prime want' from the standpoint of his characterisation elsewhere of communist society as a society distinguished by the release of the free time that in capitalist society is consumed in the production of surplus-value. For so long as the term 'labour' specifies 'work' as opposed to free time, and is taken to be the concept of an individual's in-put of time and energy in a *social* production of goods and services, as opposed to the time and energy consumed in direct, personal pursuits, then it is difficult to reconcile the notion of labour becoming life's prime want, suggestive as this is that much more time will be spent on labouring, with the notion of a society in which work is cut to a minimum and free time expanded to a maximum. What then seems to be at issue here is whether the concept of labour under communism remains in any sense specific[6] (whether, for example, it still designates a particular *form* of expenditure of time and energies in a particular *kind* of production, namely, social production), or whether it becomes a generic term for each and every activity that the individual happens to be engaged in. Even if it be allowed that the concept of the labour which becomes the 'prime want' has itself become the generic concept of everything that is done in the furtherance of self-fulfilment — in the expansion of needs — the question of its relationship to the concept of leisure, to that which is done, or more importantly, not done in 'free time' (time not spent on labour?) remains. Either there is no distinction any longer between the two, and the term 'labour' has to be understood yet even more generically as a concept of time expenditure as such, or else one retains a distinction between work and free time activities or idleness, and the relationship between them under communism remains to be explained. (Here it should be noted that the suggestion that under communism all surplus labour time increasingly comes to be necessary labour time is no solution to the problem, but merely a reformulation of it. For what Marx means by this suggestion is that an increasing proportion of social labour time will be devoted to the 'necessary means of subsistence' of the members of society — to the point, in fact, where all labour time is necessary to the reproduction of the worker. But it is precisely under such conditions that 'necessary subsistence' has come to include a vast amount of free time not spent on labour in the ordinary sense of 'work'. All social labour time becomes necessary labour time only in a society of 'richly developed' individuals, this rich development itself being dependent on the free time made available by the release from surplus labour.)

In the absence of anything more specific by way of explanation of what is meant by labour becoming life's prime want, one is bound to suspect either that 'labour' is doing duty for the concept of needs in general (in which case we are not greatly informed by being told that it becomes the prime need), or else that Marx's vision of communism is imbued with a work ethic that is insufficiently distinguished from that of bourgeois society.

Now I am not suggesting here that Marx is in some sense less than revolutionary in insisting upon the necessity of work in communist society. On the contrary, his utopian thought is realistic where that of many others is purely visionary in its recognition of the indispensability of work in all future societies, whatever 'perfection' they attain. When he tells us that no nation could survive for a day were it not to devote some time to labour he is, as he himself puts it, telling us only 'what every child knows'.[7] But there is, of course, a vast difference between assuming that some labour will be indispensable and the assumption that as society progresses towards 'perfection' labour will come to occupy an increasingly central position, to the point in fact of becoming the major need. Or, in other words, it is clear that no sense can be made of this idea unless it is further assumed that the need for work which becomes life's prime need is something so utterly different in kind from the mundane need for work that ensures a society's survival that we might want to question the reason for specifying 'labour' as the object of both these very differing needs. Now in one sense the reason is obvious enough, since from the standpoint of the labour theory of value, all time is value, and labour time is taken to be equivalent to time expended as such, and in this sense, any time expended, regardless of its crystallisation (and even if it is crystallised, so to speak, in free time), can equally be regarded as labour time. Hence, at one level, Marx's argument is perfectly consistent, but only because at that level it is also tautological, the concept of labour time being the concept of any and every expenditure of time.

But at any less abstract level, that is to say at any level at which labour time is not defined analytically in terms of time expenditure as such, and where, therefore, we allow ourselves once again to acknowledge empirical — and politically relevant — questions about the distinction between something called 'work' and something called 'free time', and about the 'ideal' proportion between the two from the standpoint of a satisfaction of human 'needs', the analytic argument that establishes the need to labour as life's prime need is utterly uninformative.

In arguing at both levels, and in not acknowledging that he does, Marx is once again inconsistent. For while from the one level it makes little sense to distinguish between labour and something which is not labour, Marx constantly places himself at the other level in order to make claims, such as that in the letter to Kugelmann cited above, about the necessity of *work* (where work means precisely the mundane business of keeping ourselves in business in order to enjoy the free time that comes our way), and in order to indulge in a number of (quite cogent) arguments about the psychology of our 'need' to work and about the ontological nature of work itself.

For how, if we place ourselves at the conceptual level at which labour is the concept of any time expenditure, are we to make sense of the argument he directs at Adam Smith for his conception of work as a 'curse':

'Tranquility' appears as an adequate state, as identical with 'freedom' and 'happiness'. It seems quite far from Smith's mind that the individual 'in his normal state of health, strength, activity, skill, facility', also needs a normal portion of work, and of the suspension of tranquility.[8]

In arguing here (and quite correctly so it seems to me) that the need to work is a quite distinct need, whose 'neediness' is a function of another, again quite distinct need, to rest, or not to work, Marx is here quite at odds with any assumption about the *primacy* of the need to work or about all time becoming necessary labour time. And when he distinguishes the pleasure of work precisely in terms of the toil and effort it requires, and argues that it cannot be made into 'fun' or 'mere amusement' as Fourier 'with *grisette*-like naivety, conceives it', since 'really free working, e.g. composing, is at the same time precisely the most damned seriousness, the most intense exertion',[9] he is himself engaged in a serious empirical and politically relevant discussion of the nature of work, and is drawing pertinent and important distinctions between it and 'free time', or idleness, or respite from work.

Unless, then, we relegate it to the level of vacuous tautology, the notion of labour being life's prime want is simply a muddle, and, furthermore, runs counter to many more subtle and incisive insights that Marx offers elsewhere upon the need to work, where he shows, for example, that the need to work and the pleasures it affords can never be isolated from the context of human needs and activities as a whole. If the effort involved in work is intrinsic to the pleasure it provides, that is only so because it exists in a relationship of contrast to the specific pleasures and pains of idleness and play. It is impossible to divorce the 'need to work' from other needs and still regard it in any informative sense as a 'need'. For that reason, it cannot be elevated above all other needs upon which it depends for its very existence as a need.

Accepting what I have referred to as Marx's empirical-psychological commentary on the nature of work and of our need to engage in it as a fruitful basis for thinking about the division of time socially and individually in an ideal society, it would seem to suggest some such picture as the following: every member of society will be required to devote a certain proportion of waking time to the work that is essential to the reproduction of society as a whole. It will be work devoted to the material production of the means of production and of the means of consumption (though both these will increasingly take the form of 'immaterial' goods and services catering to a wide range of cultural and educational needs). For the sake of argument, we might suggest that it will engage any individual for four hours per day, or two-three days of every week, or one week out of every month. This work will, ideally, itself have become a pleasure, gratifying our creative needs and our urge to devote ourselves to occupations requiring toil, effort and concentration. Relative to the time engaged in this work, the remainder of the individual's time will be 'rest' time or free time; but it will nonetheless be time that the individual can divide between 'work' and 'rest', a certain proportion of it — and maybe even most of it — being devoted to activities which, in involving toil, effort and the 'pains' and 'frustrations' of creativity, will *satisfy* the need to work and afford the *pleasures* that alone ensue from it.

Now it seems clear, once the issue is set up in those terms, that the conditions of realisation of this highly desirable society are not any abstract change in our attitude to work or any metaphysical alteration that it undergoes simply by virtue of being pursued under communist relations; they are absolutely concrete conditions, the first, and possibly the most important and difficult to fulfil, being communal agreement upon what constitutes a 'decent and humane' level of existence in the material sense, or in other words a decision upon the limitations to be imposed on material consumption. Here, from the standpoint of the 'civilising' influence of capitalist development of the productive forces, the pertinent concepts will be those precisely not of expansion and development, but those of 'retrenchment', of a 'simple' rather than 'expanded' reproduction, and even possibly of 'sacrifice', and I suggest that a genuine and realistic socialist politics must begin to talk in terms of 'civilising limits' and to recognise, and argue for, the *curbs* and *restrictions* upon material consumption that are a condition of the expanded consumption of free time and of the kind of consumption and production that free time alone permits.

The second condition is a radical transformation of the kinds of occupations in which individuals are required to engage, and of the socal organisation of labour. This, it seems, is primarily a technical rather than a political task; if we grant, that is to say, the common commitment of society to the attainment of certain goals (of which the most relevant here would be to permit as many as possible to gain as much pleasure as possible from the work they were required to contribute to the reproduction of society), then the only question that remains is how, concretely, this change in occupations can be achieved. It is a question about the material nature of the labour process, and of the different forms it could take, the alternative technologies upon which it might be based; and it is a question about the possibilities and limits of change to the division of tasks within any given labour process and likewise of changes to the hierarchical structure of distinctions between 'mental' and 'manual' labour which all existing technologies incorporate and reproduce. It is a question that is so profoundly difficult to resolve and so profoundly practical, that one would, I think, have to deem it unrecognised by a Marxism that continues to refer us to a future state where division of labour has been abolished and the 'mental' and 'physical' distinction eradicated.

Nor, clearly, is it a question simply of producing analogies for the 'desired' effects of altered technologies when the real question relates to the possibility of introducing those effects into labour processes whose products are utterly different in kind from the products of the labour processes of individual creations — whose products, for example, are steel girders and telecommunications systems, not symphonies or dissertations. In this respect, the analogy with the composition of music is less than convincing. Marx tells us that labour concerned with material production can only have the quality of creative and artistic labour if (i) it is of a social nature and (ii) it has a scientific character and is at the same time general work, i.e., if it ceases to be human effort as a definite, trained natural force, gives up its purely natural aspects and becomes the activity of a subject controlling all the forces of nature in the production process.[10] But, prima facie, nothing seems more at odds with this social, general, non-definite and all controlling form of work, then the highly individualistic, highly specific, and artistic rather than scientific character of the work involved in writing a symphony. The pleasures involved in the labour of composing music are understandable enough; what is less understandable is how they are introduced into forms of production that have nothing in common with the writing of music. Marx attempts to bridge the gap in comprehension by asking us in effect to imagine material production in the form of music production, but the sceptic is sceptical precisely on account of the difficulty in doing so.

All this invites a direct confrontation with the vexed question of the eradication of the division between mental and manual labour. It is a question far too complex for me to do justice to it here, even if I felt capable of doing so. Suffice it to say here merely that this distinction is not a product of capitalist society but as much a mark of 'civilisation' as is the oppression of women. One must distinguish, therefore, between 'altering' the system of values wherein society at large has tended to relate to intellectual activity as a superior and more intrinsically 'human' form of activity, and an alteration in the existing pattern of distribution of knowledge or 'intellectuality' and in the system of rewards which privileges its possessors and, at the best, merely compensates in material ways for those deprived of its benefits. It is difficult to understand what the first alteration might involve, and it is not, in any case, at all obvious that it is desirable. The second alteration, however, despite the enormity of the difficulties of achieving it — since it would involve massive alteration to the contemporary division of labour and distribution of social wealth, and disruption of a social system of inheritance of knowledge that is so fixed and deeply entrenched that it appears to be a product of nature itself — is an indisputable political option, and were it to be 'chosen' much could be done to put it into effect. At the same time, however, it must be remembered that any alteration of this latter kind will also entail an alteration in our very idea of what constitutes knowledge at the present time, and in our privileging of scientific knowledge over all other forms of intellectual activity. Rudolf Bahro is to be applauded for the manner in which he directly confronts the problem of the division of labour and the associated mental-manual distinction, and for offering a definite programme whereby it might be overcome.[11] But to the extent that he suggests the solution lies in allowing everyone to acquire the level of knowledge and expertise that is currently the exclusive property of elite groups, he tends to assume that this knowledge is itself a 'neutral' property that does not bear the marks of its elitist production and transmission. But the very content of science, the very nature of knowledge, are like everything else in our society, 'products' to a significant degree of the system of social relations in which they exist and whose interests they serve. In this sense, the communalisation of knowledge would seem to be necessarily linked with the emergence to prominence of knowledges that are able to recognise and explain the relationship between a given form of society and what it produces and recognises as 'knowledge' — and these knowledges will have themselves to be a communal property.

3. 'Planning to meet needs'

I suggested above that at the level at which Marx can consistently (though vacuously from the standpoint of any concrete political programme) argue for all labour becoming necessary labour, and for labour itself becoming life's 'prime want', the concept of labour time is the concept of time expenditure as such. I now want to amplify on this remark, and in doing so relate some of the themes (and their difficulties) of the *Critique of the Gotha Programme* to the equally celebrated characterisation of socialist and communist society as a society that 'plans to meet needs':

It is only where production is under the actual, predetermining control of society that the latter establishes a relation between the volume of social labour-time applied in producing definite articles, and the volume of the social want to be satisfied with these articles.[12]

(Under socialism) the social anarchy of production gives place to a social regulation of production upon a definite plan, according to the needs of the community and of each individual.[13]

The apportionment of labour time (in the society of free individuals) in accordance with a definite social plan maintains the proper proportion between the different kinds of work to be done and the various wants of the community.[14]

If the transition to socialism is the transition to a planned and rational allocation of social labour time in accordance with social needs; if it is not based on a 'plan' merely in the sense of an abstract imposition of certain goals by a central authority in the name of a collective people, but is genuinely planned in the sense that it operates in accordance with the development of the productive forces;[15] and if the possibility and desirability of such an economy derives from a real knowledge of social needs and recognition of the priority to be accorded them, then it is a transition that is made in awareness of the objective economic laws that govern any social production. These laws have emerged from their ideological concealment by the 'laws' of the market and are consciously recognised by the agents of production who plan their acts in accordance with them. At the same time, the category of 'social needs' emerges from the subordinate position it occupies in the analysis of capitalist production — where, in relation to the productive aim, needs are mere means towards the end of realising and accumulating surplus-value — to the position of dominance it must occupy in the analysis of any society which makes the satisfaction of social needs the end of social production itself.

The use-value of a product is thereupon no longer reflected in the fact that it sells, in the fact that it realises exchange-value, but is directly manifested in the fact of its production, which itself is the direct social manifestation of its 'value'. This is a 'value' which derives from the existence of the need for it. The existence of a need for a product becomes its social 'value'; or, in other words, 'need' displaces 'value' in that the *a priori* assessment of needs takes the place of the *a posteriori* adjustment of production to consumption made via the exchange on the market. Whereas, under capitalism, the use-value of a product is revealed in its exchange-value, under socialism this use-value is revealed in the allocation of social labour time to its production. Labour under socialism, therefore, is not related to as 'exchange-value', but as time expended, and the expenditure of time and social needs exist in a relationship of mutual determination: the allocation of labour time to the production of x, accords x the status of a need; the need for x determines the allocation of labour time to its production.

Under socialism, or first stage communism, where distribution is still according to labour, the members of society and its production generally are still dominated by the labour theory of value in that it is the labour time crystallised in the product (rather than any other aspect of it) which appears as what is significant about it, and which gives it is social existence and commensurability. But under communism proper, where distribution is supposedly according to need, presumably what will predominate in the way that the members of society assess their production, will be not so much the labour time involved in producing x as the fact that x is needed; and since an individual's 'value' will no longer depend on how much work (s)he does, nor on the particular quality and quantity of it (s)he fed into the system, labour power must cease to be related to as a 'special commodity' and labour time must cease to be a measure of value.

Another way of stating this point is in terms of the disappearance of the concept of value itself. The difficulty of conceptualising this disappearance is, of course, directly related to the difficulty we experience in giving solid content to Marx's statements about distribution according to need, about the rich development of individuality, about the nature and role of labour in communist society and about the relationship of the social individual to work in that society. This inconceivability of the disappearance of the concept of value is, in a sense, expressed by Marx himself in his claim that the wealth of a future society is 'the development of all human powers as such... not as measured on a *predetermined yardstick*' (my emphasis), since what he appears to have in mind here is a society whose members no longer relate to their own production, to each other as producers, and to the exchange of products, in terms of measurement of any kind.

Measurement presumes that it is possible to evaluate intrinsically different objects in terms of a third which is common to both, and it is that alone which makes the concept of value possible. It arises with exchange, and with the apparent necessity for exchanges to be equal. Whether they are in fact equal or not by their own standard of measurement is irrelevant: what is important is that the exchangers both deem their exchange to be 'fair and equal'. The exchange of capital with labour, is, for example, an equal exchange in terms of the ideology of capitalism — to effect the exchange both parties must share this ideology and relate to money as the common third between them which enables the exchange to take place. Marx exposes the actual inequality of the exchange by showing how the third which both parties believe to be the basis of their exchange, conceals the real third by reference to which the exchange is equalised — labour-time; but he can only expose it as unequal by reference to a notion of fairness or equality which is in turn dependent upon measurement of some kind, and that measurement in its turn is only sustained by the existence socially of a value relationship. Marx himself, of course, realises this when he writes in the *Critique of the Gotha Programme* that:

... labour, to serve as a measure, must be defined by its duration or intensity, otherwise it ceases to be a standard of measurement. This *equal* right is an unequal right for unequal labour. It recognises no class differences, because everyone is only a worker like everyone else; but it tacitly acknowledges unequal privileges. *It is therefore a right of inequality, in its content, like every right.* Right, by its very nature, can consist only in the application of an equal standard; but unequal individuals (and they would not be different individuals if they were not unequal) are measurable only by an equal standard insofar as they are brought under an equal point of view, are taken from one definite side only.[16]

Hence, as he goes on to say, where distribution is still according to labour, the equal right is in principle bourgeois right 'though principle and practice are no longer at loggerheads, while the exchange of equivalents in commodity exchange only exists *on the average* and not in the individual case'.

But where distribution is according to need, labour is no longer related to as the value of products; it ceases to be the measure for comparing or assessing their worth — or, if preferred, assessment, comparison, *measurement* of goods and services against each other (and, of course, also of the labour contribution of individuals) ceases to take place; and with the disappearance of the relation to products in terms of a common standard — in terms of their being taken from 'one definite side only' — the value relation disappears: the 'equal point of view' disappears, and is replaced by a relationship to products which sees them not from one definite, one-sided aspect, but in their multifaceted and specific individuality; in its material aspect, the product is a precise embodiment of certain raw materials fashioned in a certain way, capable of functioning in a certain manner; in its social aspect, it is seen, not as having value, but as satisfying a need (a likewise individual and specific need).

All this, of course, suggests the specificity of the law of value to the exchange economy. It might be illuminating in this connection to look at the account that Marx gives of the relationship between 'market' and 'individual' value. In *Capital* III, introducing the concept of market value, he writes:

On the one hand, market value is to be viewed as the average value of commodities produced in a single sphere, and, on the other, as the individual value of the commodities produced under average conditions of their respective sphere and forming the bulk of the products in that sphere.[17]

If we are to understand what Marx is saying here about the relationship between this market value and the individual (or 'simple' value) that has been the object of his analysis up to this point in *Capital*, then we must understand that hitherto he has been assuming that all exemplars of a given sort of product are produced under normal, average conditions (i.e., that the actual time taken in their production is the same as the socially average labour time needed for their production). Whereas in the earlier stages of his analysis, no account was taken of the difference between individual and social (market) value, account is now taken of the fact that different exemplars of a given product are produced under different conditions — and hence an opposition arises between their individual and their social value. In other words, as I. I. Rubin puts it, 'the concept of value is developed further and is defined more accurately as social or market value', and 'in the same way, *socially necessary* time opposes individual labour time which differs in enterprises of the same branch of production'.[18] In the commodity economy, that is to say, it is price which establishes the equivalence of commodities in abstraction from the quantity of individual labour expended in their production. Every individual commodity sells not according to its individual value, but according to its social value.

But this development of the concept of value appears to proceed only by way of exposing the incoherence of the concept of individual value. If 'value' is a social concept, what sense do we make of the notion of individual value? Certainly it expresses the actual labour time crystallised in the commodity, but how do we measure that labour time in terms of value? It might be thought that even if we cannot measure its type (for by its nature it is specific in terms of skill and intensity) we might be able to measure its individual quantity in terms of actual time expended. True, we can — we can say, for example, that x took 1 hour to produce — but this one hour cannot be expressed in terms of value unless we have some third (precisely 'socially necessary labour time') with which to compare it. We need a criterion in order to assign value, that is to say, a universal, a socially given common quality. So, when it comes down to it, individual value can only be measured by reference to market value, on the basis, that is to say, of how much more or less than the socially average labour time is incorporated in the product.

The concept of value, then, disappears when we no longer measure products one against the other with a view to their exchange, and the only remaining grounds upon which products can be said to have 'value' is that they each in their specific ways, and on the basis of the specific labours incorporated in them, satisfy needs. The concept of need can in this sense be said to displace that of value whenever distribution is no longer mediated through exchange (whether on the basis of money or time chits), but takes place directly, and is directed towards the satisfaction of needs. We would then speak of something being 'valuable' if it is used or consumed, if it satisfies a need.

But if we do assign value to products in this way on the basis of the extent to which they satisfy needs, it is clear that we are once again involved in an assessment relative to some common third, some universal abstraction — which in this case would be an abstract 'social need' where 'social need' would not be the Marxist concept of an aggregate of goods needed to reproduce society, but a generally and socially recognised notion of need in abstraction from individual and particular needs. It would be the common 'third' by reference to which alone there could be any assessment and quantitative and qualitative comparison between the objects of production in terms of the extent to which they satisfied needs. Marx appears to assume that a society which distributed according to needs would have dispensed with the need for any such common third, since it will be left to individuals themselves to determine their needs, and all value will be an individual, not a social, matter, and therefore not a matter of value. But what then is it that is common to the consumption of different individuals, to the share of social wealth they each respectively decide to be their 'rightful' allocation, that renders it a consumption satisfying *needs*, that 'equalises' between each share in terms of it equally being 'needed'? Whichever way we turn it about, we can make no sense of a distribution according to needs unless we assume what Marx appears precisely to want to avoid assuming by his appeal to that notion, namely, a criterion of needs, a concept of value, and thus, in turn, political decisions about what is 'good' for society and its individuals to consume, and therefore what it is *worth* it producing.

Marx, as I have tried to show throughout, is constantly making implicit decisions of this kind, yet equally constantly explicitly suggesting that they neither can nor should be made, since it must be left to our needs themselves, whether viewed as natural givens or as by-products of earlier productions, to decide upon our needs. This impasse, so striking in the case of 'distribution according to need', is the same as that which we must ultimately confront in the case of 'planning to meet needs', where again the 'solution' supposedly contained in this notion must itself be seen in terms of the problem it constructs.

Now clearly all that Marx initially intends us to understand by 'planning to meet needs' is that society, on the basis of an *a priori* assessment of existing levels of needs for the various products that form part of a historic, aggregate social consumption, allocates its body of social labour time available to the different departments and branches of production so as to produce each product in the quantity proportionate to the existing need for it. In this conception, the difference between a planned (socialist) economy and an unplanned (capitalist) economy would consist in the fact that one deliberately adjusts the expenditure of social labour time to the existing social needs, whereas in the other this adjustment only takes place in haphazard fashion, *post eventum*, through the market, where the level of need only becomes known at the point of sale. Though in both societies a presupposition of the allocation of social labour time to a particular branch of production will be the existence of a need (obviously not even the capitalist produces except on the assumption that the product will be needed, for without use-value, no exchange-value), it is only the socialist society that is able in principle to assess its needs with the precision that avoids any squandering or inadequate allocation of social labour time. Hence, despite the extent of 'planning to meet needs' under modern capitalism (both in the private sector through market research, and in the intervention of the State for political ends, the emergence of a state sector as a corrective to the destruction of its very conditions of existence that an unbridled competitive capitalism would effect, and so on), its continual tendency to proceed by way of crises, extremes of over and under production, and unemployment, whose by-product is enormous wastage of both social labour time and of resources, and a continued failure to meet quite ordinary needs.

In short, granted the existence of a dislocation between a body of needs that are felt at a given time and a body of needs in the sense of the aggregate products sold on the market at the same time, then a planned economy will be one that attempts to close the gap between the two. The very closing of this gap will effect certain changes as a by-product in patterns of consumption, firstly because products which represent 'use-value' or 'needs' because they happen to find a market (i.e., they sell below their value) even where the normal need for them has already been satisfied will simply not enter as needs into the calculations of a planned economy since they are precisely not needs from its standpoint; and secondly because there will be no space left for the play of capitalism's 'inventiveness' in the creation of new needs: all labour time expended on the production of commodities in the hope that they will elicit a hitherto 'undiscovered need' (and most of which is wasted even from the standpoint of capitalism since only a small proportion of new products actually manage to establish the required need) will be wasted from the standpoint of an economy whose 'planning' consists in the allocation of social labour time in as perfect a possible correspondence with *existing* needs. Or to put this another way: any needs that are evoked upon the appearance of a particular product could scarcely enter into any calculus of needs *prior* to production for there would be no expression of them: they would simply not feature as needs.

But it is at this point that we encounter an impasse between this construction to be put upon the notion of planning to meet needs, and an alternative, though related, construction that is necessarily put upon it by Marx's conception of socialist and communist societies as based on an expansion and elaboration of needs. For what is put on the agenda by this latter conception is not simply a 'plan' that plans to meet existing needs, but a 'plan' that plans what is going to be needed. Any society which simply planned to meet existing needs[19] would not, it would seem, be fostering the kind of qualitative elaboration of needs that Marx regards as the *sine qua non* of a properly planned, communist, society.

Granted, then, that this alternative construction is to be put upon the notion of 'planning to meet needs', what are we to make of it? Will this planning 'challenge' the existing body of needs (which of course would run counter to any planning that left them unquestioned and was simply devoted to their satisfaction)? Or would it confine itself to decisions about the employment of any social labour time still available after the satisfaction of existing needs — decisions to do with the elaboration and expansion of needs through the provision of previously non-existent products and services, rather than with any alteration to needs already felt and expressed by the members of society?

Such questions remain wholly abstract and in a sense imponder-able to the extent that a whole series of other related questions are left unanswered: who makes the decisions? On what basis? By what mechanisms? But these are questions which are inescapable for any society which is no longer even partially under the dictate of the law of value and its exchange relations, since in such a society, production becomes wholly determined by conscious, political choice, and the manner in which this is made, and by whom, become crucial issues. In other words, to escape from the dictate of the law of value, to plan to meet needs in this second sense, is to assume political responsibility for all decisions and actions relating to production. And that, in turn, means facing, fairly and squarely, the problem of the criterion of need; it involves decisions about what is 'valuable' (needed) and therefore worth producing.

There are two aspects of this question of responsibility and they are not easily reconciled. One relates to the provision and interpretation of *information* upon which decisions can be based. The other relates to the degree of social *participation* in those decisions and to the procedures for ensuring this. Insofar as concerns the aspect of information, it would seem that any attempt to alter, guide or direct patterns of human consumption must necessarily have to base itself upon a knowledge or set of beliefs about human potentialities and the conditions of human happiness. Where does one look to for that kind of knowledge? To the individuals themselves? To the human sciences? Well, no doubt to both, though in the case of both, there are specific considerations to be borne in mind. For where it is a case of providing information upon which to guide the planning of new needs that have yet to be experienced, one clearly cannot look directly to the stated needs of individuals. It will be a matter, rather, of inferring needs that are not expressly articulated, but might be argued to be implicit in their actions (or lack of action) and their stated feelings. But inferences of this kind obviously themselves rely upon, and can only be made in the light of, information provided by the human sciences, and this in turn poses the question of the selection and interpretation of such scientific evidence and of its translation into practical decisions.

The aspect of participation is equally problematic: assuming that maximum participation of all the members of society in decisions about the expenditure of labour time is the *sine qua non* of the democratically planned society, how best does one ensure this participation? How are conflicts at the level of individual needs to be reconciled? To the extent that such conflicts both reflect and are affected by different interpretations that individuals place upon the 'data' of their social lives, they appear to pose a problem of 'education', and this problem is in turn complicated by all the problems attaching to the provision of information: equal participation depends in a profound sense on equalisation of persons in terms of their possession of information and of the conceptual means for assessing it. How is this achieved, and can it be achieved compatibly with a democratic respect for what individuals feel to be true and correct? In short, is a democratic decision-making process compatible with any attempt to guide needs?

These are the kind of problems to which ultimately the conception of an expanding social production that plans to meet needs invites us to consider. They can usefully be viewed, I think, in terms of two different but interdependent aspects of the 'theory of needs' that I isolated right at the beginning of this book. The one concerns the problem of the *determination* of needs; the other the problem of their *satisfaction*. In other words, questions about how human beings come to have the needs that they are thought to have are rather different in kind from questions about how best to satisfy the needs that they ascribe to themselves or are credited with having. But the two concerns connect to the extent that human needs never exist as pure biological and psychological demands, but are themselves determined by the forms of satisfaction offered by a particular society. Human beings, that is to say, are determined by virtue of their biological and psychological constitution to experience certain 'general' needs, but the particular content those needs acquire, and the extent and the mode of their satisfaction, will be directly determined by the allocation of social labour time and the distribution of use-values in the 'society' of which they are members. Under a capitalist economy, what determines this allocation and distribution is the law of value rather than the immediate needs of individuals. But under socialism, where, ideally, there is no longer any gap or difference between the determinants upon the formation of needs and determinants upon the allocation of social labour, the conscious decision about the *satisfaction* of needs (the particular allocation of social labour time) is at the same time involved in a conscious *determination* of needs.

But lest it be thought that all this amounts to a statement of the theoretical and practical impossibility of any 'planning to meet needs', let me here also refer back to my earlier claim to the effect that an authentic politics of need consists precisely in a conscious recognition of these problems. In the light of that claim, I would want to insist here that any society that recognises *these* to be its problems, and in that sense *has* them, is fortunate indeed and its members to be greatly envied. Intransigent as they may seem, and even in a sense irresoluble, these problems can be seen in another sense to be resolved in the very process of active social confrontation with them. There is all the difference in the world between a society that suppresses the problems of the politics of need, and a society whose major concern is what to do about them.

4.   Marxism, the theory of needs, and current politics

Despite the highly critical arguments developed in the preceding sections of this chapter, I would not like to leave the reader with the impression that I have compromised on my initial positive judgement concerning the value of the terrain that Marxism provides for our thinking about human needs. For this value, I have wanted to argue, lies precisely in the extent to which it exposes, almost by way of its own internal inconsistencies, its aporia, the problems it conceals in the guise of its solutions, the inevitable involvement of questions concerned with the satisfaction of needs with questions concerned with their determination. In this, moreover, Marxism is uniquely valuable, there being no other body of thought which constructs, and rigorously pursues, the arguments which call in question and undermine the very grounds that sustain its critical force. There is no essential human nature, Marx tells us, and then proceeds to recommend a more truly human society; needs are evoked on the perception of products, Marx tells us, and then proceeds to analyse their determining influence on production; our needs are always historic and relative, Marx assures us, and then proceeds to specify our absolute needs for labour, for all-round development, for rich individuality. Capitalism's development of the productive forces is 'civilising' Marx claims, and then proceeds to develop all the arguments that allow us to understand the reasons for its incivility; scientific socialism is freed of moral judgements, Marx suggests, and then proceeds to argue the more equitable nature of socialist and communist society; concepts of the 'human' and 'inhuman' are relative to any society, says Marx, and then proceeds to damn the society that has reduced the mass of its human agents to the level of beasts. All this, it seems to me, is to his credit, since in constructing these 'contradictions' he expresses the complementary aspects that must be brought together, and must be thought in their conflictuality, whenever the question of human needs is fully and fruitfully posed. It is Marxism's value, then, to have revealed to us that this question has to be posed in the fullness of these tensions between relativism and essentialism, between 'forms' common to our needs and their irreducible 'contents', between nature and culture, between the 'natural' and the 'historic', between 'economics' and 'anthropology', between the development of science and human development, between the relative autonomies of the development of something called the productive forces and something called the relations of production, something called the 'economy' and something called the 'politics' of a society. Or, as we might say in terms of the framework established in the first chapter, it is its value to have exposed the impossibility of treating the question of human needs in any way that remains obedient to the distinction between 'facts' and 'values', means and ends. For in his consistent attempt to remain obedient to that distinction, and his equally consistent failure to manage to do so, Marx has more to tell us about our needs than any purely descriptive or purely normative account of these.

Now it might be said, I suppose, that to have exposed a truth in the very attempt to deny or evade it, is no great recommendation for a theory. But what matters, in fact, is not so much the inconsistencies of Marxism or even the extent of Marx's commitment to a positivistic view of science; what matters is that we should learn the lesson of those inconsistencies and see their implications from the standpoint of the very grounds upon which they are accounted 'inconsistencies'. More importantly, we must use them as the grounds themselves for deconstructing a political programme which quite rightly claims to have Marxist credentials — since Marx himself espoused it — but which must be understood now to be the product of a false consistency (the consistency of the fact-value distinction) which again Marx himself encourages us to attribute to Marxism. This political programme, adhered to hitherto by most of the European communist parties, is based on the assumed neutrality of the productive forces and on the related supposition that their development constitutes the essential pre-condition of the development of any authentic socialist society.

I have tried to show that any political programme of this kind — which takes itself to be 'realistic' and 'scientific' precisely because in principle it disallows itself to conduct any critique of the *nature* of the productive forces and thus of the nature of the consumption to which their development gives rise — is guilty of an evasion and suppression of the political dimension of the question of needs, and in this sense offers no political programme at all, or, if preferred, is engaged in mystifying the nature of politics. But I have also tried to show that while this political dimension can be evaded and mystified, it can never be eradicated, and that in this sense, the opting out of political responsibility for the question of needs which proceeds under cover of the argument that a 'scientific' socialism must have freed itself of an evaluation of our needs, itself constitutes a form of politics — it is itself the political dimension of any approach to the question of needs that adheres to the separation of its factual and normative dimensions. From this standpoint, a revolutionary politics that leaves the question of what we need to the solution provided by the develop-ment of the productive forces shares its politics with those who would conserve the society it wants to revolutionise — and differs only in its greater incoherence. For when it refuses to pass judgement upon the nature of the needs to which a capitalist development of the productive forces has given rise, it is recon-firming the judgement that capitalist society has itself conferred upon its productions; yet *this* judgement, concealed in this refusal to pass judgement, is utterly at odds with the implicit judgement upon human needs which alone provides the rationale for any attack upon capitalist relations of production. Or, in other words, a revolutionary politics directed purely at the means whereby a society promotes the ends of developing the productive forces is incoherent, for in the means whereby it does so a society is also determining the very content and nature of these forces — the 'needs' themselves. In this sense, it is not just the society that 'plans' to meet needs that is involved in a continual evaluation of its needs and a continual determination of the ends towards which it shall be a means, but also the society that evades the question of needs by reading its needs in what it in fact consumes, since it, too, is reconfirming the value of those needs in every act it undertakes as a means to satisfy them. For though it is true that only a society that consciously plans to meet (i.e., decide upon/determine) its needs has entered into a political engagement with the question of needs, it is also true that a society which leaves the 'planning' of its needs to the dictate of economic forces 'beyond its control' is in its particular way engaged in a politics of the suppression of the politics of needs, and a revolutionary politics must understand and make this truth explicit rather than continue to rely on the very arguments that allow it to remain concealed.

But if the attempt, whether on the right or on the left, to evade the question of human needs, or to defer it to an ever receding future, is theoretically incoherent, then we might expect the 'facts' of politics to constantly belie it. And this is precisely what we do discover. The impossibility of evading the question of human needs is finding expression today in a wide range of choosings-positings of 'value', which however uncoordinated they may be, however powerless and ineffective at the present time, are authentically political in that they directly confront the question of needs and commit themselves upon it in full recognition of the non-neutrality of the ends that supposedly make a necessity of all our current means. Worker militancy directed at the conditions, the nature and the very purpose of work today, as distinct from the rates at which it is paid, is an instance of this commitment; so, too, is the formation of ecology parties and of the various pressure groups concerned with specific forms of development of the productive forces (use of nuclear energy, development of road and of air transport, and so on) and with their effects on the environment and upon the health and safety of human beings; so, too, is the women's movement in its sustained attack on one of the most central and pernicious forms of the division of labour, together with all its effects; so, too, is a wide range of radical and alternative networks attempting to cater to needs on socialist and collective principles, and to establish a counter-culture within, but always at odds with, the existing framework of social relations; and so, too, is that quintessential expression of the politics of need — the campaign for nuclear disarmament; dormant for a decade, but now renascent and drawing upon the advantage of a more clearsighted understanding of the importance and dimensions of its task, this movement commits itself on the question of human needs in simple, but quite fundamental terms: welfare, not warfare.

These initiatives, moreover, bring into prominence not only the interrelationship between means and ends and the oppressive nature of any politics that tries to deny it, but also the inter-relationship between the exercise of individual political power and the exercise of State power. Anyone who has been active in any of these causes will know that the main task is not so much to persuade other ordinary mortals of the sanity of their programmes as to restore to them a sense of their individual powers of action in situations over which they appear to have no control. It is a task of explaining the function of their unit of political 'voice' in the calculus of modern politics, where silent resistance amounts to tacit consent and tacit consent to active compliance in the power politics that seems to make a nonsense of all individual dissent; it is a task of persuading them of the double blow that is dealt to that politics by every unit of silence that is withdrawn and converted to noisy protest. One and one still makes two even in the context where it seems that 'no one' makes politics.

Let me, then, briefly in conclusion state my own commitment. I believe that the vast majority of people in Britain, as elsewhere, possess a potential for fulfilment that is so under-realised that it is deprived even of the forms of existence and possibilities of self-understanding that might allow it to be experienced as existing. There is a lack even of the means to understand the sense of lack and what it is that it lacks. In this sense, the positive commentary on needs that finds explicit expression in the organised politics of left-wing resistance has its counterpart in another commentary. This is the implicit, negative, and as yet much more pervasive commentary on needs that exists only in the silence of the failure to vote, of the empty factory 'suggestions' box, of the yawn that greets the television screen, of the millions of conversations that might have been had, and the equally numerous unheard exchanges in the doctor's surgery. For it is not just the articulated language of revolt and the reasoned attack on capitalist society that bespeaks our needs and the 'truth' about them that our decision and choice of them makes true, but the private and unarticulated language of inner conflict that every individual must daily hear and listen to as the condition of the production of the silence of boredom, apathy, neurosis and despair.

In a world that for too long now has tried to say 'no' on the grounds of rationality itself to the practical or logical possibility of this truth, these languages, and even the very differences between them, remain testimony to the possibility and indeed the necessity of saying 'yes'. For failure to speak now may well prove fatal for the future. If we continue to allow the 'natural' forces of social progress to treat our lives as 'cheap as beasts', we can be sure that in the end there will be neither gorgeous apparel, nor warmth, nor any reasoning upon true need.

Notes

1 K. Marx, F. Engels, *Selected Works,* London, Lawrence and Wishart, 1968, pp. 320-1.

2 C. Castoriadis, *The Crossroads in the Labyrinth, loc. cit.*

3 Aristotle, after all, anticipated him by some years. Here, again, I must refer the reader to Castoriadis' discussion. Castoriadis, indeed, approaches the *Critique of the Gotha Programme* as an attempt to answer Aristotle's original problem rather than as a statement of a novel kind about social justice, *op. cit., loc. cit.*

4 *Ibid.*

5 Admittedly both these formulae are borrowed by Marx who, it might be argued, was under no illusion here that he was appealing precisely to *slogans* rather than attempting an elaborate theorisation of communist society, and that it is therefore a little pedantic to quibble over a mere *façon de parler*. But at the very least, one would have to think twice before excusing Marx for such slip-shod forms of expression in the context of what is itself a most relentless exercise in linguistic analysis of the inanities underlying Lasalle's thoughtless remarks.

6 A question evaded, it seems to me, by Lucien Sève in his interesting discussion of Marx's claims about the need to work (*Man in Marxist Theory*, op. cit., pp. 326-31), for while Sève appreciates that there must be a difference between our ordinary understanding of the term 'labour' and that of which Marx can say it is the 'prime want', he nonetheless wants to argue that this is the difference between 'alienated' and 'unalienated' labour. But that is really only a more elaborate way of dodging the question that I am suggesting is dodged by Marx in his original formulation, and Sève's whole argument seems to be predetermined by his unshakeable conviction that the statement of the *Critique of the Gotha Programme* must represent the solution to the problems of communism, rather than the posing of them.

7 K. Marx, Letter to L. Kugelmann, 11 July 1868.

8 K. Marx, *Grundrisse, op. cit.,* p. 611.

9 *Ibid.*

10 *Ibid.*, pp. 611-12.

11 R. Bahro, *The Alternative in Eastern Europe*, London, New Left Books, 1978.

12 K. Marx, *Capital, op. cit.,* Vol. III, p. 187.

13 F. Engels, *Anti-Dühring*, London, Lawrence and Wishart, 1969, p. 332.

14 K. Marx, *Capital, op. cit.,* Vol. I, P. 85.

15 I.e., the goals of the plan are in fact realised, and production is rational to the extent that productive forces are consciously and effectively wielded in the interests of a planned economy.

16 *Selected Works, op. cit.,* p. 320.

17 K. Marx, *Capital, op. cit.,* Vol. III, p. 178.

18 I. I. Rubin, *Essays on Marx's Theory of Value*, Montreal, Black Rose Books, 1973, p. 174.

19 Itself a hard enough task, given the practical difficulties of assessing needs: the 'plan' of all existing socialist economies is deficient to the extent that they are unable to assess needs *a priori* in a full and socially effective manner. The persistence of the market and the distribution by means of money under socialist economies is the index of this failure — it indicates the still *a posteriori* nature of the assessment of needs in that it is only if a given product is sold that its status as satisfying a need can be ascertained.

Index of Names